MARRIAGE AND DIVORCE
A CONTEMPORARY PERSPECTIVE

THE GUILFORD FAMILY THERAPY SERIES
ALAN S. GURMAN, EDITOR

MARRIAGE AND DIVORCE
A CONTEMPORARY PERSPECTIVE

EDITED BY

CAROL C. NADELSON AND DEREK C. POLONSKY
TUFTS UNIVERSITY SCHOOL OF MEDICINE

THE GUILFORD PRESS

NEW YORK   LONDON

© 1984 The Guilford Press
A Division of Guilford Publications, Inc.
200 Park Avenue South, New York, N.Y. 10003

Printed in the United States of America

Library of Congress Cataloging in Publication Data

Main entry under title:

Marriage and divorce, a contemporary perspective.

  (The Guilford family therapy series)
  Includes indexes.
  1. Marriage—Addresses, essays, lectures.
2. Marriage counseling—Addresses, essays, lectures.
3. Divorce—Addresses, essays, lectures. I. Nadelson,
Carol C. II. Polonsky, Derek C. III. Series. [DNLM:
1. Marriage. 2. Divorce. 3. Family therapy.
4. Marital therapy. WM 55 M3588]
HQ728.M286 1984   306.8′1   83-1567
ISBN 0-89862-047-3

Contributors

DAVID A. BERKOWITZ, MD, Department of Psychiatry, Tufts University School of Medicine, Boston, Massachusetts, and Faculty, Boston Psychoanalytic Society and Institute, Boston, Massachusetts

LEE BIRK, MD, Department of Psychiatry, Harvard Medical School, Boston, Massachusetts, and Learning Therapies, Inc., Newton, Massachusetts

OLIVER BJORKSTEN, MD, Department of Psychiatry and Behavioral Sciences, Medical University of South Carolina, Charleston, South Carolina

RUTH A. BRANDWEIN, PhD, School of Social Welfare, State University of New York at Stony Brook, Stony Brook, New York

ROBERT DICKES, MD, Department of Psychiatry, State University of New York–Downstate Medical Center, Brooklyn, New York, and Department of Psychiatry, New York University School of Medicine, New York, New York

SHARON W. FOSTER, MA, Eating Disorders Program, University of Wisconsin Center for Health Sciences, Madison, Wisconsin

ALAN S. GURMAN, PhD, Department of Psychiatry and Psychiatric Outpatient Clinic, University of Wisconsin Medical School, Madison, Wisconsin

JANCIS V. F. LONG, PhD, Faculty, Washington School of Psychiatry, Washington, D.C.

MARY ALICE MATHEWS, MD, Department of Psychiatry, Harvard Medical School, Boston, Massachusetts

ELIZABETH H. MAURY, PhD, Exceptional Parents Unlimited/Association for Retarded Citizens, Fresno, California, and Central San Joaquin Medical Education Program of the University of California at San Francisco Medical School, Fresno, California.

NORMAN I. MOSS, MD, Department of Psychiatry, Harvard Medical School, Boston, Massachusetts, and Department of Psychiatry, Beth Israel Hospital, Boston, Massachusetts

CAROL C. NADELSON, MD, Department of Psychiatry, Tufts University School of Medicine, Boston, Massachusetts

DEREK C. POLONSKY, MD, Department of Psychiatry, Tufts University School of Medicine, Boston, Massachusetts

CONTRIBUTORS

THOMAS J. STEWART, PhD, Department of Family Medicine, Medical University of South Carolina, Charleston, South Carolina

LORA HEIMS TESSMAN, PhD, Psychiatric Service, Medical Department, Massachusetts Institute of Technology, Cambridge, Massachusetts, and private practice of psychotherapy and consultation, Newton, Massachusetts

JUDITH WALLERSTEIN, PhD, School of Social Welfare and School of Law, University of California at Berkeley, Berkeley, California, and Center for the Family in Transition, Corte Madera, California

HARVEY S. WAXMAN, PhD, Department of Psychiatry, Beth Israel Hospital, Boston, Massachusetts, and Department of Psychiatry, Harvard Medical School, Boston, Massachusetts

Preface

Concerns about the viability of marriage and the family have led to pronouncements about the death of each, and the destruction of morality in our society as a result. Our interest in looking at the realities of contemporary marriage derives from a view that it is important to have accurate data, to understand their implications, and to place these data in the context of evolving theoretical and therapeutic formulations.

In the first two chapters, Bjorksten and Stewart have undertaken to review the significant ways in which marriages today differ from those in the past. They examine the importance of commitment in dyadic relationships. Foster and Gurman have reviewed the complexities of current social developments and point to the significance of these for therapists who work with couples. The successful integration of a contemporary trend into a theoretical approach requires that a therapist does not label new patterns as psychopathologic when changes may reflect different attitudes and expectations. Although our own values may be at variance with some of the directions we observe, we must nevertheless examine their impact. For example, the fact that almost 50% of marital partners have an extramarital affair at some point in their marriage is a reality explored in the chapter by Waxman and Long. In his chapter on marital dynamics, Berkowitz discusses collusions in marriage and the relevance of projective identification. Elaborating on recent theories of continuing phases of adult development, Nadelson, Polonsky, and Mathews place the stages of the marital cycle in the context of individual adult life cycles. Birk describes the development of an innovative approach to the technical aspects of group couples therapy that incorporates separate meetings of husbands and wives with joint meetings.

A new treatment modality that has evoked considerable interest is sex therapy. In many situations it provides a relatively short-term effective treatment for patients, but we have learned that there is enormous complexity behind the simple descriptions in the literature. The chapter by Dickes presents an approach to the integration of sex therapy into a more traditional therapeutic framework, and Polonsky and Nadelson describe their approach to couples who present with a "sexual" symptom but whose evaluation indicates that a more complex problem must be addressed.

In the final section of the book, some dimensions of marital dissolution are explored. There has been much written in the popular press about the "epidemic" of divorce and for that reason a section dealing with the effects of divorce on mothers, fathers, children, and families is included. Maury and Brandwein, in their discussion of the impact of divorce on the woman, consider internal conflicts as well as the cultural pressures. In the chapter by Tessman, the intrapsychic "quest" for the lost parent is elucidated, and Wallerstein's chapter describes a long-term study that details the effects of parental divorce and makes it possible to make some predictions of outcome. This section will be particularly useful for therapists who work with couples or individuals who are separating. The reconstituted or blended family, where couples who have divorced remarry other partners and bring with them the children of previous marriages, is the focus of Moss's chapter on the complexities of the melding together of two families. He emphasizes the force of the rivalries that continue to exist.

In editing this book we have made the assumption that the reader is familiar with basic aspects of couples evaluation and therapy, including concepts of mutual projection and projective identification. We have decided to focus on significant shifts in contemporary society and to examine their impact on marriage and families, rather than to undertake an exhaustive review of the entire subject. We hope the data and the perspectives presented will be useful to clinicians from all mental health disciplines and to all of those who have an interest in contemporary trends in marriage.

Carol C. Nadelson
Derek C. Polonsky

Contents

SECTION III. MARITAL DISSOLUTION

MARRIAGE AND DIVORCE
A CONTEMPORARY PERSPECTIVE

Contemporary Marriage

CHAPTER ONE

Contemporary Trends in American Marriage

OLIVER BJORKSTEN
THOMAS J. STEWART

The understanding of current trends in marriage today is extremely complex and highly charged. Gone are the days when marriage was a clearly defined entity with a distinct beginning and ending and easily understood rules for behavior. Marriage today seems to be the scapegoat of many societal ills. Both liberals and conservatives point to the "deterioration of marriage" as an institution.

This unusual agreement has been commented on by John Demos:

> To study the history of the American family is to conduct a rescue mission into the dreamland of our national self-concept. No subject is more closely bound up with a sense of a difficult present and our nostalgia for a happier past. How often, in reference to contemporary problems, does the diagnostic finger point in the direction of family life. Significantly, this emphasis comes from both the right and the left. Conservatives detect a loosening of the bonds of family, a poisonous infiltration of permissiveness. Time was, they contend, when domestic life established sound patterns of authority which served to guarantee an orderly society. On the other side, counterculture spokesmen decry a damaging trend toward rigid and alienating nuclear households. It is their aim to recapture the spirit, if not the exact form, of an extended family system alleged typical of the premodern era. These perspectives differ greatly as to substance, but there is a common perjorative thrust. In both cases, the story of the family through time is the story of decline and decay, but the reality of family in the past is something else again. (1977, p. 59)

Oliver Bjorksten. Department of Psychiatry and Behavioral Sciences, Medical University of South Carolina, Charleston, South Carolina.

Thomas J. Stewart. Department of Family Medicine, Medical University of South Carolina, Charleston, South Carolina.

To what reality does John Demos allude? It is the purpose of this chapter to review some of the trends in marriage over the last 100 years with a special emphasis on the last two decades, and then suggest possible future trends. Clearly, there are a number of potential pitfalls in our effort. It is very easy to abstract statistics out of context in order to demonstrate a particular point that the authors personally favor. In an effort to ameliorate this tendency, we will assume a historical perspective as frequently as possible in order to convey the overall context in which current trends seem to lie. Moreover, since it is difficult to make predictions based on cross-sectional data long-term trends are more pertinent to our purpose.

Statistical information on such issues as courtship, marriage, divorce, postmarital relationships, child bearing, and population trends are voluminous and complex. Such groups as singles, which on the surface seem homogeneous, are in fact extremely heterogeneous, and include such subgroups as those who have never been married, those who have been widowed or divorced one time, or those who have been widowed or divorced numerous times, and so on. Thus, statistics relating specifically to the state of "singlehood" can be misleading unless they are broken down into subclassifications of the population under consideration.

Marriage as an institution does not exist in isolation but rather interfaces with many other social phenomena including the economy, work environment, government, social movements and ideologies, mobility patterns, automation, computerization, mass communication, and even energy consumption. To consider marriage as an institution while ignoring these other factors can lead to an erroneous understanding and static view of the current status of marriage. It is our opinion that marriage today can best be viewed as a dynamic process interacting in the larger context of society but also cycling between singlehood, marriage, divorce, postmarital relationships, and, eventually, marriage again. This dynamic view will be presented in considerable detail below.

As individual freedom of choice appears to be increasing in our society and rigid societal dictates for behavior are falling away, personal agendas for life-style become more significant in predicting marital trends than they have been in the past. The traditional binary concept of marriage, that is, you are or you are not, has fallen away to a large variety of relationship options that are yet additional manifestations of what Alvin Toffler (1970) refers to as "overchoice." From our consideration of marriage as an institution today, it appears that large numbers of individuals are choosing many of these alternative pathways in their relationships. Although this creates the illusion of disarray in family life, in the decades to come we will discover which of these alternatives are viable for the existing social conditions and which are not. Just as marriage appears to be changing its form in our present era, so future changes in marriage might be useful adaptations to different social conditions.

As an example, it is apparent that the social realities in the United States today are seriously affecting expectations that young people have regarding marriage. Our current economic belt tightening means that newlyweds today will probably have to revise some of their economic and marital expectations downward as it becomes necessary to conserve energy, live in smaller houses, and have greater access to information via the mass media. The little white house with the picket fence of the Norman Rockwell portrait, mowing the lawn Saturday morning, and all the associated fantasies may require reconsideration by young American adults.

There are numerous specific trends that are currently affecting marriage and which will probably do so to an even greater extent in the future. Some of these trends include:

1. The changing function of marriage to a more personal institution for fulfillment and happiness rather than simply procreation, thus leading to an increased diversity of marital styles.
2. The changing role of women in society that will have dramatic ramifications with respect to child care, marital style, and economics.
3. Changing patterns of sexuality and attitudes toward sex have already altered courtship patterns substantially and may very well change the motivations for marriage itself.
4. Marital roles are dramatically changing, not only in the methods by which role differentiation occurs (i.e., by negotiation rather than tradition), but also by the degree of competence in which the roles are fulfilled. The more diversity there is in these marital styles the fewer role models there are for newlyweds to consider, the fewer marital skills will be preserved and passed forward.
5. Recent demographic trends have already affected marriage substantially and will continue to do so in the future. The truncation of child-care years for women, the increased number of never-married individuals, the postponement of marriage to a later age, the increasing number of women in the work force, the declining number of children per family, and the doubling of the number of years that marriage partners can expect to be alone without children, are all going to increase in the future.
6. Children and child-rearing practices, including cooperative parenting arrangements, postdivorce relationships, and child-care centers, are already changing marital relationships substantially and will continue to do so.
7. Divorce is increasing statistically, although the overall rate of marital dissolutions (due to death, desertions, and divorce) has remained constant for over 100 years. Yet this high divorce rate, while relieving marital pressures on the one hand, is spewing forth large numbers of single individuals with their children, many of whom

5

will remarry. Some of these individuals, veterans in the marriage arena, are at the forefront in creating new and innovative family relationships.

8. Postdivorce relationships, a hitherto little-studied phenomenon, are becoming a major statistical trend in this country. At this point, these individuals are practically disenfranchised by government and mental health policymakers.

9. Mass media, especially television, are having a major impact on Americans in general and upon family life in particular, not only by what they are portraying, but also by what individual viewers are not doing when they are watching television.

10. Finally, encroachment on high-quality family time appears to be an important trend in family life, that is, the intrusion into high-quality communication and intimacy periods in the family life by such things as work demands, organization of schedules, role differentiation, television, and the increasing tendency for people to look for personal gratification outside the home.

From this cursory overview, it should be apparent that forces affecting marriage both from within and without are significant. Probably the most conspicuous observation is that at present there is an enormous flux in marriage at the aggregate and at the individual couple levels. This flux will certainly lead to some quite predictable trends for the future, but many will be unpredictable. The crunch comes in the application of our understanding of marriage to the clinical situation. We can no longer talk about "marital therapy" in a generic way, but rather "therapies" of individuals in relationships that might be vastly different from our image of the traditional nuclear family. Our stereotyped assumptions about the little house with the white picket fence must give way to the social realities of more compact living units and our assumptions about power relationships within families must be reconsidered in the light of the large numbers of blended families that are occurring today. We can no longer make the assumption that the single-breadwinner nuclear family is the most prevalent form of family life in this country, since, at most, 16% of the American population lives in such a household arrangement. Clinicians must be prepared to consider more complex postdivorce family relationships, which, ironically, seem to resemble the mythical extended family of bygone times. Intrapsychic concepts, which have validity in the context of the nuclear family, must be reconsidered in the light of the startling changes in the family composition in this country and may eventually have to give way in part to a broader systems approach. Finally, an important ramification of these trends is that meaningful clinical research can no longer be designed by blindly using such concepts as "the representative sample," but may instead have to carefully examine specified subgroups of the population in an effort to understand their specific conflicts and difficulties.

There are a number of important ramifications for psychotherapists and marital therapists of these considerations:

1. It is incumbent on therapists dealing with couples to fully educate themselves about the spectrum of possible relationships that "normal" people can realistically and legitimately engage in today so that they will have a better ability to decide which issues are interpersonal and which are intrapsychic.

2. As types of relationships become more heterogenous, therapists are going to be presented with a much larger variety of relationship problems, which may be extremely difficult to understand in traditional psychiatric and psychological terms.

3. Functional issues in relationships are changing rapidly from traditional ones to more innovative ones, thus the therapeutic tasks in dealing with these families become more complex. For example, the stereotypic authority structure in the traditional nuclear family is quite easy to understand; however, the power relationships in the blended family can be quite intricate. What is the power that a stepfather or mother has over his or her new partner and children, and by exerting that authority what potential conflicts does he or she face with the new partner and ex-spouse? Further, what kinds of sibling rivalries evolve in the context of blended families?

4. As more innovative relationship styles become prevalent and workable, patients are faced with more "realistic" alternatives for the management of their lives that make the task of the therapist all the more difficult in helping the patient decide on a life pattern that is most suitable. As patients traditionally look to therapists for advice, the therapists can be faced with an equally difficult problem of overchoice.

5. Traditionally, the therapist has assumed a primarily analytic and passive role in therapy, helping the patient to understand his or her own motivations, which can eventually lead the patient to make his or her own personal decisions. Today, and in the future, the therapist will probably need to assume at least two other important functions: that of education and negotiation. As the therapist becomes more familiar with the wide variety of relationship styles, it may be important to convey this information to patients to permit them broader latitude of choice, and as these more complex relationships are being treated by therapists, more superficial negotiation skills may at times be more appropriate in the resolution of the difficulties than traditional psychotherapy skills.

DATA BASE

This section includes a review of selected data considered in historical perspective, elaboration of a model that portrays the elements of being single, married, divorced, and remarried, and a discussion of the impact and resulting dynamics for marriages and families as institutions.

Patterns and Trends

Prior to considering recent changes that have occurred in marriage, it seems appropriate to identify areas in which little or no change has occurred. Some indicators that have remained stable over time are:

1. A two-generation nuclear family or some variation of it as the most prevalent form of family composition;
2. The proportion of people getting married;
3. The proportion of married women choosing to have children;
4. The proportion of all marriages dissolved (by divorce, death, and other reasons).

In reviewing the literature regarding marriage and the family as institutions in America, one cannot avoid being struck by the underlying assumption that families and marriages in America's past were somehow more stable, more responsive, larger, and more functional. Unfortunately, this presumption of the "good old days of American families" is as common among professionals as it is in the general public. Indeed, the historical and contemporary data available to us now indicate that the nuclear family including two generations has been the basic unit in European and American societies over the past several centuries. Laslett (1976), Shorter (1977), Demos (1970), and others have revealed that France, England, and the United States have had the two-generation nuclear family as the dominant form for centuries. The very small percentage of American families that have three or more generations living together in the same household (about 7–8%) has remained stable for the past two centuries (Bengston & DeTerre, 1980). Factors such as high mortality rates and movement to frontier lands obviously adversely affected the availability of multiple generations of a family.

The assumption that families were more stable and composed of multiple generations in the past has been referred to as the "world we have lost" syndrome (Goode, 1963) and as the "classical family of western nostalgia" (Davis, 1972). It is important to appreciate the fact that a great deal of mythical thinking remains about marriage and family living in America's past and present.

Table 1-1 reflects data collected on cohorts of women over roughly 100-year period in American history. This table shows the general stability of the percent of women who marry and the percent of women who marry and have children. It is noted from the table that though there are minor fluctuations, women who were born in the period 1846–1855 married and had children as often as those women born in the period 1936–1940. Contemporary women continue to marry as often as they did in previous years even though the circumstances now are substantially different from those

Table 1-1. Percentages Ever-Married and Childless, and Mean Children per Mother, Women Born 1846–1940, by Birth Cohort

Year of birth	Data source		Total number of women (1000s)	Ever-married (%)	Childless among ever-married (%)	Average number of children per mother
	Census year	Age at survey				
1846–1855	1910	55–64	2385	92.7	8.2	5.71
1856–1865	1910	45–54	3868	91.3	9.2	5.33
1866–1875	1910	35–44	5500	88.4	11.1	4.55
	1940	65–74	3173	90.4	13.2	4.35
1876–1885	1940	55–64	5122	91.0	15.2	4.02
1886–1890	1940	50–54	3469	91.3	15.2	3.75
1891–1895	1940	45–49	3987	91.4	15.4	3.62
1896–1900	1940	40–44	4271	90.2	16.2	3.30
	1950	50–54	4077	92.3	18.6	3.32
1901–1905	1950	45–49	4480	92.0	20.4	3.13
1906–1910	1950	40–44	5083	91.8	20.0	2.96
	1960	50–54	4927	92.4	20.6	2.97
1911–1915	1960	45–49	5560	93.5	18.2	2.94
1916–1920	1960	40–44	5898	93.9	14.1	2.99
	1970	50–54	5735	94.3	13.8	3.02
1921–1925	1970	45–49	6250	94.7	10.6	3.20
1926–1930	1970	40–44	6154	94.6	8.6	3.39
1931–1935	1970	35–39	5711	94.1	7.3	3.42
1936–1940	1970	30–34	5852	92.6	8.3	3.06

Note. From Bane (1976, p. 145).

of 100 years ago. Similarly, though there is fluctuation, women in both cohorts decided to have (or not have) children with the same frequency.

Although a great deal of discussion is devoted to America's rising divorce rates, it is important to consider the larger context of marital dissolution (consisting of death, desertion, and divorce). Table 1-2 indicates that over the past century, while death has declined as a factor in marital dissolution, divorce has substantially risen, so that the overall marital dissolution rate has remained essentially constant for 100 years. Thus, use of divorce data alone to suggest deterioration is misleading since total dissolution rates have remained constant. An interesting reciprocal relationship between divorce and desertion has been noted: as divorce rates have risen, the desertion rates have probably declined (desertion data, unfortunately, are not available) due to the increased ease of divorce.

What has changed? A convenient way for understanding the changing

9

Table 1-2. Annual Marital Dissolutions by Death and Legal Divorce, and Rates per 1000 Existing Marriages, 1890–1970

| Year | Dissolutions per year | | Dissolutions per 1000 existing marriages | | | Divorces % of total dissolutions |
	Deaths	Divorces	Deaths	Divorces	Combined	
1860–1864	197,200	7,170	32.1	1.2	33.3	3.5
1865–1869	207,000	10,529	31.1	1.6	32.7	4.8
1870–1874	226,400	12,417	30.3	1.7	32.0	5.2
1875–1879	238,600	15,574	28.7	1.9	30.6	6.1
1880–1884	285,400	21,747	30.6	2.3	33.0	7.1
1885–1889	290,400	27,466	27.6	2.6	30.2	8.6
1890–1894	334,800	36,123	28.3	3.1	31.3	9.7
1895–1899	328,800	45,462	24.9	3.4	28.4	12.1
1900–1904	390,800	61,868	26.5	4.2	30.6	13.7
1905–1909	427,400	74,626	25.4	4.4	29.8	14.9
1910–1914	453,600	91,695	23.7	4.8	28.5	16.8
1915–1919	551,000	119,529	26.0	5.6	31.6	17.8
1920–1924	504,200	164,917	21.9	7.2	29.0	24.6
1925–1929	573,200	193,218	22.6	7.6	30.3	25.2
1930–1934	590,800	183,441	21.9	6.8	28.7	23.7
1935–1939	634,600	239,600	21.9	8.3	30.2	27.4
1940–1944	656,400	330,557	20.4	10.3	30.7	33.5
1945–1949	681,200	485,641	19.2	13.7	32.8	41.6
1950–1954	692,400	385,429	18.2	10.0	28.3	35.9
1955–1959	733,600	385,385	18.3	9.2	27.8	34.2
1960–1964	n.a.	419,600	n.a.	9.6	n.a.	n.a.
1965–1969	n.a.	544,800	n.a.	11.7	n.a.	n.a.
1960	790,400	393,000	18.9	9.4	28.3	33.2
1961	789,200	414,000	18.7	9.8	28.6	34.4
1965	820,800	479,000	18.5	10.8	29.4	36.9
1970	908,200	715,000	19.3	15.2	34.5	44.0

Note. From Davis (1972, p. 256).

profile of marriage and family living is to consider those changes that are internal and external to marriage and family as institutions.

The external changes are:

1. The age profile in America;
2. Mortality rates with a decline in deaths and an increase in longevity and life expectancy;
3. An increasingly heterogeneous composition of population;

4. Patterns of sexual experience;
5. The increase of the importance and visibility of women in the labor force;
6. The growing importance of social institutions, agencies, and media in family life.

One of the most important but least acknowledged changes in modern American life has been the gradual aging of our population. As a consequence of what is termed the "demographic transition, graphically shown in Figure 1-1, Scanzoni and Scanzoni described it as follows:

> The demographic transition is the central event in the recent history of human population. It begins with a decline in the death rate, precipitated by advances in medicine (particularly in public health), nutrition, or both. Some years later the birth rate also declines, primarily because of changes in the perceived value of having children. Before the transition the birth rate is constant but the death rate varies; afterward the death rate is constant but the birth rate fluctuates. The demographic transition usually accompanies the modernization of nations; it began in Europe and the United States late in the eighteenth century and early in the nineteenth, but in the underdeveloped nations it began only much later, often in the twentieth century. In the developed countries the transition is now substantially complete, but in much of the rest of the world only mortality has been reduced; the fertility rate remains high. In the interim between the drop in mortality and fertility population has increased rapidly. (1981, p. 557)

Table 1-3 shows projections of the proportion of older people in the U.S. population up to the year 2000.

One of the major contributors to the profound demographic change referred to as the "aging of America" is the equally dramatic change in

Fig. 1-1. The demographic transition. From Scanzoni and Scanzoni (1981, p. 557).

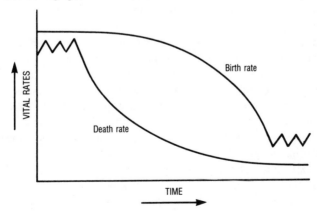

Table 1-3. *Number and Proportions of the Older Age Groups, 1980–2000*

| | 1980 | | 1990 | | 2000 | |
Age	Number (millions)	Proportion of total population	Number (millions)	Proportion of total population	Number (millions)	Proportion of total population
55 years +	45,570	20.5	49,412	20.0	53,537	20.4
60 years +	34,267	15.4	39,127	16.0	40,589	15.5
65 years +	24,523	11.0	28,933	11.7	30,600	11.7
75 years +	9,112	4.1	11,402	4.7	13,521	5.2

Note. From Siegel (1976, pp. 3, 8).

mortality patterns. In 1900 average life expectancy was 49.2 years but in 1974 had climbed to 71.9 years. A variation on the theme of declining mortality in this century has been the sex mortality differential (the difference in male–female life expectancy at birth). Using the comparable dates above, it is clear that the survivability of women has improved over that of men—in 1900 the differential favoring women was 2.9 years and in 1973 was 7.7 years. This circumstance was greatly affected by improvements in maternal mortality and the detection and treatment of cancer in female reproductive organs. One of the results of the mortality differential is the substantial increase in the likelihood that any couple or family will have a surviving member of the older generation and that that member will be a female above age 75 (Bengston & DeTerre, 1980). As a result of the more general availability of multiple generations of families, intergenerational relations have become more of a factor in this century. Marriages are now in a position to be greatly affected by interactions with and developments in the older generations of the families of both partners. Issues such as geographic availability to a parent(s), their economic and health-care situations are important considerations for many young and middle-year couples and individuals.

The realities for older couples and families are profound. Table 1-4, which portrays the projected family life cycle experiences of women in the previous century and contemporary women, indicates that a great deal of time in one's life is now spent in postparental circumstances. Women who have lived and functioned in a traditional arrangement are confronted today with as much as 20 to 40 years of life after children have grown and departed, a circumstance that may have dramatic implications regarding quality of life and divorce in this group.

A casual glance through popular women's books and magazines indicates that there is a general recognition of this pattern. Women in their 40s and above receive messages about "changing gears," entering occupations, and making themselves more attractive. The data on increasing enrollment of older women in colleges and universities are also indicative of the choices and activities of women during this period.

The sex mortality differential also points to the fact that women are the greater survivors and are therefore represented much more in the older and widowed categories. Widowhood has substantially different implications for women than for men. The pool of individuals available for women above age 55 who are widowed is small. The pool for men is much greater, and widowed men are consequently much more likely to be remarried following the death of a spouse. Widows then are much more likely to settle into a stable period of singlehood following the death of their spouse. However, there have been indications of experimentation and of attempts to develop alternatives such as group living arrangements among older women.

Life circumstances dictate to a great extent the choices and activities of older couples and individuals. Issues dealing with income, housing transportation and health care have become much more salient for this group. Current controversies about the funding base and the provision of benefits under the Social Security Act reflect the importance of these issues to the older population and the growing political power of older people in America.

Another external change, or perhaps more accurately a continuing phenomenon, in the United States is the heterogeneity of the total population. The attention devoted to the immigration of large numbers of Cubans, Vietnamese, Thais, Haitians, and Mexicans into the United States is only one facet of our heterogeneous population base. America always has been and continues to be a pluralistic society. It seems that the idea of America as a melting pot is more of an idea than a reality. Cultural and ethnic variations of marital and family arrangements and patterns are still distinct. Though the

Table 1-4. Hypothetical Life Cycles: Mean Ages at Major Events of Women in Mid-Nineteenth and Mid-Twentieth Centuries

	Year of birth	
	1846–1855 (six children)	1946–1955 (two children)
First marriage	22.0	20.8
Birth of first child	23.5	22.3
Birth of last child	36.0	24.8
First marriage of last child	58.9	47.7
Death of spouse	56.4	67.7
Own death	60.7	77.1

Note. From Bane (1976, p. 25).

difference between blacks and whites on such indicators as fertility rates, proportion of women who marry, and proportion who divorce has decreased during the past two decades, these distinctions are still conspicuous (as seen in Table 1-5). Similarly, the experiences of Spanish-speaking individuals differ not only from whites but also from blacks in America. Table 1-5 reflects some of the differences.

Sexual experiences and attitudes have changed markedly over the past three decades. Perhaps the most telling data in this area come from adolescent and college age youth. Recent surveys of adolescents indicate that there is a lifetime prevalence of permarital coitus of 31% for whites and 63% for black youths. Comparative studies indicate that these percentages have increased from earlier studies and that the rate of increase among whites is greater than that among blacks (Zelnick & Kantner, 1972, 1977). Reviews of the epidemiology of premarital sex in the United States indicate that there has been a general trend toward more permissive sexual attitudes among all segments and age groups of the population (Clayton & Bokemeier, 1980; Yankelovich, 1981). Coupled with the increased likelihood that individuals who enter marriage will probably have lived with their partner before marriage, sexual experience is much more widespread and diverse than at any time in our past. Similarly, there is much more attention devoted to satisfaction and the role of sexuality within marriage and in relationships generally. The growth of professional activity and associations in the area of sex therapy as well as innovations in therapeutic techniques are only two indicators of the changes occurring in this area.

Prior to the immigration of large numbers of Europeans into the United States during the last half of the nineteenth century, women were a major element in the American labor force. However, the arrival of large numbers of emigré men and the rapid growth of heavy industry in that period reduced the demand for and the role of women in the workplace.

Table 1-5. *Selected Fertility and Household Data for Black, White, and Spanish-Speaking Women*

	White	Black	Spanish origin
Percentage childless among ever-married women, ages 15–44 (1978)	19.7	11.3	14.8
Percentage of births with low birth weights (1977)	5.9	11.9	n.a.
Percentage of unwanted births to all mothers, ages 15–44 (1976)	9.5	25.8	n.a.
Persons per household (1978)	2.8 (all)	3.1	3.5

Note. From U.S. Department of Commerce (1981, pp. 46, 66–68).

Table 1-6. *Participation of Women in the Labor Force by Marital Status, 1890-1970*

Year	Percentage of total work force	Single	Married	Widowed/divorced
1890	18.2	68.2	13.9	17.9
1900	20.1	66.2	15.4	18.4
1910	n.a.	60.2	24.7	15.0
1920	22.7	77.0	23.0	n.a.
1930	23.6	53.9	28.9	17.2
1940	25.8	49.0	35.9	15.0
1950	29.9	31.9	52.2	16.0
1960	35.7	23.6	60.7	15.7
1970	41.4	22.5	62.3	15.0

Note. From Gordon (1978, p. 83).

Table 1-6 reveals that from 1890 to 1970 women have evolved as a growing percentage of the total work force. A parallel development has been the relative growth of married women and the decline of single women in the composition of the labor force. A typical pattern earlier in this century was that of a young single woman working in industry prior to marriage and dropping out of the labor force after marriage. The more typical pattern today is that a woman will continue to be active in the labor force both before and after marriage and even during her child-bearing years. The number and proportion of women with children in the labor force grows annually. Day care as an institution and practice in America is the by-product of this phenomenon. Interestingly, the 1980 White House Conference on Families had many areas of conflict between conservative and liberal factions (abortions, the role of government, adolescent sexuality), but the continued and growing role of women in the labor force and the need for sound day-care programs for the children of working mothers was accepted by both groups. The only argument was whether or not day care as an institution should be supported primarily by government (the liberal position) or by the families and industries (the conservative position) (White House Conference on Families, 1980).

Another consideration regarding women in the labor force is the rising educational level of women in America. The educational attainment level of women is catching up with that of men. Figure 1-2 shows the rise in women receiving professional degrees in the United States as one indicator of this trend. Women now approach one-third of the proportion of doctorates awarded annually and considering the relatively brief historical period shown

15

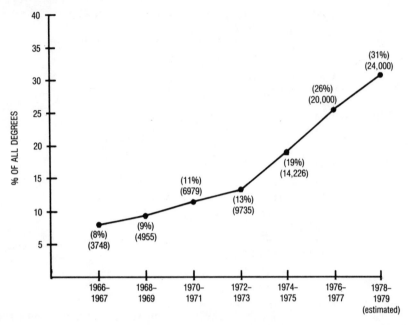

Fig. 1-2. Percentage of professional degrees awarded to women (1966–1979). From Melville (1980, p. 235).

in Figure 1-2 (1966–1979), the data are even more striking. The link between educational level and women in the labor force is important because the more education women have, the more likely they are to be working.

Changing work patterns for women have promoted such phenomena as dual-career marriages and changing sex roles in marriages. Though some recent studies show that married women who are working continue to handle the large majority of traditional household tasks, the impetus toward equality or less highly structured roles in marriages is clearly present (House & Garden Louis Harris Study, 1981; Waite, 1981).

A final external influence and source of change for American marriages and families is the general rubric of social institutions. These include governments, broadcast and print media, schools, social services, and so on. Again, referring to the themes evident in the 1980 White House Conference on Families (White House Conference on Families, 1980), one of the most central issues was the conflict over the role of the federal and state governments in the lives of families. Conservatives cited the need for decreasing governmental involvement and reliance on other institutions such as churches and extended families. Liberals recommended a continuing and highly visible role for the federal and state governments in such areas as divorce, law reform, abortions, and day care.

The past 25 years have been a period in which a minor revolution occurred in the establishment of legal relations between married couples, families and governments, government agencies and court systems. In the 1950s no more than a handful of states had laws defining and setting legal grounds for child abuse and neglect—in 1982 essentially all states have rather specific and tested laws in that area. Family and children's courts evolved in that period as well. Consequently, the legal rights and obligations of parents, children, and spouses have been codified systematically for the first time in American history.

Other institutions have been identified as having profound impact upon marriages and families. Perhaps the most notable after governments are the broadcast and print media. The growth of magazines that appeal to specific segments of the population and describe particular life-styles and images is remarkable (*Playboy, Penthouse, Ms., Redbook, Cosmopolitan, Playgirl, Viva, Family Circle*, to mention only a few). The rise of television in America is a modern legend (with fully 97% of American households having a television set in 1979 as contrasted with 96% having telephones (U.S. Department of Commerce, 1981). The images of families portrayed in prime-time shows such as "The Waltons," "Little House on the Prairie," and "Eight Is Enough" are countered by the portrayal of wife beating, "swinging," divorce, marital conflict, and extramarital sexuality in soap operas. Of major significance is the relative discordance of these portrayals and the realities of contemporary life. Enough alarm and concern has been expressed about the amount of time spent viewing television (national average is approximately 3 hours per day per person), particularly for children, that even television broadcast associations now sponsor viewer messages to parents urging the monitoring of their children's television viewing. Television is one of the most potent influences in marriage and family life today and, for that matter, in almost all other arenas of attitude and behavior. The external factors discussed above, from the demographic transition to social institutions, greatly influence the environment in which marriages are formed, survive, or dissolved.

The major internal changes of marriage are:

1. Courtship and mate-selection patterns have changed dramatically;
2. General birth rates have declined and the number of children per family has also declined;
3. The life cycle of families (i.e., the pattern of family life over time);
4. Divorce rates have increased substantially;
5. The remarriage rates for individuals who have divorced or who are widowed have also increased substantially;
6. Alternative living arrangements both in and out of marriage have increased and become more visible (cohabitation, experimental marriages).

In a recent review of the research conducted on courtship and mate selection in the 1970s, it was noted that the dating behavior so typical of the 1950s—boy calls girl, girl says "yes," boy picks up girl at her home, they "go out" to a movie and later "go steady" if all goes well—has changed markedly (Murstein, 1980). Current surveys of dating among high school and college students reflect less structure in the process—couples frequently meet somewhere mutually acceptable, and often do not plan to do anything sepcific such as going to a movie or dancing. Recent advertisements have depicted women calling men for dates or women dropping gifts off at men's apartments, reflecting the general acceptability of women being more initiating in the courtship process.

The most important phenomenon in the process of courtship in the past decade has been the resurgence of the ancient tradition of cohabitation. Trial marriage was practiced widely in Ireland in the 1500s but eventually declined. Though it is impossible to precisely establish the extent of cohabitation today, estimates indicate that almost 4% of unmarried adults are living with an unrelated member of the opposite sex (in actual numbers, about 2 million) (Ramey, 1978). Some surveys reveal that as many as 30–35% of men and women report that at one time or another they have lived with a member of the opposite sex for an extended period of time. It is clear that more women and men today are likely to have experience in living with or having an active sexual relationship with either their marriage partner or someone else prior to marriage. This trend is part of the contemporary pattern in which dating and courtship are not seen as necessarily leading to the goal of marriage, but rather as opportunities to obtain training and experience in intimate relationships (McCall, 1966).

One of the major elements of the demographic transition was noted to be declining birth rates in industrial societies. The declining birth rate in the United States has been a source of concern to some observers of American families and has been interpreted as one indicator of the "failure" of family life in America. Taken in perspective, the data indicate a continuing commitment to children in marriages and families; yet, there are clearly fewer children per family unit. Table 1-1 portrays the fluctuations in the proportion of married women choosing to have children and also reveals that the cohorts of women who were born during and following the Depression years have lower percentages of childlessness. The majority of married women still *choose* to have children, but they tend to have fewer children than women in earlier generations (19 out of 20 married couples still have a child). The word "choose" is critical when considering parenthood today. Parenthood by choice is a very recent phenomenon, permitted by contraceptive technology. Figure 1-3 depicts the movement from the "baby boom" years (1945–1960) to the "birth dearth" years (1965–1980) and reflects a variety of influences including contraception, changing attitudes, and economic and other factors.

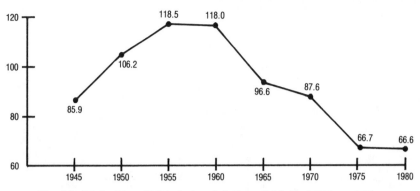

Fig. 1-3. "Baby boom"/"birth dearth." From Melville (1980, p. 329).

The decline in number of children per married woman is noted among both black and white women and also crosses educational levels. The trend is toward smaller family size in essentially all segments of the population.

Perhaps the most remarkable change in marriage and family living in this century is the radical change in the family life cycle of women. The family life cycle is a depiction of the timing of particular events in marriage and child rearing as seen in Table 1-4. It is clear that with the decline in the number of children, there has been a truncation of the proportion of years women spent with children at home and with the family, as compared with the nineteenth century. Contemporary men and women face greater life expectancy and consequently spend more time as an older couple without children. These older childless couples are faced with a major adaptation away from parenting and back to dyadic intimacy and, thus, are greatly concerned with issues related to quality of life. It is not surprising that some couples fail in this reorientation leading to increasing divorce rates in older age groups.

The categories of marital status (singlehood, marriage, divorce, widowhood, and remarriage) are often portrayed as discrete categories which are, by implication, stable. Our review suggests a more dynamic view of marital activity, in which movement from one status to another is an important characteristic. To depict this flow, we offer Figures 1-4 and 1-5 as schematic representations of this marital movement. We elect to use raw data (U.S. Department of Commerce, 1981) to minimize the confusion that occasionally accompanies the use of percentages and to indicate the magnitude of phenomena.

Of the 156,200,000 adults over 18 years old in the United States, 31,400,000 are marriageable singles. A constant 8–9% of singles historically never marry. In a given year (1979), there were 2,331,337 marriages involving 4,662,674 individuals, contributing to the total number of married people in

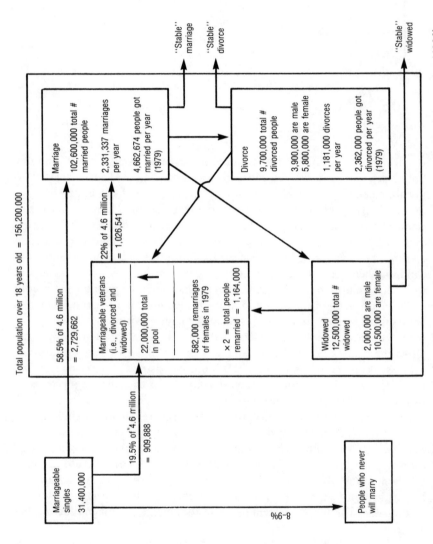

Fig. 1-4. The marital cycle. Data from Glick (1980) and U.S. Department of Commerce (1981).

Total population over 18 years old = 156,200,000

Marriage

102,600,000 total # married people

2,331,337 marriages per year

4,662,674 people got married per year (1979)

58.5% of 4.6 million = 2,729,662

22% of 4.6 million = 1,026,541

Divorce

9,700,000 total # divorced people

3,900,000 are male
5,800,000 are female

1,181,000 divorces per year

2,362,000 people got divorced per year (1979)

Marriageable veterans (i.e., divorced and widowed)

22,000,000 total in pool

582,000 remarriages of females in 1979

× 2 = total people remarried = 1,164,000

Widowed

12,500,000 total # widowed

2,000,000 are male
10,500,000 are female

"Stable" marriage

"Stable" divorce

"Stable" widowed

19.5% of 4.6 million = 909,888

Marriageable singles

31,400,000

People who never will marry

8-6%

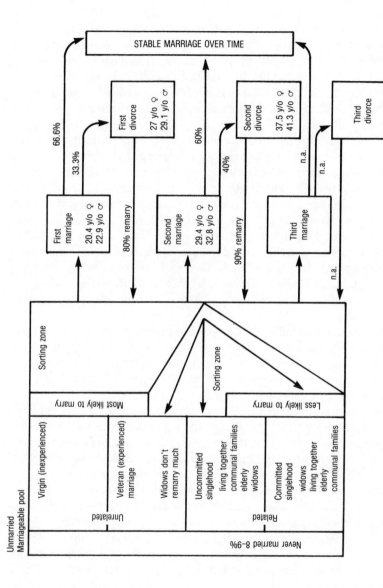

Fig. 1-5. Cycles and decision-making regarding singlehood, marriage, divorce, and remarriage. Data from Glick (1980) and U.S. Department of Health and Human Services (1973a, 1980). n.a. = not available at this time.

21

the United States (102,600,000). Marriages involving never-married single people constituted an estimated 58.5% (2,729,662 people) of the marriages performed that year. Interestingly, marriages between an individual with previous marriage experience (divorce or widowed) and a never-married single made up 19.5% (i.e., 909,888 people) of the total number of marriages. On the other hand, marriages in which both partners had previous marital experience comprised 22% (i.e., 1,026,541 people) of the total number of marriages.

There are three outcomes of marriage: stable marriage, divorce, or dissolution due to the death of a partner. It is very difficult to calculate the number of "stable" marriages since one would have to follow marriages for many years to determine the outcome. However, in 1979, 1,181,000 divorces occurred involving 2,362,000 individuals. These divorces contributed to the known 9,700,000 people who are currently divorced. At present, 12,500,000 people are widowed in the United States, and of these, 2,000,000 are men and 10,500,000 are women. Thus, adding the total number of divorced and widowed people, there are about 22,000,000 "veterans" of marriage who are in the remarriage market. In contrast with these 22 million "remarriageable" people, there are only 31.4 million marriageable singles. Since the pool of singles is decreasing, and there seems to be no decrease in the veteran pool, it would appear that the sizes of these two pools are converging. Today, a never-married single person has a 33% chance of marrying a divorced person, but a divorced person has a 50% chance of marrying a never-married single person.

While there are 22 million in the remarriage pool, there are only 582,000 remarriages of women each year, suggesting that 1,164,000 total people remarry each year. Of these remarriages, the vast majority are divorced rather than widowed people. In fact, divorced persons remarry at least four times more actively than widowed persons do.

Thus, one can see that there is a considerable amount of marital "activity" in the United States which does not just stop with divorce. In considering the impact of divorce on our society it is necessary to also consider the remarriage rate, especially over time. Longitudinally at least 80% of divorced people will remarry, leading to a relatively small number of "stable" divorces.

While Figure 1-4 is a first pass at the marital pool, Figure 1-5 is a closer examination of a cohort of married people. In this figure, it can be seen that the marriage pool is considerably more complex than as portrayed in Figure 1-4. For example, the status of singlehood is by no means homogeneous. Rather, there are at least four categories of single individuals. First, there are virgin (maritally inexperienced) individuals, who are not presently in any primary relationship. Second, there are divorcees (maritally experienced individuals), who are also not in primary nonmarital relationships. Both these groups are considered to be highly marriageable and actively seeking a marital partner. By contrast, there are two groups of individuals who may be considered related in that they are presently engaged in a close emotional relationship with another individual. The first of these groups may be considered "uncommitted singles" in that, although they are in a serious relationship with another individual, they are not committed to singlehood and can easily move into the pool of those interested in becoming married. Included in this group are people who are living together, communal families, widows, and the elderly. By contrast, there are groups of individuals who relate intimately with others but are committed to *not* marrying. This group includes people who are living together, the elderly, some communal families, and some widows. Finally, approximately 9% of singles never marry.

It is clear that within this group of single individuals there is a considerable amount of movement between categories; for example, a virgin (inexperienced, unrelated individual) might decide to enter into a living arrangement with another person, which would put him or her into the category of unrelated, uncommitted single. These people may eventually dissolve their relationship only to reenter a different aspect of the single marriageable pool of individuals. The main point is that there is a great deal of dynamic activity within the group of single marriageable individuals.

When individuals decide to marry for the first time, which the majority of virgin, inexperienced singles do, they generally do so at age 20.4 for women and 22.9 for men. As can been seen in Figure 1-5, 66.6% of these individuals will remain in a stable marital relationship while 33.3% will divorce. When they do so, the average age for women is 27 and for men 29.1. Eighty percent of those divorced then re-enter the marital pool and face the problem of sorting themselves into the various categories that have been delineated. Some become unrelated veterans while others become related veterans who are either committed to singlehood or not committed to singlehood. How this sorting process occurs is unclear at the present time but is extremely interesting. Conversely, how individuals sort themselves in the other direction, that is, from the single marriageable pool, in the direction of becoming married, is also relatively unclear except as shown on Figure 1-4. It is of interest that fully 20% of individuals decide after the first divorce not to remarry at all and form a stable pool of unmarried individuals.

Although all are traumatized by divorce, 80% of individuals decide to try it again and marry for a second time at an average age for women at 29.4 and for men 32.8. Of these second marriages, 60% end in a stable relationship over time while 40% divorce for a second time at an average age of 37.5 for women and 41.3 for men. Ninety percent of these two-time divorcees re-enter the marital pool and will remarry, while 10% drop out of the marital system altogether to remain committed singles. This process of remarriage and divorce continues, but unfortunately figures are unavailable at present for the numbers who marry for a third time and divorce for a third time or subsequent times.

It is important to emphasize that the data base for Figure 1-4 is considerably different than for Figure 1-5. Figure 1-4 uses as a data base overall statistics for the entire population while Figure 1-5 uses cohort data so that each aspect of the figure is comparable within it.

One of the most striking implications of Figures 1-4 and 1-5 is that although there appears to be a considerable amount of movement within the marital cycle, the number of marital dropouts appears relatively small. Only 23% of individuals divorced once or twice truly drop out of the marital pool while 77% decide to continue working at marriages, albeit with a new partner. Thus, it is difficult to escape the conclusion that marriage as a system appears to be quite strong and viable in our culture and the emphasis today is on searching for the best possible marital partner.

FIRST MARRIAGES

One of the most remarkable things about marriage in the United States is its continuing high rate. The United States is second only to Egypt in regard to marital frequency, and slightly over 90% of all individuals will be married at one time or another. It is important to distinguish between first marriage and remarriage. Our discussion at this point will focus primarily on first marriages. Most first marriages still occur prior to age 30. However, demographers and other observers of marital trends indicate that people are delaying marriage more and marriages are becoming more concentrated in the age range of 25–44. Figures 1-6 indicates the arrangement in which the "virgin" and "veteran" singles tend to marry. The most common pattern is for two virgin singles to marry (58.5%). However, there seems to be a growing

Fig. 1-6. *Marriages by marriage order. From U.S. Department of Health and Human Services (1979, p. 2).*

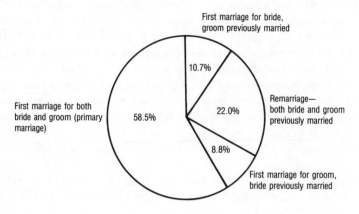

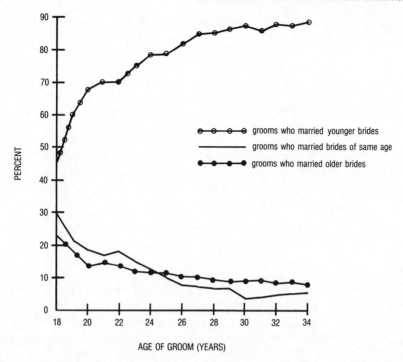

Fig. 1-7. Grooms who married younger brides, brides of same age, and older brides, when both married for the first time (by age of groom). From U.S. Department of Health and Human Services (1979, p. 4).

interaction between subpopulations in the pool so that veterans and virgin singles are marrying more frequently than in the past.

Another first-marriage constant over time is that women generally marry older men and men continue to marry younger women except at the early ages. The most likely time for a man to marry an older women is at the ages 18–24 (see Figure 1-7). This has important implications for pool activity. The large majority of men tend to marry women younger than themselves the first time and that pattern holds for remarriages as well (71.6% for first marriages and 70.7% for remarriages). However, it appears that if it is the groom's first marriage or remarriage and the bride's first marriage, 89% of men marry a younger woman. Conversely, if it is a bride's remarriage to a "virgin" groom, she has an equal chance of marrying an older or younger man—50.1%.

Table 1-7 indicates the age distribution for first marriages for brides and grooms. It is noted in this table that the greatest amount of activity occurs prior to age 24 for both men and women. Though a great deal of discussion has gone on recently regarding teenage marriages and the relatively greater

25

Table 1-7. *Distribution of First Marriages by Age of Bride and Groom*

Age	1976 (%)		1968 (%)	
	Bride	Groom	Bride	Groom
Under 18 years	11.9	2.1	12.3	1.8
18–19 years	26.4	15.4	29.2	16.1
20–24 years	44.8	52.2	46.2	56.6
25–29 years	11.6	21.0	7.8	16.7
30–34 years	2.7	5.2	1.9	4.3
35–44 years	1.6	2.7	1.6	3.0
45 years and over	.9	1.4	.9	1.5

Note. From U.S. Department of Health and Human Services (1979, p. 5).

risk for divorce of younger people, historically we can see in Table 1-8 that the proportion of females who marry prior to age 19 continues to be fairly stable over time (on average 11–12%). The notable historical trend has been the increasing number of young males who get married under age 19. In 1890, a negligible proportion of men were married during the age 15–19 (.5%), whereas in 1970, 4.1% of men were married prior to age 19.

As discussed earlier, it was noted that there has been a substantial increase in educational level for women in contemporary America. It has been

Table 1-8. *Percentage of Teenage Population Ever-Married, by Sex and Age, United States, 1890–1970*

Year	Female			Male		
	15–19 years	15–17 years	18–19 years	15–19 years	15–17 years	18–19 years
1970	11.9	4.7	23.4	4.1	1.4	8.7
1960	16.1	6.8	32.1	3.9	1.2	8.9
1950	17.1	7.2	31.1	3.3	1.1	6.6
1940	11.9	4.6	22.2	1.7	.4	3.7
1930	13.1	5.4	24.6	1.8	.3	4.1
1920	12.9	5.2	24.6	2.1	.5	4.7
1910	11.7	—	—	1.2	—	—
1900	11.2	—	—	1.0	—	—
1890	9.7	—	—	.5	—	—

Note. From U.S. Department of Health and Human Services (1973b, p. 2).

suggested by a number of researchers that the increase in time spent in education for women has influenced the general trend toward delay in years to marriage. The rapid growth of educational levels for women influences their choice of careers, entry into the labor market, and the general level of their feelings of security in their ability to develop their own economic base, with the resulting change in marital agenda. It should be noted that well educated women are most likely to accept either a life of singlehood or a stable marriage. Women with postcollege education usually enter a marital arrangement at a rather late age and remain very stable in that relationship and are at less risk for divorce than are less-educated women. Thus, the overall trend in marriage appears to be that of postponement with subsequent stability, probably due in part to an increased level of maturity and security of individuals entering into a marital situation. Across the board there tends to be more marital dissolution when people marry at a young age, whether they are male or female, and the more years they remain in the marriage, the less likely they are to divorce. Interestingly, the median duration of marriage in this country is only 6.7 years, but this figure is misleading if one does not keep in mind the high divorce rate of young individuals who marry and the low divorce rate of older individuals.

DIVORCE

Much has been made of the increasingly high divorce rates in the United States. However, these divorce rates are part of an international trend, particularly in Western industrialized countries. The United States, as indicated in Table 1-9, has the highest divorce rate of the countries indicated— 5.07 per 1000 population as of 1976. It should be mentioned that a number of other countries are closing the gap on the United States (notably, Canada [2.34], England and Wales [2.56], Germany [2.67], Denmark [2.58], Sweden [2.64]). It can be noted that from 1930 to 1976 a number of other countries (e.g., Canada) had a more rapid rate of increase than has the United States.

Another important consideration in looking at divorce rates as well as marriage rates is the matter of choosing the type of data one will use for comparison and reading of trends and patterns. A variety of rates are used to consider divorces. One of the most common is the crude divorce rate (divorces as a part of total population). However, use of a crude divorce rate is a bit of a problem in that it considers all individuals in the population, not just those who are at risk for divorce. Table 1-10 compares three of the major divorce indicators—the crude divorce rate per 1000 total population, divorces per 100 marriages performed, and divorces per 1000 married female population. The last is the most commonly used, refined divorce rate. Table 1-10 reveals widely varying rates of change for the United States during the period of 1920–1970. The crude divorce rate shows a much greater cumulative percent change than

Table 1-9. *Divorces per 1000 Population in Selected Countries*

	1910	1930	1940	1950	1960	1970	1976
United States	1.0	1.50	2.00	2.50	2.08	3.50	5.07
Canada	<.05	.08	.21	.40	.39	1.36	2.34
Mexico	[a]	.10	.22	.31	.43	.59	.27
England and Wales	.05	.09	.18	.69	.51	1.20	2.56
Norway	.20	.31	.32	.71	.66	.88	1.52
Sweden	.10	.36	.55	1.14	1.20	1.61	2.64
Denmark	.30	.65	.91	1.61	1.46	1.94	2.58
Finland	.10	.32	.36	.91	.82	1.79	2.14
Netherlands	.20	.36	.33	.64	.49	.79	1.52
Germany[b]	.30	.63	.92	2.47	1.34	1.61	2.67
Switzerland	.40	.67	.73	.90	.87	1.04	1.51
France	.30	.49	.28	.58	.66	.79	1.20
Japan	1.10	.79	.67	1.01	.74	.94	1.11

Note. From United Nations (1960, p. 464ff.; 1970, p. 676ff.; 1980, p. 471ff.).
[a]Data not available.
[b]Rates for 1910 and 1930 for all Germany, later rates for East Germany only.

does divorces per 1000 married female population. There is no question that there is a rapid rate of change in the United States. However, a refined rate is a more sensitive tool and generally to be preferred.

One of the continuing trends that has been noted in divorce data is the differential by race. Black men and women continue to be at greater risk for divorce than are whites. Additionally, individuals in lower socioeconomic groups also have higher divorce rates than those in higher socioeconomic categories. There has been some modification of this general trend in the late 1970s, but these differences continue to be pronounced (Scanzoni & Scanzoni, 1981).

Table 1-11 exhibits the cumulative percent divorced for both first marriages and remarriages considered by their anniversary dates. Figure 1-8 reveals the expected duration of first marriage and the percentage of first marriages that eventually end in divorce. It also demonstrates the general proposition that the longer one remains married, the more likely it is that the marriage will remain stable over time. Both tables portray the cumulative effect that duration of marriage has on divorce rates, that is, decreasing likelihood.

One of the most commonly expressed concerns about the increasing divorce rate in the United States is that of its impact upon children. Over time, the percent of divorce decrees involving children has grown to include approximately 61% of all divorces as of 1968. The average number of children

Table 1-10. Comparison of Types of Divorce Rates, United States, 1920–1970

Year	Number of divorces	Cumulative % change	Divorces per 1000 total population	Cumulative % change	Divorces per 100 marriages performed	Cumulative % change	Divorces per 1000 married female population	Cumulative % change
1920	170,505	—	1.6	—	13.4	—	8.0	—
1930	195,961	14.9	1.6	0.0	17.4	29.9	7.5	6.2
1940	264,000	54.8	2.0	25.0	16.5	23.1	8.8	10.0
1950	385,144	125.9	2.6	62.5	23.0	71.6	10.3	28.8
1960	393,000	130.5	2.2	37.5	25.8	92.5	9.2	15.0
1970	708,000	319.3	3.5	118.8	32.8	144.8	14.9	82.5

Note. From U.S. Department of Health and Human Services (1978, pp. 23–24).

Table 1-11. Cumulative Percent Divorced, by Marriage Order and Anniversary, United States, 1975

Anniversary	First marriages (%)	Remarriages (%)
5th	16.3	23.6
10th	30.0	36.4
15th	37.4	42.7
25th	44.5	47.3
50th	47.3	48.9

Note. From U.S. Department of Health and Human Services (1980, p. 12).

per divorce from 1955 through 1978 has not changed substantially and was 1.0 child per divorce in 1977. This figure has obviously been affected by the declining birth rate; however, the total trend must be considered in terms of the general increase in divorce itself in the context of marital pool activity. A large portion of these children will be involved in remarriages and subsequent family arrangements, that is, stepfamilies or blended families. It is estimated

Fig. 1-8. Expected duration of first marriage and percentage of intact first marriages that will end in divorce (by duration of marriage, United States, 1975). From U.S. Department of Health and Human Services (1980, p. 11).

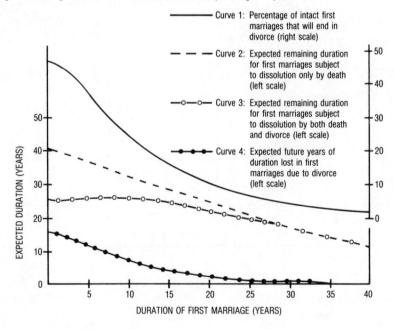

that stepfamilies make up 10% to 15% of all households in the United States (Espinoza & Newman, 1979). In 1978, it was estimated that 10% of all children under 18 were living with both a natural parent and a stepparent (Glick, 1980).

Any discussion of divorce in America must include several caveats. The first caveat is that divorce rates are considered generically in the category of total marital dissolutions. Table 1-1 revealed that historically the portion of the total marital dissolutions in the United States has remained stable over the past century. Currently death accounts for less and divorce accounts for more dissolved marriages than earlier. The second caveat has to do with the general impact of the liberalization of divorce laws upon the total divorce activity in the United States. Divorce law liberalization has reduced economic and time (required waiting periods) barriers and has made divorce accessible and realistic for a much broader range of the population. The divorce "gates" have opened and essentially a population "rush" has occurred. This backlog will eventually be processed through divorce courts and the divorce rates will not increase as rapidly as they have in the last two decades.

The increasing frequency of divorce in our society has led to an overall change in attitude. Rather than being viewed as the heinous act of marital disintegration, it is seen as a way of adjusting to an unpleasant interpersonal situation. No longer do individuals enter marriage with absolutely no thought of dissolution; the actress Sissy Spacek mentioned in *Parade Magazine* (July 1981) that she had placed the amount of the divorce filing fee in California in a bank account "in case it didn't work out." This attitude is not uncommon. Graham Spanier has summed up American attitudes about divorce succinctly:

> Divorce is a response to an unsuccessful marriage relationship in which the spouses reject each other; *they are usually not rejecting the idea of marriage or the family per se.* Thus, divorce is not so much a statement about the viability of married life or about family stability, but rather a realization of poor mate selection, lack of personal commitment, disenchantment with one's partner, or some other personal or social problem surrounding a particular relationship. Persons approaching divorce usually report that they are no longer in love, that they have grown apart, or that they do not get along with each other anymore. (1981, p. 61)

REMARRIAGE

Remarriage was not seriously considered as a phenomenon related to marriage and divorce until the 1960s and the 1970s when it became so prevalent that it could not be ignored. One of the most notable activities occurring during the past two to three decades is the substantial increase in the rate of remarriage at almost all age levels. Earlier in the century, remarriage was most commonly a phenomenon among widowed individuals. Figure 1-9 indicates the general activity of divorced men and women and widowed men and women for the period 1963–1969. Among all four groups, we see a substantial

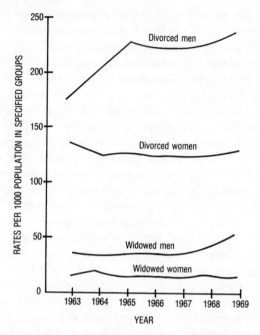

Fig. 1-9. Remarriage rates of widowed and divorced men and women (by marriage-registration area, 1963–1969). From U.S. Department of Health and Human Services (1973a).

but gradual rise in the 1960s, with divorced men being the most active and, as might be expected given the relative oversupply of the group, widowed women being the least active. Table 1-12 portrays current and more specific rates, namely remarriage rate by brides per 1000. We know that from 1960 to 1977 the proportion of increase of remarriage among brides is well over 200%. It is also noted in Table 1-12 that the median age at remarriage has begun to fall substantially both for men and women.

Table 1-12. Remarriage Rates and Median Age at Remarriage, 1960–1977

	1960	1965	1970	1977
Remarriage rate for brides per 1000	197	305	393	532
Median age at remarriage				
Men	n.a.	39.6	37.5	34.9
Women	n.a.	35.5	33.3	31.4

Note. From U.S. Department of Commerce (1981, p. 81).

As indicated in the earlier discussion about the number and proportion of children involved in divorce in America, an obvious concern is the impact of the number of children on a woman's chances for remarriage. Table 1-13 indicates the relative probabilities of remarriage considered by age at divorce, the number of children at divorce, and years since the divorce. The trend in this table, though not very strong, is that for women under 25, the more children she has, the more adversely her prospects for remarriage are affected. Further, the longer she has been divorced, the more likely she is to get remarried, whether or not she has children—so that if she has no children she has a 96% chance of remarrying within 20 years, but if she has three or more children she has a 90% chance of being remarried within 20 years. Surprisingly, this effect is reversed for women over the age of 35: The more children a woman in this category has, the greater are her chances of remarrying. Thus, a woman in this age group who has no children has a 44% chance of remarrying within 20 years, but if she has three or more children has an 82% chance of remarrying within this same time period. One possible interpretation of these figures is that a woman's chance of remarriage in these various age categories—with or without children—has more to do with men's marital agenda than with women's age or parental status. For example, young males might be less interested in marrying a woman with children, while men in older age groups might be very happy to have a ready-made family. The psychological health and overall happiness seems to be the same for remarried individuals as it is for those in first marriages.

Kingsley Davis sums up the remarriage situation in terms that resemble Spanier's comments on divorce:

> The significance of the brisk rate of remarriage is plain; it means that the American people do not have a high and rising rate of legal divorce and annulment because they're losing interest in marriage and a family. Rather, they have such a high rate because they desire a compatible and satisfactory family. Thus, despite a high legal divorce rate, a high proportion is married—higher than in any other industrial society. Americans expect a great deal out of the state of wedlock and when a particular marriage proves unsatisfactory, they seek to dissolve it and try again. (1972, p. 262)

MARITAL ATTITUDES AND STYLE

Peoples' attitudes and behavior are inextricably connected. A prevalent and routine behavior pattern leads to beliefs about that particular behavior, and if for any reason the behavior pattern changes, the individual is put in a state of cognitive dissonance that usually is resolved by attitudinal change. Once attitudes about the behavior have changed, even more diverse, behavioral alternatives are permitted, and this in turn can lead to further attitudinal changes. An excellent example is divorce. Earlier in the century, when

Table 1-13. *Cumulative Probabilities of Remarriage and Median Durations to Remarriage, by Age at Divorce and Number of Children at Divorce (White Women without Postmarital Births)*

	Woman's age at divorce											
	<25			25–34			35–44			45+		
	Children			Children			Children			Children		
Years since divorce	0	1–2	3+	0	1–2	3+	0	1–2	3+	0	1–2	3+
1	.2300	.2370	.2038	.1734	.2020	.1824	.0988	.1375	.0932	.0274	.0213	.0678
5	.7753	.7228	.6639	.5603	.5714	.5681	.2991	.3980	.3609	.1423	.2102	.2139
10	.9178	.8376	.7919	.7164	.7086	.7201	.3600	.5266	.5956	.2085	.2275	.3081
15	.9397	.8934	.8514	.7677	.7887	.7799	.4056	.5877	.7661	—[b]	—	—
20	.9601	.9325	.9009	.8130	.8230	.8131	.4453	.6052	.8264	—	—	—
Median duration to remarriage (years)[a]	2.12	2.20	2.65	2.61	2.73	2.49	3.68	3.04	4.72	—	—	—

Note. From Koo and Suchindran (1980, p. 506).

[a]Life table median duration is the duration at which 50% of women had remarried, among those who had remarried in 20 years.

[b]Insufficient number of cases.

34

divorce rates were extremely low, it was seen as a highly deviant behavior and the prevalent attitude about it was negative and unaccepting. For whatever reasons divorce rates have increased, the result has been a shifting attitude about divorce, so that today it is certainly not deviant and might even be thought acceptable, even expectable in some circles. As this attitude toward divorce has shifted, the emotional and legal impediments to it have gradually fallen away, making the behavior easier. This same kind of attitudinal and behavioral interrelationship can be seen in many aspects of marriage, including role differentiation, child care, alternative relationship styles, and remarriage itself. Since marital styles and attitudes can best be considered feedback circuits, we will make no attempt to assign a causal relationship from one to the other, since we are unaware of evidence which points in either direction.

Experimentation in relationship styles is an old tradition in America as manifested by the Oneida Community marital experiments, the Mormon church, and various utopian community experiments. What seems to have changed in recent years is not the experimentation itself, but the broad acceptance of experimental relationship styles by large numbers of individuals not associated with particular religious or philosophical orientations. Table 1-14 shows the tremendous diversity of marital styles and the gradually declining traditional forms as manifested by a change from 1970 to 1978 in the percentage of married couples with children under 18—the figures being respectively 40.3% in 1970 and 32.4% in 1978. During the same time span, there has been a 6% increase in the total number of nonfamily households and a 2% increase in the number of one-parent families. Table 1-15 is a breakdown of the kinds of nontraditional family living arrangements in the United States as of 1975. James Ramey (1978) points to four major societal changes that have promoted experimental family forms. First, the demographic revolution, as manifested by the increased longevity of people,

Table 1-14. Composition of U.S. Households in the 1970s

Type of household	1970 (%)	1975 (%)	1978 (%)
Family households			
Married couple—no children under 18	30.3	30.6	29.9
Married couple—children under 18	40.3	35.4	32.4
One parent with children under 18	5.3	6.7	7.3
Other (e.g., extended)	5.6	5.4	5.3
Total	81.2	78.1	74.9
Nonfamily households			
Persons living alone	17.1	19.6	22.0
Other	1.7	2.3	3.1
Total	18.8	21.9	25.1

Note. From Macklin (1980, p. 905).

Table 1-15. Distribution of Adults in American Households, 1975

Heading single-parent families	16%
Other single, widowed, separated, or divorced persons	21
Living in child-free or post-child-rearing marriages	23
Living in dual-breadwinner nuclear families	16
Living in single-breadwinner nuclear families	13
Living in no-breadwinner nuclear families	1
Living in extended families	6
Living in experimental families or cohabiting	4
	100%

Note. From Ramey (1978, p. 1).

implies an increasing concern with personal happiness because of the greater duration of life to be lived. Second, the biological revolution, as manifested by the development of good contraception in this century, has permitted greater sexual freedom. Third, the economic revolution has provided for greater personal security and thus a refocusing of attention on individual happiness. And finally, the communication revolution implies the more pervasive spread of new and innovative ideas among larger groups of individuals.

The most accurate generalization about current marital style in the United States is that there is none. Traditional single-breadwinner nuclear families only account for 13% of all households. Thus, the stereotypic family, as frequently portrayed on television, is a fringe minority and, in fact, dual-breadwinner families (those with working mothers and fathers) account for 16% of the total households of the country (and seem to have different living arrangements and marital norms). A far more frequent marital style in this country (23%) are those couples without children, either because they have never had them or because the children have left home. In fact, single-parent families (16%) are more common than traditional nuclear ones. Clearly, any discussion of marital dynamics must be specific to the particular type and circumstances of the household under consideration. Needless to say, this disqualifies a tremendous amount of the currently available literature on marriage.

Stepfamilies, often known as blended families, have been estimated to comprise 10–15% of all households in the United States and 10% of all children under eighteen were reported to be living in this kind of arrangement (Espinoza & Newman, 1979). Research on blended families seems to suggest that, as compared with "intact families," stepfathers have a more negative image of themselves as fathers, are more passive in exercising control, and unlike their wives and stepchildren, rate their stepchildren's happiness as lower than do natural parents. However, a study of the long-term effects of stepfather families on stepchildren, using national probability data, has found new differences between individuals raised in stepfather families and in intact families (Wilson, Zurcher, McAdams, & Curtis, 1975). Duberman (1975), in a study of 88 blended families, found that "stepmothers are less likely than stepfathers to establish good relationships with younger stepchildren," and that, in regard to the quality of the family relationship, "45% of the families [were] high in family integration, 34% moderate, and 21% low."

Binuclear or joint-custody arrangements seems to be increasing in this country with a considerable amount of support from the judicial system. This kind of arrangement facilitates parent–child contact even in the postdivorce period, but is predicated on the previous marital partners successful resolution of conflicts that often had led to the divorce in the first place. Steinman found that, although most parents found joint custody satisfactory despite the difficulties, the children's experience of it was somewhat more mixed (Steinman, 1981). Most children did not like the fact that their parents were divorced at all, but seemed to value the joint custody arrangement in that they had access to both their parents. One-third of these children felt burdened by such demands of coparenting as the transfer back and forth between homes with all its attendant difficulty. Steinman concludes that the most crucial components for joint custody appear to be the attitudes, values, and behaviors of the parents in a situation. Thus, as expected, cooperative, respectful parents seem to have children who adjusted better to coparenting than those who are still conflicted. Interestingly, Ahrons (1981) found that, in a sample of 108 divorced parents (54 pairs), 85% maintained direct contact with each other (usually by telephone at least once a month), and that the more contact that the couple maintained, the more often they were supportive and cooperative with each other. One major pitfall in coparenting found in the study is that both males and females perceive themselves to be underbenefited in that they saw themselves as more supportive and accommodating than their partner. This perception can easily flare into conflict as each partner tries to achieve what they feel to be a fair level of involvement, which traditionally and stereotypically differs between men and women. Finally, therapists must reexamine their attitudes toward postmarital relationships since, traditionally, they have been viewed as efforts by one or the other partner to hang on to the marital relationship. Although this is certainly true in some cases, clearly it is impossible for coparenting to occur unless individuals are willing to continue relating to each other at some level and, as this study has shown, the more contact the couple has, the more smoothly the coparental relationship is apt to proceed.

In our concept of the family, we are coming to the position today in which we must not only consider grandmothers and grandfathers, uncles, aunts, and cousins, but now also coparents and stepparents as legitimate members of the extended family. This is a radically new idea about which there is a dearth of objective information, norms, and guidelines.

One of the most conspicuous changes in marital style that has occurred over the last 20 years and that is a direct result of these new emerging relationship patterns is the increasing negotiation of marital role differentiation, which now occurs routinely. Traditionally, marital roles were clear-cut and were accepted as part of the marital package. If they were unacceptable, one simply did not marry. Not so today. Given the diversity of relationship patterns, including single-parent homes, coparenting relationships, dual-career families, and various other experimental family forms, nogotiating who does what is an expected part of the marital adjustment. In his Stimulus Value Role Conceptualization of Courtship, Bernard Murstein (1971) has stressed the importance of this role negotiation during the courtship phase. While the courtship period has traditionally been a testing time to discover whether one genuinely enjoys one's partner, finds him or her sufficiently attractive, supportive, and companionable, Murstein is suggesting that one must also examine the partners' role expectations as a valid criterion to decide whether or not to proceed with marriage.

DISCUSSION AND CONCLUSIONS

Our discussion will focus on three areas: first, a recapitulation of the important demographic trends in marriage; second, attitudinal and marital style trends, and finally, a discussion of some ways to synthesize the information which we have presented.

Demographic Trends

Demographically, marriage appears to be a highly active state involving "movement" of at least 19% of the population at any given time between the states of singlehood to marriage, marriage to divorce, divorce to remarriage. Despite this high activity level, it is quite clear that marriage as a goal is still highly desirable by most people, as manifested by opinion surveys as well as the remarriage rate. Although this marital pool activity seems on the surface to be something quite new, and in fact the increasing divorce rate is rather new, we suspect that it represents a fairly old and rather constant phenomenon, as demonstrated by the stability of the overall marital dissolution rate for the last 100 years. Further, the vitality of marriage is manifested by the consistency with which people have married over the last 100 years (a fairly constant 92% for women). What does appear to be changing is the overall age of Americans; with larger numbers of older individuals, there will be many more people in the empty-nest stage of the life cycle (increasing from virtually no years 100 years ago to as many as an expected 30 years for people born in 1945). This aging of the population affects not only this later phase of marriage but also the size of the pool of marriageable single individuals, since the birthrate is declining and their numbers are gradually diminishing relative to other groups in the population. One of the most important implications is that single individuals will have to look beyond other singles for marital partners and this helps to explain the dramatic rise in single individuals marrying divorcees (19.5%). Whether it is cause or effect, this change is directly related to the attitudes regarding divorce, in that today divorce is seen as much more socially acceptable than in the past. This facilitates the direction that demographic changes have been taking.

Our review supports the notion that most individuals in this country wish to form intimate and usually marital relationships rather than to remain single. This can be seen by the consistency of the percentage of single individuals over the last 100 years—approximately 9%—and also by the relatively small number of divorced individuals who choose to remain divorced as a stable life-style (approximately 8% of all divorcees). In fact, 80% of individuals who have been divorced for the first time will remarry, and 90% of individuals divorced the second time will remarry.

What appears to be changing most is the relative caution with which people marry and the tendency toward smaller family size. There has been an increased latency to marriage, an increased delay from marriage to the birth of the first child, and a decrease in the number of children that a couple have, although the percentage of women having children has remained constant for 100 years. Thus, the desire of most people to have children seems to have remained consistent; only the number of children per family seems to have changed. Interestingly, this is congruent with the European pattern of marriage, in which people tend to marry at an older age and have fewer children. It appears that the people of this country are becoming concerned more with the quality of life than with quantitative issues. This may help to account for such trends as fewer children per marriage.

Finally, one of the most important trends in recent years has been toward the heterogeneity of marital style as manifested by the rapidly declining number of individuals who are in a single-breadwinner nuclear family—considered the traditional mode of marriage by most Americans. This change has probably been due primarily to the increased numbers of women in the work force, which places pressure on men to participate more in homemaking activities and parenting.

Aside from that, a major demographic shift has been the increasing divorce rate, which, in general, is closely associated with children in that there is an average of one child per divorce. This statistic, coupled with the 41% remarriage rate by divorcees overall, leads to the conclusion that the number of blended families is rapidly increasing and, in fact, becoming a major phenomenon. This will have tremendous therapeutic implications for family therapists, marital therapists, and child psychiatrists, who will be forced, in rapidly increasing numbers, to deal with this new family form.

Attitudinal and Marital Style Trends

In general, attitudinal shifts can best be characterized as an acceptance of known demographic changes that have already occurred and are in process. This means an increased acceptance of divorce and remarriage, an increased acceptance of the concept of the blended family and other kinds of post-divorce relationships, a decreased feeling of centrality of children in a relationship, and a decreased willingness to remain in a dysfunctional or nonfulfilling marital relationship. Although the ideal of being married and relating intimately to another person remains extremely viable, there has been a significant attitudinal shift in that people are willing to change partners or marital styles in order to make this institution work for them. Further, the attitude of "the sanctity of marriage" seems to be diminishing significantly; rather, marriage is viewed as a means to an end. It appears that there is a massive change in attitudes about working women. From its prior status as a relatively innovative, risky endeavor, it is now viewed as the norm. It is extremely interesting that the ratio of single versus married women in the work force has virtually reversed itself over the last 100 years. Today married women compose the large majority (62%) of women in the labor force. Interestingly, both conservatives and liberals have come to gradually accept women in the work force along with the implication that increased day-care facilities are necessary. The only point of contention appears to be who should provide those facilities: industry, government or the individual. Thus, attitudes toward child rearing are also undergoing rather massive changes in that more utilization of day-care facilities is being seen and accepted as a necessity.

Another significant attitudinal shift in this country has been the "normalization" of sexuality, especially premarital sexuality. As people come to accept the sexuality of women, and to see premarital sexual relations as acceptable and even as expected, there is less motivation to marry for sexual reasons than has been true in the past. Further, the increased degree of sexual experience by men and women early in their lives also implies greater understanding of and utilization of contraception which may have important implications with respect to family size. One of the ramifications of this changing attitude regarding sexuality is the demystification of sex, so that sexual gratification becomes an expected part of a relationship for both men and women rather than for men only.

One of the more important areas of attitudinal change has to do with child custody. In the last century, children were typically viewed as the father's property and were thus awarded to fathers in divorce cases. This attitude changed during the earlier part of this century when children's rights became an important concern. It was felt that interests could best be served by maternal care during the formative years. Interestingly, there seems to be a shift in custody awards today, still consistent with the concept of the child's best interest, but not necessarily always interpreted to mean sole maternal custody. Instead, today there are an increasing number of joint-custody awards and it is predicted that this trend will continue in the future. Clearly, this represents a major shift in legal thinking as well as in cultural norms, with the result that, today, fathers as well as mothers are seen as required parent figures and capable of meeting important needs of children.

Another attitude shift with direct legal implications is the movement away from an adversarial concept of divorce and toward the idea of "no fault" divorce. Previously, a divorce always implied that one partner or the other had failed in his or her marital duties in some specific fashion, for example, infidelity, alcoholism, physical abuse, and so on. Today it is recognized that marital dissolution is often the result of both partners' actions and the law is increasingly providing for that contingency with radically new divorce procedures. An important implication of the recent judicial change in the way divorce is viewed is that it seems to reflect an increased nonbinary view of marriage; that is, the attitude that one either is married or isn't married and that no other state, in essence, exists. Rather, today, the attitude is more toward functionality, with a wide variety of family and marital configurations.

A major attitudinal change seen in younger Americans, especially those of the baby boom generation, is that of "security" rather than of deprivation and/or tragedy. Individuals raised in the depression era viewed life as difficult, security as tenuous and by no means taken for granted, and had as their goal simple acquisition of goods and services to provide for the possibility of tragic circumstances. Those born since World War II, that is, during the baby boom, have been blessed with a very long period of stable economic conditions and, in general, a high degree of affluence. Thus, they have never experienced the personal deprivation that their parents had and so this does not figure strongly in their thinking about life. Their orientation is more toward quality of life than quantitative issues. From this point of view it can be seen that the stability and continuity of marriage, while terribly crucial in a depression-era family, would be less so in an environment of affluence, since there is higher potential for economic security whether or not one is married. This is especially true in the thinking of women though not necessarily in the reality of their employment capability.

Marriage today is carried out differently than in previous times and the cause-and-effect relationship between marital style and demographic trend is unclear. Undoubtedly, there is some feedback system in which personal style changes lead to attitudinal ones, which, in turn, are reflected in behavior as measured by statistical data. These demographic shifts are then picked up, communicated, and serve to alter attitudes, which, in turn, lead to personal style changes. Be that as it may, today there are a number of important differences in marriage from previous times. Probably the most conspicuous difference is the increased number of years that couples will spend in the empty nest period. Thus, the focus and orientation of people in these years will necessarily change from child-rearing issues to personal fulfillment ones, such as the quality of the relationship, professional and work achievement, leisure time, and personal comfort. Some manifestations of this trend can be seen in retirement communities in Florida and the Southwest where the major orientation is toward the development of high-quality life-styles for people in this age group.

Such issues as power and decision making, which traditionally had been highly structured (the woman makes decisions regarding home and children while the man makes economic and external decisions), today are distributed more reciprocally in the typical dual-breadwinner home. Even though the couple can easily agree that equal breadwinners should have equal decision-making power, the change from traditional to a more modern distribution of power is not easy, since expectations of marital roles seem to have changed more slowly than actual marital behaviors (House & Garden Louis Harris Study, 1981; Waite, 1981). This tends to lead to a high degree of marital strain in some "liberated" marriages even though there is complete rational agreement on these issues (Scanzoni & Scanzoni, 1981).

The prevalence of dual-career families and attempts to improve each partner's breadwinning capacity seems to have led to a reevaluation of child-care arrangements in the United States, as indicated by an enormous rise in the use of day-care facilities. Further, the obvious end-of-day fatigue that each partner feels can have a dramatic effect on parenting practices and can certainly encourage the use of television as a soporific for children. Further, this fatigue also promotes the increased consumption of all commodities and techniques that make housework easier and less burdensome, such as pre-pared foods, high-technology kitchen and laundry room machinery. The increasing consumption and utilization of these items can have a dramatic and deleterious effect on the competence with which each marital partner fulfills his or her negotiated marital role. This topic will be covered in greater detail below.

Recent changes in the way that people court each other seems to have had an impact on marriage itself. As sexual attitudes and behaviors have become liberalized, a majority of Americans are sexually experienced before marriage—almost always with their marital partner. Sex per se, as a motivation for marriage, has diminished substantially. Many individuals have lived in a cohabitation arrangement prior to marriage, either with their subsequent marital partner or with someone else, so they have at least some idea of what an intimate living arrangement is like prior to a full commitment to it. What is new, therefore, is that individuals entering marriage are not doing so as blindly as they did in the past and thus are more apt to be selective about not only their partner but also the style in which the relationship proceeds. Regardless of these changes, however, it is clear that Americans are overwhelmingly committed to the institution of marriage in general and to intimate relationships of any kind. The only issue appears to be how to go about making these relationships work well and finding a suitable partner.

Role Competence

The confluence of a variety of social factors seem to have led to an increased prevalence of role incompetence in marital relationships. "Role incompetence," as used here, is defined as a lack of mastery of whatever role function an individual has agreed to perform, regardless of what that particular function happens to be. Thus, the various chores and jobs that are necessary to make any relationship work are carried out at a mediocre level of competence, so that neither partner can take pride in the process or in a product of his or her efforts. One can see the possibility that this mediocre performance of actual incompetence can lead either or both partners to a sense of failure, hopelessness, and demoralization in the functioning of the relationship and that this feeling, in turn, can further diminish the motivation to achieve role mastery.

It appears that there are a variety of reasons for role incompetence. First, male and female role functions are more ambiguous today than they were in the past. Because more role issues are negotiable, there is more role negotiation, which, if not clearly resolved, can lead to uncertainty as to who is supposed to do what. This uncertainty in itself can lead to devaluation of the other person's effort, as well as mixed motivation about one's own functioning. The conflict between work outside the home and homemaking that women face today is a particularly poignant example of the kind of dilemma that can result. The simple factor of physical exhaustion can lead to role assumption by default; that is, if a woman is simply too tired at the end of the day to perform a particular function, her partner might assume it only to help her out and not really be motivated to master it.

Marital dysfunction itself can lead to sabotaging of either or both partners' efforts at role competency. Probably the best example is a power struggle between marital partners, in which one partner, using a zero-sum game assumption, deliberately sabotages the other's efforts, in an attempt to "win." A common offshoot of a couple's power difficulties is diminished communication, which leads to difficulties in decision making especially as regards to role functions, support of the other person's efforts, and problem perception. The kinds of marital dysfunctions that can contribute to role dysfunction are too numerous to elaborate here, but can be an important factor in role incompetence.

A third major cause of role incompetence is time encroachment. With the majority of women working, with the increased utilization of day-care facilities and school, and with the amount of television viewing in which the American public engages, there is remarkably little time left over for people to gain mastery of home and family role functions. Even the marketing thrust of media advertisements is often in a direction contrary to valuing homemaking functions and, in fact, frequently devalues them. Most advertisements view the making of meals, the cleaning of the house, and similar jobs as disagreeable chores and major burdens, rather than as opportunities for the family to interact with each other or to improve the aesthetic condition of the household.

The tremendous mobility of the American people is probably another factor contributing to role incompetence in that, by frequent moves, some families never get beyond the level of the mere establishment of the household. It requires a certain length of time in a stable homelife before true role mastery has the potential for development.

The impact of television as a factor in time encroachment cannot be underestimated. The average American watches television for at least 6 hours a day, and, the lower the socioeconomic group, the more hours of television per day watched (U.S. Department of Commerce, 1981). Television not only promotes a number of attitudes that are contrary to the development of role competency, but, as a medium, keeps people from talking, playing games and sports, and generally interacting. Families spend hours watching television in parallel with each other, but not interacting except when they bump into each other in the kitchen to get a snack during advertisements. Television characters are often unrealistic models—their problems are often dealt with superficially; the mechanisms by which resolution is reached, as portrayed on television, are extremely superficial, mysterious or coincidental. Chronic television use can seriously interfere with attention span. In this country, we are rapidly developing a 12-minute mentality—the time between advertisements. More important than the period between advertisements is the frequency of scene changes on most television programs. If one watches a television program carefully, one will notice that there is usually a change of scene or a change of camera angle at least every 15 to 30 seconds. This, of course, is designed to enhance the novelty and interest of the program. However, viewers become so accustomed to this constantly novel and interesting presentation that any serious discussion that does not have this built-in variety quickly becomes boring and the viewer inattentive. An excellent example of this phenomenon is that dialogue between individuals especially on educational television seems boring, not because of the topic but because of viewer expectation of novelty. As a participant on a number of television talk shows, one of the authors has been continually frustrated by his inability to discuss not only his point but also some of its implications and ramifications due to the incredible pressure that talk-show hosts feel to keep the program "moving along" and the very short periods of time available between advertisements or changes of topic.

There are a number of attitudes prevalent in America today that contribute to role incompetence. Generally speaking, there is a massive devaluation of the homemaking function (General Mills American Family Report, 1981). Thus, any man or woman who is interested in developing role mastery in the home is fighting against the tide of public opinion that this endeavor has little value. Linked to this devaluation is the assumption that most of life's major satisfaction will occur outside the home, thus leading to the idea that housework should be finished as quickly as possible to leave time for other, more important things. This desire for "personal freedom" leads to a diminution of such rituals in the home as sitting down for dinner at six o'clock, eating breakfast together, and so on. The unfortunate part of this diminution of home rituals is that it also diminishes the number of opportunities for the family to get together as a unit and interact, whether it be for pleasure or problem solving. Finally, there tends to be a product orientation rather than a process orientation; that is, people tend to be more interested in having dinner than in the process of making it, would rather have a clean house than be engaged in the process of cleaning it. This product orientation in essence removes the positive aspects of doing the chores, since it is no longer seen as an opportunity for interaction, but rather an odious task endured. The ramifications on early-childhood education should be conspicuous; that is, if the child is used to seeing dinner put on the table, he or she may never learn how it got there. A process orientation, while not only focusing on the dinner itself, teaches children how to go about getting dinner on the table. Needless to say, all products designed to ease the burdens of the homemaker, such as prepared foods, high-technology kitchens and cleaning items, serve to deprive children of the opportunity to learn how these functions are carried out in a more elementary fashion.

Finally, one of the most important and saddest causes for the increasing level of role incompetence is our nonutilization of available resources for the development of role competence—elderly people. It is well known that America has been a "youth-oriented society" that either directly or indirectly devalues the knowledge and experience of the elderly; yet clearly these individuals are our best resource for learning how to do the various role functions that make relationships work. They may not be sophisticated in high-technology housekeeping, but probably are more adept at making cherry pies, negotiating differences of opinion, simply talking with each other, and entertaining each other with conversation. A particularly poignant example struck one of the authors when he was watching the evening news with his 90-year-old grandmother-in-law: Each time a particularly interesting news item was presented, the grandmother would turn to him and begin a rather interesting and intelligent discussion of that particular item, which she viewed as a stimulus for conversation and interchange. Unfortunately, the news did not pause long enough for them to explore each item, but continued rattling on instead, so that each of her attempts at making conversation was frustrated as the author, going under the assumption that they would discuss any or all of it later, continued to watch the news so as "not to miss anything." The result was that grandmother was frustrated because the author was fairly unresponsive to her efforts at conversation, and the author was frustrated because grandmother kept interrupting the news. The conclusion we must reach is that rather than talking about role competence as an absolute, it is probably a relative phenomenon. Clearly, the author was much more competent at watching television news, because he continued to remain silent and wait for the next item, but was incompetent when it came to sustaining a conversation with grandmother. On the other hand, the grandmother was extremely incompetent when it came to watching the news, because she kept interrupting but was clearly much more competent as the initiator of interesting conversation.

So far, by role competence issues, we have indicated such things as the common household chores of cleaning, cooking, decorating, and child care, and entertainment and family rituals such as birthdays, holidays and even certain weekend activities. However, role competence goes beyond these concrete activities and includes such things as conversational ability, the ability to entertain children on car trips, decision and negotiating skills, communication skills, and so on. Although we are choosing to focus primarily on the more concrete aspects of role functioning, in all probability our comments could be generalized to the broader ones as well (Bossard & Bolle, 1956; Davey & Paolucci, 1980).

CASE EXAMPLE

A 31-year-old-female physician presented herself for the treatment of sexual dysfunction. She gave a history of having been married to her husband, also a physician aged 31, for 7 years. Their early marital adjustment was excellent, and their sexual functioning was fine in all spheres. Approximately 4 years ago, the patient's husband became physically sick and the couple had to stop their sexual relationship for a number of weeks. After he recovered from his illness, the patient noted an inability to achieve orgasm even though she was capable of becoming sexually aroused to a certain extent. This problem tended to increase in severity so that by the time she presented herself to the therapist, she was neither sexually aroused nor orgasmic with her husband although capable of arousal and orgasm by masturbation.

The patient claimed that her marital relationship was excellent, that she and her husband got along well, had not major areas of conflict, and enjoyed their very busy life-style a great deal. Upon further questioning, the patient revealed that she was feeling quite lonely and that her husband did not pay enough attention to her, although he tended to include her in group activities such as parties and outings. Neither the patient nor the husband had major psychopathology although each of them could be considered mildly obsessive as a personality style. The patient did admit to being mildly sexually inhibited, although she had been capable of a fulfilling sexual life with her husband prior to the onset of her dysfunction.

The patient's husband was superficially cooperative and was concerned about his wife's dysfunction. In fact, he had tried numerous sex therapy maneuvers based on the work of Masters and Johnsons to help her, but to no avail. The couple complained that they were both extremely busy because of their medical work loads, and frequently missed each other since they had call schedules that did not always coincide. It seemed to the therapist that the first order of business, before any other specific therapeutic activity could take place, was to create a situation in which the couple merely spent time with each other. To that end, the couple was asked to spend 3 or 4 hours together alone, doing nothing but being together. The first week the couple was able to spend 2 hours in each other's presence, but that frequency of contact deteriorated over the next several weeks so that the couple was literally unable to spend any substantial period of time together except when they went to bed exhausted at the end of their day's work. After 6 weeks in therapy, the couple left the area to establish medical practices elsewhere and were lost to therapy. The most important point of this case presentation is that probably the "pathologic" factor involved in the sexual dysfunction and marital disability was the lack of time that the couple spent together and, by implication, the low priority that each of them put on spending personal time with each other. This low priority was reflected by the woman's feelings of resentment toward her husband, which manifested itself by her sexual dysfunction. This case highlights the importance of time spent together as part of maintaining role competency.

Children

Children, as a factor in relationships, have been alluded to on a number of occasions in this chapter. The major trends relate to the truncation of the child-rearing years, the delay in couples having children, and the diminution in numbers of children per couple, although the total of couples having children remains relatively constant. Probably the most outstanding trend has to do with children and divorce. As the number of children per couple diminishes and the divorce rate increases, the number of children involved in divorces will increase. In fact, this can be seen in Table 1-16 in which 6.4 divorces per 1000 children were seen in 1953 and 11.9 divorces occurred per 1000 children in 1969 (U.S. Department of Commerce, 1981). Looking at this 16-year change from a child's point of view can be quite confusing. However, from a parent's point of view the number of children per divorce has remained constant. Thus in 1970, 1.22 children were involved in each divorce and in 1977 1.03 children were involved per divorce (U.S. Department of Commerce, 1981). This figure can be somewhat misleading, however, because the number of children per family is decreasing while the

Table 1-16. *Number of Children per 1000 Divorces and Mean Number per Divorce*

	1960	1970	1977
Children involved per 1000 divorces	463	870	1095
Mean number of children involved per divorce	1.18	1.22	1.00

Note. From U.S. Department of Commerce (1981, p. 81).

overall divorce rate is increasing. In summary, the most conspicuous conclusion that can be drawn from this information is that, because more and more children are involved in the divorce and remarriage process, they probably do not represent the same impediment to marital dissolution that they once did.

Children are frequently involved in remarriage as well as divorce and the impact that children have on a woman's likelihood to remarry has already been discussed and portrayed in Table 1-13.

The folk wisdom of bygone days and the comments that clinicians frequently hear from patients, that children are a major consideration in keeping a marriage together, seems to be changing in tenor from an absolute interdiction to divorce to a problem needing to be solved by two parents who plan to separate anyhow. This naturally leads to alternative postdivorce relationships including coparenting, blended families, and other parenting styles to which we have already alluded.

A Closer Look at the Baby Boom Generation

The focus of our consideration so far has been general in the sense that population and cohort data have been used as the basis for our comments. The advantage of this approach is that it gives an excellent overall perspective of demographic changes in our country, but lacks the specificity that is sometimes most interesting to clinicians. For that reason, it may be well to examine at least one specific segment of the population for the purpose of gaining some limited insight into that group. The study we have chosen to examine was commissioned by *House and Garden Magazine* (1981) and implemented by the Louis Harris and Associates Company. It involved "in person" interviews with 1218 men and women from August 14 to September 8, 1980, of college-educated men and women aged 25-40 with household incomes of $20,000 or more. This standing sample consists of 31% in the 25-29 age bracket, 36% between 30-35, 33% between 35-40. Fifty-one percent of the sample were women, while 49% were men. Fifty-two percent had some college training, 26% were college graduates, 22% held post-graduate degrees. Sixty-six percent of the sample were married with children, another 14% were married without children, 12% were single but living with someone other than a mate, 4% were single but living with a mate, and 4% were single and living alone.

The ten major areas of investigation will be briefly reviewed.

1. This generation feels that it is unique (53%) and generally enjoying a better quality of human experience than their parents did (58%). While many feel they have had better education (35%), feel freer to express themselves (29%), and have greater material comfort (27%), they also feel that they face disadvantages that other generations escaped, such as pressing social problems (52%), material and economic problems (41%), and problems of the outside world (41%). In general, they feel they are better off than their parents in that they can establish the way of life they want (51%), have their own home (37%), and achieve a satisfactory balance between work and leisure (35%). However, they feel that they are worse off than their parents in terms of their political leadership (45%) and in the kind of world their children will inherit (39%).

2. The second major finding was that this generation feels that owning one's own home is still one of life's most important goals (82%) and 80% had already achieved that. Interestingly, when thinking in terms of the considerations that people use in deciding on a home, 94% felt that the quality of the home was most important, while 84% felt that a reasonable mortgage rate was, and 80% thought that the efficiency of heating was an important consideration. Regardless of what this generation wishes it had, the reality of what they do have is also quite interesting in that 92% of the sample believed that their present house or apartment provided them with a sense of peace of mind, 91% found their home "a place you can really call home," and 84% felt that their home was a "proper environment in which to raise children."

3. The area of investigation related to sex-role differentiation revealed that there is much more sharing in work and homemaking activities than has been true in the past. As a group, this generation is committed to work, in that 95% of the males and 72% of the females are employed. Interestingly, only 31% of all the households maintain the traditional mold of a one full-time breadwinner family. This commitment to work has ramifications with respect to in-home relationships. Only 50% of the sample designated the man as the head of the household, and 39% said that it was shared between man and woman. That the family life is shared is shown by the following statistics: Seventy-two percent of the sample report sharing the decision about how money is to be spent, 75% report sharing decision making regarding shopping for furniture and major household items, 52% regarding decorating decisions, 53% regarding yard or garden work, 47% painting and minor repairs, 45%

cleaning the house, 37% paying the bills and keeping the records, 37% shopping for food, and 35% cooking. Fully 45% of the men in this sample are involved in cooking on a regular basis.

4. Of this generation which emphasizes the importance of relationships, this group listed as its three top priorities having good, close friends (46%), having a good family life (41%), and having a strong and close relationship with somebody else (32%); they prefer to spend free time with their friends or loved ones (53%). What satisfies them most in their personal lives is the quality of the relationships with their mate (70%) and having a comfortable circle of family and friends (53%).

5. This generation is committed to having children. Seventy-two percent had one or more and feel that 2.33% children is the ideal number. However, children don't seem to have the same importance in the relationships as they once did. Forty-three percent of the sample felt that children were not vital to the family structure—a position supported primarily by the women (47%) and younger people aged 25–59 (49%). Women (43%) more than men felt that a home could be fulfilling even when children were not present. The strong career motivation that has already been mentioned seems to affect these peoples' attitude toward child rearing. Fifty-six percent of them do not believe that having children is a full-time responsibility or that it is wrong for both parents to work, and 55% feel that working parents can give children the attention they deserve. These parents seem to be somewhat more permissive in that 40% believe in raising their children in a less strict atmosphere, but also 34% believe in spending more time with them and being more involved in their activities. Parents include children in household responsibilities to a large extent. Ninety-three percent include children in cleaning-up activities, 46% in kitchen and meal duties, and 41% in outdoor work.

6. The sixth major finding had to do with the importance of time as a factor in daily life. Forty-five percent of the sample felt that they had less time at present than they did previously to accomplish the things they wanted to do, and 42% reported having too little time to do the things they would like. When asked to describe the source of the time pressure, equal numbers felt that the bind was due to job, housework, or leisure activities. As one might expect, women complained more often about job and household time difficulties, while men about the lack of leisure time. Regardless of the time bind, 59% of the sample still do not view the pace of life as being too fast and 30% believe that the pace is about as they would like it. However, if given an extra 10 hours a week, 53% said that they would spend it with their families and friends, 39% would devote it to cultural activities, and 24% to personal ones.

7. The baby boom generation is extremely sophisticated when it comes to money matters and seems to be coping moderately well with inflation by cutting back on luxuries (67%). They are particularly interested in invest-

ments in the future, and often (75%) view their home as their prime investment, while 36% own stock, 31% savings certificates, 27% art and antiques, and 21% own shares in money funds. Most interesting, however, is that 92% of the families agree that "people place too much emphasis on material possessions these days, and not enough on the other things that make life worthwhile." This group is most interested in the quality of their material possessions rather than simply the quantity of them.

8. The eighth major finding of the study is that this generation is extremely concerned about the energy problem (64%) acknowledging that it is "very serious." Virtually all of the samples (98%) are positive about improving the situation by turning off their lights at home, closing doors, lowering heating in certain rooms, and 88% say they have been actively engaging in these kinds of activities. Surprisingly, 71% of the sample claimed that they are actually driving 55 miles an hour or less in their cars.

9. This generation is oriented toward aesthetics and has, as a major motivation, the improvement of their homes to make them more attractive and pleasing. Eighty-four percent served as their own interior decorators and 62% felt deeply concerned with the aesthetics of their home. At present, 83% say they have enough living space in their home, but 40% say they have too little storage, and that this is generally due (76%) to the lack of storage space not to the existing space being cluttered up.

10. Finally, it appears that the top priority for the baby boom generation is "the human condition, both for themselves and those they care about." As has already been said, they are extremely concerned about having a good family, close friend, and group relationships, and a pleasant home, and are quite willing to achieve this by commuting longer distances. Seventy-seven percent would prefer to shop personally in stores where they can see the items themselves and 79% want to handle more of the chores around the house themselves rather than buying services. Surprisingly, 74% prefer to prepare meals at home and 85% would prefer to cook meals themselves using the healthful ingredients they select. More important than any other specific activity, the baby boom generation feels (61%) that they would rather spend time with family and friends.

This in-depth look at one particular sample of upper middle class Americans seems to confirm some of the points already elaborated, such as the strong interest in relationships and the commitment to marriage as an institution even though it may not work out with a particular partner. Further, it supports the notion that while children are desirable they are less important as a factor in maintaining relationships and appear to be less of a central focus to the parent's lives. The increased degree to which men and women share careers leads to an increased amount of sharing of household responsibilities and the centrality of homes in this generation's view of its own satisfaction is striking. Finally, what stands out most conspicuously is that this generation is concerned with the *quality* of goods, services, relationships—rather than with mere quantity, a marked contrast to their parent's generation and a theme that is likely to continue in the future. This study strongly supports the notion that marriage as an institution, and family life are strong, highly valued, and in little danger of deterioration although certainly open to negotiation and readjustment even if that means divorce and remarriage.

Dual-career families are rapidly increasing in numbers, which means that men have had to participate in household activities and parenting out of necessity and seem to be statistically doing so at a high level. Interestingly, women are often somewhat reluctant to accept men's participation in household chores, but in our view this is a transient shift that should soon diminish in frequency. As a consequence of both partners sustaining employment, there is an increased reliance on ancillary day-care facilities and a different style of relating to children when they are with the family. Both partners come home from work tired and have to share child-care and household activities more evenly, and generally have less time in which to do so. A natural consequence of this increased participation by both partners in work and household duties is the relative increase in negotiated marital structure versus prescribed structure. Previously role differentiation in marriage was prescribed by social custom and involved males working outside and females working in the household. As this structure is diminishing, there is increased need for both marital partners to negotiate who does what in the household and in the workplace. Thus, the entire mechanism of decision making and power structure in marital relationships is changed. Decisions now are more frequently made by negotiation and power is more symmetrical than in the past.

The increased divorce rate and the self-sufficiency of women has led to a much more tentative view of marriage. Most people today do not necessarily assume that marriage is as permanent as they once did. This caution may, to a certain extent, be self-protective but also may be a consequence of increased independence on the part of women. Regardless of why it occurred, an important implication of the assumption of possible marital change is on the limit of tolerance that individuals have toward marital disharmony. It appears today that people are much less tolerant of poor and especially nonintimate marital relationships than they once were and are unwilling to tolerate that state for as long as they once did. Thus, the threshold to divorce appears to be lowering. An important clinical implication of this is that we would expect, in the years to come, fewer and fewer women will present themselves to mental health facilities with the "trapped wife syndrome," since their ability to be self-sufficient and their willingness to change should increase.

It is entirely possible that, as one might predict using Seligman's (1975) notion of learned helplessness, as people feel more in control of their marital situation, they will suffer from less reactive forms of depression.

An important trend that has been alluded to earlier is that of shifting role competence. Today older, more traditional forms of role competency are gradually being lost as the household is becoming increasingly mechanized and as people use television as a form of family anesthesia. In general, people hold more of a "product orientation" than a process one, so that they are more concerned with having dinner than making it. The result is that traditional household activities, which provided a context for family members to relate to each other, are gradually diminishing, and, when people do relate, they seem to do so in parallel, as when they are watching television. Television appears to play an increasingly important role in family relationships today, a fact that is of considerable concern to family and marital therapists. The impact of television on families appears primarily due to "default" in that it creates reduced circumstances for communication. It tends, in general, to put people in a relatively passive mental state, acts as a very convenient soporific for children, diminishes family communication, and tends to portray rather unrealistic images of family life—not only in terms of how people relate to each other, but also in terms of socioeconomic and ethnic considerations.

Americans have always been a highly mobile people and large population migrations are nothing new in this country. Thus, the recent "move to the Sunbelt" is only one of many social migrations that we have seen in the course of our history. Therefore, attempts at using geographic mobility patterns as explanatory constructs in family and social change appear not to stand up very well. An important implication of this finding is that Americans appear to be quite able to reestablish themselves in new geographic locations, develop support groups, and integrate themselves into new social circumstances. Even so, we suspect that this social integration might occur in a slightly different pattern today than in previous times. It seems possible that this integration may occur today more by the active efforts on the part of individuals (i.e., achieved integration) than merely as a result of their socioeconomic or marital status (prescribed integration). This means that, in previous times, there tended to be more stratification of social groups based on marital status, so that single young marrieds with babies, older marrieds, people with older children, and other such groups would stratify and relate to each other easily in a somewhat prescribed fashion. Today there appears to be more heterogeneity of social networks.

Many of these conclusions can be seen in Table 1-17, which compares traditional with contemporary marriage.

Toward a Synthesis

In the book *Change* Watzlawick, Weakland, and Fisch (1974) describe two different kinds of change, "one that occurs within a given system which itself remains unchanged," and "one whose occurrence changes the system itself."

Table 1-17. Comparison of Traditional with Contemporary Marriage

Traditional marriage	Contemporary trends
1. "Prescribed" structure	"Negotiated" structure
2. "Product" orientation	"Process" and outcome orientation
3. Decision by "status" (i.e., by head of household)	Decision by negotiation
4. Complementary power structure; influence within power structure	Symmetrical power structure; therefore, increased power struggles of *peer* nature *about* power structure
5. Binary concept of marriage and divorce; first choice (i.e., marriage) "sanctified; change per se seen as bad	Systemic view of marriage and divorce, seeking relatedness with best possible partner *even if change necessary*
6. Assumption of permanence	Assumption of adaptation and change
7. Assumption of tragedy; "hoarding mentality"	Assumption of security; "quality mentality"
8. Conferred integration into reference groups	Achieved integration into reference groups
9. Role modeling more narrow and personal	Role modeling more based on "expertise" via mass media

These kinds of changes are designated "first order" and "second order" changes respectively. First order changes are those from state to state within a system and can be exemplified by changes that occur in a machine. For example, the rotating flywheel in an automobile engine changes its position as it goes around, but always does so on its own designated circular path. There is no doubt that the location of a spot on the flywheel changes as the wheel goes around, and if one wished to quantify the amount of change that had occurred, one could do so by measuring the revolutions per minute of the spot on the flywheel. Extending this analogy to marriage, if one agrees that it is the job of the parent to take care of the children, then any change in how the parents take care of the children is considered a first order change, since the system itself is not undergoing any transformation.

Second order change is a change of the system itself, from transformation to transformation. So, for example, if one took the flywheel from the automobile and used that as a weight in a new machine, that would be a transformation from one machine (or system) to a new one. In marriage if one took the view that parents should not take care of their children at all, it would be a second order change of parenting attitudes.

Second order change is a change of the system itself, from transformation to transformation. So, for example, if one took the flywheel from the automobile and used that as a weight in a new machine, that would be a transformation from one machine (or system) to a new one. In marriage if one took the view that parents should not take care of their children at all, it would be a second order change of parenting attitudes.

Second order changes occur frequently in life whenever some unpredictable events alter the system, especially one involving rules of personal or social behavior. When this happens, an interesting process ensues, that is that second order changes become first order. Going back to our machine analogy, originally first order changes of the flywheel could be conceptualized as different locations on its circular path. Second order changes could be viewed as using the flywheel in different machines. Finally, once one has the idea firmly established that the flywheel can be used for many different purposes, then that idea, which used to be a second order change, now becomes first order because any of its new applications can be seen as the abstraction: a flywheel can be used for many purposes in building machines. The particular purpose to which the flywheel is put is only a first order change within that more general abstraction. The point to be emphasized is that as second order changes continue, people abstract the change process per se so that eventually second order changes become first order. Another way of saying this is that the more one gains perspective in a situation or in a system, the more that changes can be seen to be first order.

We have embarked on this digression in order to explain what we feel has happened socially and culturally to the marital system over the last 20 to 30 years. In earlier times, marriage was viewed as a "final state" or a "haven in a heartless world" with the implication that it was probably permanent and that any change from the state of marriage would represent a major change in a person's system and therefore could be considered a second order change. Even within the state of marriage, first order changes were extremely limited to only the different ways of performing the highly prescribed traditional sex roles that men and women believed in. Changing those sex-role activities themselves at that time was certainly as important second order change. As those changes in marital style became more accepted, they have gradually become first order changes, so that today we accept negotiated marital style and dual-breadwinner families with equanimity, but older individuals can still remember the turmoil they felt as they experienced these changes as second order. The state of marriage itself seems to have undergone the same process. Previously it was felt that divorce represented a major second order change for an individual, but as divorce has become increasingly prevalent and accepted, it is seen more as a change within the marital system (which now includes marriage, divorce, and remarriage) than of the system itself. This broadened view of the marital process means that many marital changes that used to be considered second order changes are now increasingly thought to be first order changes. What is interesting is how consistently people in our country still cling to the idea of relatedness and marriage as a desirable goal. Clearly the institution or system itself is very strong and healthy; all that seems to have changed is our perspective on that system. As our perspective broadens, we view "minor" changes such as remarriage as merely first order changes, but the system itself remains relatively unchanged. In the past there has generally not been a systemic view of marriage, divorce, and remarriage such as we are seeing today, and this is most conspicuous in the absence of any numerical data that reflect changes in the system itself. We have made a first attempt at a systemic view of marriage in Figure 1-5, which reveals that 19% of the population is in marital movement at any given time. It would be extremely interesting to examine how this percentage has changed in the past and how it will change in the future. Further, we feel it is vitally important to develop other quantitative indexes of the overall marital system.

Generally speaking, first order changes are not associated with nearly as much stress as are second order changes. Second order changes are much less predictable, are unsystematic, illogical and capricious. Thus an important implication of our view of marriage is that as marital movement is increasingly seen as first order change, the degree of stress associated with these changes should diminish in the future. We anticipate that our children and grandchildren should experience much less stress as they experience first order marital changes than individuals in our generation, many of whom still experience these changes as second order, will feel.

Seligman (1975), in his book *Helplessness*, describes the effect of uncontrollability and unpredictability on individuals, relating uncontrollability to the onset of depression and unpredictability to the onset of anxiety. It is our feeling that his work is of great importance in understanding some of the marital shifts that are occurring in our country today. As women become more self-sufficient in the workplace and at home, and as their power within relationships increases, we would expect that there will be an increased tendency for sexual differentiation to be negotiable and, hence, less prescribed than in the past. This has its good as well as its bad sides. On the good side, women should feel an increasing sense of control over their environment, which, at least in theory, should diminish the likelihood that they will become depressed as a result of relationship factors. On the other hand, as marital roles become more negotiated and less certain, we would expect that both men and women will experience less predictability in the relationship and hence more anxiety. An important implication that Seligman refers to is that animals in general search for "safety signals," that is, factors in their environment that are highly predictable and signal that nothing particularly bad will happen. Following this line of reasoning, we would guess that people in increasingly ambiguous relationships will also seek safety signals, which may take the form of increased television abuse and outside unconflicted activities and relationships that can be relied on in spite of their status in the marital system. A broader perspective of the marital system is another important safety signal for the individual since a broadened view of the marital status implies that the system itself is constant and stable although one's particular situation within the system might change. In conclusion, marriage in the past has been seen as a stable institution to which individuals could retreat from the stresses and changes of the world. Changes in marital status were viewed as second order changes and associated with high degrees of stress. What has changed and probably will continue to change in the future is that transitions in marital status will seem less significant and more of a first order variety that will be associated with much less stress. While the institution of marriage itself seems to be viable, the conduct of marriage is becoming increasingly negotiable and consequently ambiguous, and this situation, we expect, will be associated with higher degrees of anxiety and lower degrees of depression. It is important for mental health professionals to discard the view that marriage, divorce, and remarriage are isolated states and instead adopt a more systemic view of these conditions as processes within a larger marital system that has remained robust for at least 100 years in this country.

REFERENCES

Ahrons, C. R. The continuing co-parental relationship between divorced spouses. *American Journal of Orthopsychiatry*, 1981, *51*, 415–428.

Bane, M. *Here to stay*. New York: Basic Books, 1976.

Bengston, V., & DeTerre, E. Aging and family relations. *Marriage and Family Review*, 1980, *3* (1/2), 51–76.

Bossard, J. H. S., & Bolle, E. S. *Rituals in family living*. Philadelphia: University of Pennsylvania Press, 1956.

Clayton, R. R., & Bokemeier, J. L. Premarital sex in the seventies. *Journal of Marriage and the Family*, 1980, *42*, 759–775.

Davey, A. J., & Paolucci, B. Family interaction: a study of shared times and activities. *Family Relations*, January 1980, *29*, 43–49.

Davis, K. The American family in relation to demographic change. In C. F. Westoff & R. Parke (Eds.), *Demographic and social aspects of population growth* (Vol. 1). Washington, D.C.: U.S. Government Printing Office, 1972.

Demos, J. *A little commonwealth*. New York: Oxford University Press, 1970.

Demos, J. The American family in past time. In A. Skolnick & J. Skolnick (Eds.), *Family in transition* (2nd ed.). Boston: Little, Brown, 1977.

Duberman, K. *The reconstituted family*. Chicago: Nelson Hall, 1975.

Espinoza, R., & Newman, Y. *Step-parenting* (DHEW #ADM 78-579). Washington, D.C.: U.S. Government Printing Office, 1979.

General Mills American Family Report, 1980–1981. *Families at work*. New York: Louis Harris Associates, 1981.

Glick, P. Remarriage: Some recent changes and variations. *Journal of Family Issues*, December 1980, *1*, 455–469.

Goode, W. *World revolution and family patterns*. New York: Free Press, 1963.

Gordon, M. *The American family: Past, present and future*. New York: Random House, 1978.

House and Garden Louis Harris Study. *How the baby boom generation is living.* New York: Conde Nast, 1981.

Koo, H. P., & Suchindran, C. M. Effects of children on women's remarriage prospects. *Journal of Family Issues*, December 1980, *1*, 497–575.

Laslett, P. Societal development and aging. In R. Binstock & E. Shanas (Eds.), *Handbook of aging and the social sciences.* New York: Van Nostrand Reinhold, 1976.

Macklin, E. D. Nontraditional family forms. *Journal of Marriage and the Family*, November 1980, *42*(4), 905–922.

McCall, M. M. Courtship and social exchange. In B. Farber (Ed.), *Kinship and family organization.* New York: Wiley, 1966.

Melville, K. *Marriage and family today* (2nd. ed.). New York: Random House, 1980.

Murstein, B. (Ed.). *Theories of attraction and love.* New York: Springer, 1971.

Murstein, B. Mate selection in the 1970's. *Journal of Marriage and the Family*, November 1980, *42*, 777–791.

Parade Magazine. July 19, 1981.

Ramey, J. Experimental family forms—the family of the future. *Marriage and Family Review*, 1978, *1*(1), 1–7.

Scanzoni, J., & Scanzoni, L. *Men, women and change* (2nd. ed.). New York: McGraw-Hill, 1981.

Seligman, M. *Helplessness: On depression, development and death.* San Francisco: W. H. Freeman, 1975.

Shorter, E. *The making of the modern family*, New York: Basic Books, 1977.

Siegel, J. S. Demographic aspects of aging and the older population in the United States. *Current Population Reports, Special Studies.* Washington, D.C.: United States Bureau of the Census, 1976.

Spanier, G. The changing profile of the American family. *Journal of Family Practice*, 1981, *13*(1), 61–69.

Steinman, S. The experience of children in joint custody arrangement. *American Journal of Orthopsychiatry*, July 1981, *51*, 403–414.

Toffler, A. *Future shock.* New York: Random House, 1970.

United Nations, Department of International Economic and Social Affairs. *Demographic Yearbook*, Issue 10. New York: United Nations, 1960.

United Nations, Department of International Economic and Social Affairs. *Demographic Yearbook*, Issue 20. New York: United Nations, 1970.

United Nations, Department of International Economic and Social Affairs. *Demographic Yearbook*, Issue 30. New York: United Nations, 1980.

United States Department of Commerce, Bureau of the Census. *Statistical Abstract of the United States—1980.* Washington, D.C.: U.S. Government Printing Office, 1981.

United States Department of Health and Human Services. Remarriages. *Vital and Health Statistics*, December 1973, Series 21(25), 1–27. (a)

United States Department of Health and Human Services. Teenagers: Marriages, divorces, parenthood and morality. *Vital and Health Statistics*, August 1973, Series 21(23), 2–42. (b).

United States Department of Health and Human Services. *Vital and Health Statistics*, March 1978, Series 21 (29), 23–24.

United States Department of Health and Human Services. Divorces: Analysis of changes. *Vital and Health Statistics*, March 1978, Series 21 (29), 1–81.

United States Department of Health and Human Services. National estimates of marital dissolution and survivorship. *Vital and Health Statistics*, November 1980, Series 3(19), 1–31.

Waite, L. J. U.S. Women at work. *Population Bulletin*, May 1981, *36*, 1–43.

Watzlawick, P., Weakland, J., & Fisch, R. *Change.* New York: W. W. Norton, 1974.

White House Conference on Families—Listening to America's Families. *Action for the 80's: The report to the President, Congress, and families of the nation.* Washington, D.C.: White House Conference of Families, 1980.

Wilson, K. L., Zurcher, L. S., McAdams, D. C., & Curtis, R. L. Stepfathers and stepchildren: an exploratory analysis from two national surveys. *Journal of Marriage and the Family*, August 1975, *37*, 526–539.

Yankelovich, D. *New roles: Searching for self-fulfillment in a world turned upside down.* New York: Random House, 1981.

Zelnick, M., & Kentner, J. F. Sexual and contraceptive experience of young unmarried women in the U.S., 1976 and 1971. *Family Planning Perspectives*, March 1977, *9*, 55–71.

Zelnick, M., & Kentner, J. F. Sexuality, contraception and pregnancy among unwed females in the U.S. In C. F. Westoff & R. Parke (Eds.), *Demographic and social aspects of population growth* (Vol. 1). Washington, D.C.: U.S. Government Printing Office, 1972.

CHAPTER TWO

Marriage and Health

THOMAS J. STEWART
OLIVER BJORKSTEN

Strikingly different mortality and morbidity patterns for marital statuses have been consistently observed over the past four decades. The variations are clearest in regard to mortality: mortality rates are lower for (1) married versus unmarried people; (2) married people with children versus married without children; and (3) nonmarried household heads versus those who have no other household members. These differences can also be seen in selected morbidity indicators, such as hospitalization rates, occurrence of acute and chronic conditions, and utilization of physicians.

Thus, from the standpoint of health these data give new significance to the assessment of marital happiness and stability as well as the overall institution of marriage. Marital status can be one very important variable in dealing with patients who have stress-related illnesses and also in the assessment of an individual's overall risk of developing illness.

The purpose of this chapter is to review and discuss mortality and morbidity data in relation to the various marital statuses; to examine the nature of the relationship demonstrated by the data; to project the impact of changing circumstances in relationships on general health care; and, finally, to suggest possible clinical implications of these data.

In one of the major recent analyses of national mortality, a report published by the National Center for Health Statistics revealed that during the decades of the 1940s through the 1960s the same pattern emerged (Carter & Glick, 1970). Although there were variations both by sex and by race. In considering mortality data by marital status it was clear that those who were

Thomas J. Stewart. Department of Family Medicine, Medical University of South Carolina, Charleston, South Carolina.

Oliver Bjorksten. Department of Psychiatry and Behavioral Sciences, Medical University of South Carolina, Charleston, South Carolina.

currently married were in a favored position. In any comparison by marital status, married men and women compared more favorable with those who were single, widowed, or divorced. Figure 2-1 is an adaptation of the data from that report and indicates that distinct mortality differences still exist between men and women and between white and nonwhite Americans. However, the third distinction in the table is very clear: for both men and women, those who were married have more favorable mortality figures than those in other categories. This trend is not as distinct for women as it is for men. The data for the 1959–1961 period indicate that unmarried men had death rates that were generally 135% higher than those of married men, whereas unmarried women had death rates that averaged only 67% higher than those for married women. In a sense, being married was twice as advantageous for men as it was for women.

Married men tend to have different causes of death than single, widowed, or divorced men. Similar variations are seen for women, although the categories are somewhat different. Tables 2-1 and 2-2 indicate causes of death for white and nonwhite men and white and nonwhite women for the period 1959–1961. Table 2-1 shows that death rates from nearly all causes are lower for married than for unmarried persons. White married men and women have in common four of the five leading causes of death: coronary heart disease and other myocardial degeneration, motor vehicle accidents, cancer of the digestive system, and vascular lesions or stroke. Unmarried men are considered to have excessively high rates in such categories as: tuberculosis, cirrhosis of the liver, accidental fire or explosion, pneumonia, homicide, accidental falls, suicide, syphilis, and motor vehicle accidents. Table 2-1 also demonstrates

Fig. 2-1. Death rate per 100,000 persons 15–64 years old, by marital status, standardized for age, United States, 1959–1961. From Carter and Glick (1970, p. 341).

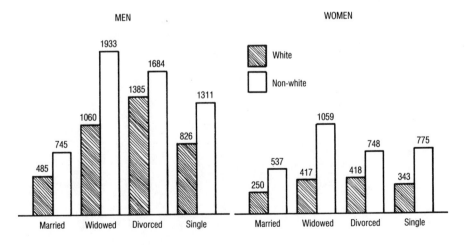

Table 2-1. *Average Annual Death Rates per 100,000 Men 15-64 Years Old from Selected Causes, by Marital Status and Color, Standardized for Age, United States, 1959-1961*

Cause of death	Death rate for white men				Death rate for non-white men			
	Single	Married	Widowed	Divorced	Single	Married	Widowed	Divorced
Coronary disease and other myocardial (heart) degeneration	237	176	275	362	231	142	328	298
Motor vehicle accidents	54	35	142	128	62	43	103	81
Cancer of respiratory system	32	28	43	65	44	29	56	75
Cancer of digestive organs	38	27	39	48	62	42	90	88
Vascular lesions (stroke)	42	24	46	58	105	73	176	132
Suicide	32	17	92	73	16	10	41	21
Cancer of lymph glands and of blood-making tissue	13	12	11	16	13	11	15	18
Cirrhosis of liver	31	11	48	79	40	12	39	53
Rheumatic fever (heart)	14	10	21	19	14	8	16	19
Hypertensive heart disease	16	8	16	20	68	49	106	90
Pneumonia	31	6	25	44	68	22	78	69
Diabetes mellitus	13	6	12	17	18	11	22	22
Homicide	7	4	16	30	79	51	152	129
Chronic nephritis	7	4	7	7	18	11	26	21
Accidental falls	12	4	11	23	19	7	23	19
Tuberculosis, all forms	17	3	18	30	50	15	62	54
Cancer of prostate gland	3	3	3	4	7	8	15	12
Accidental fire or explosion	6	2	18	16	15	5	24	16
Syphilis	2	1	2	4	10	6	14	15

Note. From Carter and Glick (1970, p. 345).

Table 2-2. *Average Annual Death Rates per 100,000 Women 15–64 Years Old from Selected Causes, by Marital Status and Color, Standardized for Age, United States, 1959–1961*

Cause of death	Death rate for white women				Death rate for non-white women			
	Single	Married	Widowed	Divorced	Single	Married	Widowed	Divorced
Coronary disease and other myocardial (heart) degeneration	51	44	67	62	112	83	165	113
Cancer of breast	29	21	21	23	26	19	28	27
Cancer of digestive organs	24	20	24	23	33	25	41	35
Vascular lesions (stroke)	23	19	31	28	89	72	147	82
Motor vehicle accidents	11	11	47	35	13	10	25	20
Rheumatic fever (heart)	14	10	15	13	14	8	12	13
Cancer of lymph glands and of blood-making tissue	9	8	9	8	7	7	9	13
Hypertensive heart disease	8	7	10	9	63	50	97	56
Cancer of cervix	4	7	13	18	22	17	34	27
Diabetes mellitus	7	7	11	8	24	20	36	22
Cirrhosis of liver	6	7	15	20	20	9	23	20
Cancer of ovary	12	7	8	8	8	6	9	8
Suicide	8	6	12	21	3	3	6	5
Cancer of respiratory system	5	5	6	7	6	5	9	10
Pneumonia	15	4	7	10	11	12	31	22
Chronic nephritis	4	3	5	4	14	11	16	11
Homicide	1	2	7	9	17	14	33	25
Tuberculosis, all forms	5	2	4	5	24	8	19	16
Accidental fire or explosion	2	1	6	4	6	4	11	5

Note. From Carter and Glick, (1970, p. 345).

that divorced men have the highest mortality rates for almost any category for white men, the only exception being that widowed white men have higher rates of suicide and deaths from accidental fires and explosions. Among nonwhite men this pattern is not as pronounced, and in many instances widowed nonwhite men are the group with highest mortality rates. For both white and nonwhite women the widowed category has the highest rates in most instances. It is interesting that for white women a notable exception is that divorced women are more likely to commit suicide than any of the other three groups.

Kobrin and Hendershot (1977) conducted a more recent analysis of mortality data using figures from the period 1966–1968 and found essentially the same pattern. However, they include a refinement that considered death rates not only by marital status but also by the presence or absence of children. Table 2-3 indicates that the patterns observed from the earlier data held. In Table 2-3, the ratio of deaths for nonmarried to married men in the age range 35–44 is a remarkably high 3:12. The ratios for females, though not as pronounced, are in the same direction indicating the favorable position of married compared with nonmarried individuals. Table 2-4 elaborates on the picture of mortality among the married by distinguishing between the presence and absence of children. From this table, we can see that those who have children under the age of 18 and living in the household are in a more favorable position than those who do not. It is interesting to note that for women the pattern is stronger than for men. It is also noted that these differentials decline with progression into higher age categories. Indeed, married men over 55 with children in the home tend to have a higher mortality rate than do men without children in the household.

The findings reported by Kobrin and Hendershot are also supported by an analysis conducted by Veevers (1973) that looked at the presence or

Table 2-3. Deaths per 100,000 by Age, According to Sex and Marital Status, United States, 1966–1968

Martial status and sex	Age			
	35–44	45–54	55–64	65–74
Male				
Married	323	814	2042	4456
Nonmarried	1008	2125	4276	5944
Ratio, nonmarried to married	3.12	2.61	2.09	1.33
Female				
Married	212	464	910	2379
Nonmarried	408	757	1278	2595
Ratio, nonmarried to married	1.92	1.63	1.40	1.09

Note. From Kobrin and Hendershot (1977, p. 741).

Table 2-4. *Deaths per 100,000 by Age, According to*
Sex and Presence of Children, Married Persons,
United States, 1966–1968

Presence of children and sex	Age		
	35–44	45–54	55–64
Male			
Children under 18 present	268	695	2118
Children under 18 absent	557	892	1930
Ratio, absent to present	2.1	1.3	.9
Female			
Children under 18 present	160	331	777[a]
Children under 18 absent	378	523	567
Ratio, absent to present	2.4	1.6	1.1
Ratio, female to male ratios	1.1	1.2	1.2

Note. From Kobrin and Hendershot (1977, p. 742).
[a] <100 deaths.

absence of children in terms of suicide rates. Veevers found that not only were there distinctions in national suicide rates between the married and the unmarried but that there were also distinctions among the married with or without children. Individuals having children currently in the household had substantially lower suicide rates than did those married individuals without children living in the household.

The few available widowhood studies provide a further refinement when considering mortality and marital status. In three earlier studies made in Great Britain in the 1950s and 1960s it was noted that widows and widowers were at substantially greater risk for mortality and selected morbidity indicators than were comparable married individuals (Cox & Ford, 1964; Parkes, Benjamin, & Fitzgerald, 1969; Young, Benjamin, & Wallis, 1963). A recent study of widow and widowers in a rural area in Maryland has elaborated on the earlier findings in Great Britain to indicate that for women in this sample the relationship was not quite as strong as it was for men, that is, mortality rates were significantly higher for widowed males than for females (Helsing, Szklo, & Comstock, 1981). Their findings indicated that the death of a husband had little effect on women's mortality rates. The earlier British studies had indicated that the death of a surviving widow or widower was much more likely to follow in a very brief time after the death of their spouse. However, this finding was not observed in the Maryland study, which indicated that rates for the surviving widow or widower did not accelerate in the months immediately following the death of the spouse. Widowhood was seen in this study as being much more difficult for men. The overall mortality rate was 26% higher for widowers than for married men, with a comparable 3.8% difference in the rates between widows and married women. For those widowers in the age range 55–64, the mortality rate was almost 60% higher than for married men in the same age group.

One of the most interesting findings of the Maryland study was the role of remarriage following widowhood and its impact upon the mortality rates. Helsing *et al.* (1981) determined that mortality rates among widowed males who remarried were very much lower than among those who did not remarry. But the same relationship was not observed among widowed females who did or did not remarry. The researchers were so impressed by the role of remarriage that they commented:

> If, for example, it can be demonstrated that the association between remarriage and reduced mortality is a causal one, changes in social security and income tax laws to encourage marriage of the widowed would be justified as public health measures. (Helsing *et al.*, 1981, p. 808)

MORBIDITY, UTILIZATION OF HEALTH SERVICES, AND INSTITUTIONALIZATION

The picture of marital status, morbidity, utilization of services, and hospitalizations is not quite as clear-cut as the one of mortality. Using data from the 1960s, Ortmeyer (1974) provided the following synopsis in his analysis of the data in these general areas. The findings were based upon self-reported data about health conditions obtained during the 1960 census and data from the Annual Health Interview Survey of the National Center for Health Statistics.

Synopsis of Self-Reported Health Conditions

- Divorced or separated persons show age-adjusted estimates equaling or exceeding those for any other marital status for:
  1. Men and women reporting one or more chronic conditions;
  2. Men and women merely limited in their usual work (partly disabled);
  3. Women suffering all types of injuries;
  4. Average annual number of physician visits per user, by men and by women;
  5. Average annual number of visits to dentists per user by men.
- Widowed persons show age-adjusted estimates equaling or exceeding those for any other marital status for:
  1. Women reporting one or more chronic conditions;
  2. Men and women entirely unable to do their usual work;
  3. Women merely limited in their usual work;
  4. Women limited only in nonwork activities;
  5. Proportion of men with one or more hospital stays;

6. Average number of days in hospital in one year for male and female users;

7. Average annual number of visits to dentists by female users.

- Married persons show age-adjusted estimates equal to or less than any other marital status for:

1. Males and females entirely unable to do their usual work;
2. Males merely limited in usual work;
3. Females injured at locations other than places of work and home;
4. Average number of hospital days annually for hospitalized males and females;
5. Average annual number of physician (or of dentist) visits by males with at least one such visit.

- Single (never-married) persons show age-adjusted estimates equal to or less than any other marital status for:

1. Males and females reporting one or more chronic conditions;
2. Females merely limited in usual work;
3. Males and females limited only in nonwork activities;
4. Females with any of four types of injury;
5. Males and females injured by moving motor vehicles, injured at work, and injured at home;
6. Proportions of males and of females hospitalized during a year;
7. Proportions of males and of females using physicians' services during a year;
8. Proportions of females using dentists' services during year.

- Lowest proportions with no reported chronic conditions or activity limitations were estimated for divorced or separated males and for either widowed or divorced or separated females.

- Lowest proportions reporting any type of injury for males were estimated for the widowed.

- Fewest annual physicians visits per user among females were estimated for the widowed.

- Lowest proportions of users of dentists' services were estimated for widowed males for divorced or separated females.

- The most limited insurance coverages, both for hospital and surgical expenses, were estimated for divorced or separated males and females.

Verbrugge (1979) utilized both 1960 and 1970 census data as well as the Health Interview Survey to provide a more recent portrait. She found that divorced and separated individuals had the worst health status, with highest rates of acute conditions, of chronic conditions that limit social activity, and of disability for health problems. Widowed people rank next in terms of health status, followed by single people. Overall, married people reflected the healthiest profile, having low rates of chronic limitation and disability. The hospital stays of married people tended to be short. Single people had the highest rates of residence in health-care institutions and married individuals had the lowest rates. Table 2-5 is adapted from Verbrugge and indicates differences on selected indicators for morbidity, disability, utilization of health services, and hospitalization rates.

PROFILES FOR VARIOUS MARRIAGE STATUS CATEGORIES

Divorced and Separated People

Divorced and separated people appear least healthy of all marital groups. They have the highest rates of acute and limiting chronic conditions. Health-examination data show them second only to widowed people in prevalence of chronic conditions. They suffer the most partial work disability and ranked second in complete work disability. When ill or injured, divorced and

Table 2-5. Marital Differentials in Health

	Age-adjusted rates[a]		
	High	Intermediate	Low
Acute conditions			
Incidence rates	Sep, D	(W, S, M)	
Chronic conditions			
Prevalence rates (health exam, survey)	W	D, Sep, M	S
Short-term disability			
Restricted activity rates (all conditions)	Sep	W, D	M, S
Restricted activity rates (acute conditions)	Sep	D, W, M	S
Bed disability rates (acute)	Sep	D, W, M	S
Work-loss rates (acute)	D/Sep	W, M	S
Restricted activity days per acute condition	Sep	D, W, M	S
Bed disability days per acute condition	Sep	D, W	M, S
Long-term disability			
Limiting chronic condition	Sep	D, W, S	M
Major-activity limitation	Sep	D, W, S	M
Partial work disability	D/Sep	W, S	M
Complete work disability	W	D/Sep, S	M
Duration of work disability	S	(D/Sep, W, M)	
Utilization of health services			
Physician visits per year	Sep, D, W	M	M
Dental visits per year, and any visit in past year	S	M	FM
Any hospital stay in past year	Sep, D, W	M	S
Hospital discharge rates	Sep, D	W, M	S
Length of hospital stay	Sep	D, W, S	M
Institutionalization			
Health institution rates	S	D, Sep, W	M

Note. From Verbrugge (1979, p. 280).

[a]M, married; S, single; D, divorced; Sep, separated; W, widowed; D/Sep, divorced and separated together; FM, formerly married. Marital categories are ranked in descending order in each column. Parentheses indicate that rates for the categories are essentially the same.

separated people take the most disability days per condition particularly for injuries. They have the highest average physician utilization rates and the longest hospital stays. Unfortunately, they are also the group most likely not to have health insurance coverage.

Widowed

Widowed people rank second overall for health problems. Although not bothered much by key conditions, they have the highest prevalence rates of chronic illnesses and generally are more limited by them. They have the highest percentage in complete work disability and rank second for partial work disability. Short-term disability per condition is intermediate, but physician and hospital utilization are almost as high as for divorced and separated people. The average length of stay for hospital episodes is intermediate.

Singles

The profile for single people is especially interesting. Noninstitutionalized single people are unremarkable for acute conditions (with the exception of high injury rates for males). The rates of limiting chronic conditions and work disabling conditions are rather low. They also have among the lowest prevalence rates for many chronic conditions. They take the least time off for health problems and have the lowest utilization of physician and hospital services. On the other hand, institutionalization rates for single people are very high and they enter institutions (both psychiatric and general) at relatively young ages. Single people report more physical impairments and paralysis.

Married

Married people appear to be the healthiest marital group. They have rather low rates of acute conditions and the lowest rates of limiting chronic conditions and work-disabling conditions. Complete work disability tends to be recent for men. Married people have intermediate chronic prevalence rates, but conditions seldom restrict their social involvement.

ATTEMPTS TO EXPLAIN DIFFERENCES IN MORBIDITY AND MORTALITY BY MARITAL STATUS

At present, the relationship of marital status to health is not clearly understood and the relationship seems somewhat complex. It does appear that the group at highest risk are those who are separated and divorced as opposed to people who have never been married at all, thus suggesting that the transition from marriage to singlehood is a key factor as opposed to the status of singlehood itself. On the other hand, the strikingly low morbidity and mortality of married groups as compared with that of single individuals suggests that there is something about the state of marriage itself that is beneficial to overall health status. It appears that the key issue is to understand what it is about marriage that protects individuals from illness, and what it is about separation or divorce that hurts an individual's status.

The two most prominent hypotheses that have been developed to explain the differences between the health of married and unmarried individuals are the selection and protection hypotheses. The essence of the selection hypothesis is captured in a brief quote from Carter and Glick:

> The process of selection in marriage tends, no doubt, to leave persons with ill health—in other words, poor mortality risks—among the unmarried. Moreover, it may also leave among the unmarried those who are prone to take more chances that endanger their lives than married persons would ordinarily take in their jobs and in their recreation, because they have no spouse and probably no children to protect, or because they are so inclined by temperament or long standing habit. On the other hand, unmarried persons may be overly careful about their health or conduct to the point of withdrawal from the usual forms of sociable contact where potential marital partners ordinarily meet. (1970, p. 344)

The selection hypothesis indicates that healthier people get into marriage in the first place and remain married.

The protection hypothesis, on the other hand, describes a favored set of circumstances that protect the married individual. These can include a broad range of protective factors: regular diet, the availability of another individual to diagnose and treat small illnesses and allow the individual to enter the sick role, the availability of regular human contact, and other factors. Basically, the protection hypothesis indicates that marital status is one of numerous indicators of social integration into a community or society. The protective function of marriage relative to health was recognized as early as the nineteenth century by Emile Durkheim (1951) in his classic study of suicide rates in Europe. He indicated that marital status was one of the most important contributors and proposed the notion of the protective status of marriage. In a recent formulation, Antonovsky (1979) indicated that marital status is one of the most important social ties that contributed to one's general feeling that the world is coherent and predictable (a state important in reducing the serious consequences of stress).

Interestingly, there are studies that tend to support both arguments. Carter and Glick (1970) seem to favor a selection hypothesis in their analysis of mortality and morbidity data. Verbrugge's study pointed to protection and selection processes at work for married people:

Compared to other marital groups, married people probably have relatively safe lifestyles and are less vulnerable to injuries and chronic ailments. The conditions they do develop may be less incapacitating. Married people are also selected for good health: severely ill or disabled people have trouble marrying at all and married people who incur a severe health problem may become divorced or separated. But several illness behavior factors act to make married people appear healthy: they often have responsibilities to dependents and cannot afford to lose work time or completely abandon a job when ill. Despite health problems, they continue to work and thus report low limitation and work disability. Dependents may be able to give home care to ill family members, which shortens hospital stays. Both family responsibilities and opportunities for home care deter entry of married persons into institutions. Those who do enter them tend to be very ill and are likely to stay permanently. This prospect may encourage an "outside" spouse to file for divorce or legal separation, which acts to deflate institution resident rates for married people. (1979, p. 285)

Kobrin and Hendershot also conclude that it is likely that both protection and selection factors are at work when considering the health of married and unmarried individuals, though they tended to favor the protection hypothesis when considering mortality data alone.

The findings were interpreted as showing greater evidence for the hypothesis that protection against death is supported by different kinds of social ties, rather than the hypothesis that mortality differences result from a selection process. Persons with high status social ties (heads of families for both men and women) are most protected; persons with few social ties (men living alone) or only low status ties (women living as dependents in families) have highest mortality; persons with other kinds of ties (dependent men, women alone) have mortality levels between the other groups of their sex. . . . It is true that the major increases in living alone are occurring within two groups: younger men and older women. These data suggest that this trend should cause less concern for the older women, who have mortality rates which are quite low relative both to older living arrangements and to the married, and greater at concern for the younger men who seem to be trading the low mortality of living at home for the double mortality rates of living alone. (1977, p. 744)

James Lynch's book, *Broken Heart: The Medical Consequences of Loneliness*, is a detailed elaboration of the protective aspects of marriage. Lynch concluded that the matter of living alone contributed substantially to the secondary gain sought by single people in illness episodes:

For many isolated and lonely individuals, illness itself becomes the only legitimate method for gaining attention. Many lonely people experience very real secondary gain by getting ill: at least for a brief period of time during hospitalization they are flooded with compassion provided by hospital staffs, nurses and physicians who care for them, inadvertently providing something that is missing in their lives—human attention. (1977, p. 209)

Though it never explicitly stated in Lynch's book, there are a number of implicit references to the physical and emotional nurturing that is more likely to occur in marriage than in other relationships. In Harlow's work with primates the issue of contact comfort is central.

In considering the above discussion, it is important to distinguish between illness and illness behavior. Illness behavior refers to the manner in which a patient plays out the "sick role." In his work on illness behavior, David Mechanic has suggested that there are high variations in patients' stoicism, complaining behavior, objective reports of distress, and dependency on help givers. It is entirely possible that, as Lynch has suggested, marital status may be closely related to illness behavior. This may work in a positive way for married inidividuals who might be highly motivated to continue gainful employment and minimize their incapacity from illness in order to continue child-rearing duties and other marital behaviors. Conversely, one can easily argue that married individuals have a potentially greater ability to achieve secondary gain from their symptoms because of the availability of a helping spouse. The data do not support this latter possibility, however. For single individuals, who less frequently have a nurturing social support system, dependent needs and secondary gains may be manifested by more frequent visits to physicians and by prolonged hospital stays.

Verbrugge and Kobrin and Hendershot have speculated on how marriage protects individuals against the manifestations of illness. It is tempting to add to their list of factors the concept of "contract comfort" suggested by the work of Harry Harlow and Rene Spitz (Harlow & Zimmerman, 1959; Spitz, 1945). It has been shown in developing primates (Harlow) as well as humans (Spitz) that infants require a certain amount of physical contact for normal, healthy development, both physically and psychologically. John Bowlby (1960) has referred to the continued significance of attachment into adulthood as well as the potentially devastating effects of loss with specific respect to illness behavior. It is tempting to suggest that one of the protective aspects of marriage is contact comfort or attachment bonds and that separation and divorce, which imply the breaking of these attachments, are in themselves the specific factors that predispose to morbidity and mortality. This speculation has important clinical implications since it would suggest that remarriage can once again protect the individual by re-forming attachment bonds and providing contact comfort, and that divorced and separated individuals may be experiencing significant degrees of depression, which can potentially be treated by the physician.

HEALTH CARE IMPLICATIONS OF CONTEMPORARY CHANGES IN MARRIAGE PATTERNS

In our earlier chapter we referred to the demographic transition and the impact that this has upon the general aging of the American population. As life expectancy improved, more individuals can be expected to live to age 65 and beyond. The increases in the proportion of individuals who are older will clearly lead to increases in degenerative diseases, chronic diseases such as diabetes mellitus and hypertension, and organic brain syndromes associated with aging. It is quite likely that in several decades organic brain syndromes will be one of this country's most pressing health-care problems. Similarly, it is highly probable that relatively new areas such as sexuality among the aging and life quality issues will receive more attention than at present.

Landon Jones, in a book about the impact of the baby boom generation on America, predicts that the baby boom generation (the massive number of individuals born between 1945 and 1960) will probably press for greater emphasis on biomedical research on the entire aging process.

> The generations that kept pediatricians busy in the 50's and 60's and psychiatrists busy in the 70's and 80's will eventually do the same for gerontologists. It is not inconceivable that their investigation of the underlying genetic and cellular mechanisms of old age could conceivably produce the same sort of breakthrough for the baby boom elderly that Jonas Salk did for the baby boom children. (1980, p. 382)

Ernest Gruenberg (1977) has indicated that this process of increasing human longevity to the point that organic brain syndromes and degenerative processes become critical health and social issues, is the ultimate irony of health care in the modern world.

As pointed out earlier, divorce rates have been climbing and will probably continue to climb in the near future, then level off some time in the 1990s. When considering the rise in the number of divorced people in America today, one of the most ready hypotheses that comes to mind is that mortality rates might also increase. If there were a fixed relationship between not being married and an increased risk for mortality and selected morbidity indicators, then we might predict that with rising divorce rates mortality and morbidity rates would also rise. However, that is probably an oversimplification. Factors such as increasing biomedical technology and improved nutrition will continue to affect mortality rates. Another qualification of this predicted development relates to the studies that have attempted to elaborate on the relationship between being divorced, separated, widowed, or single and increased risk for mortality and health problems. For example, Fenwick and Barresi (1981) concluded in their study of a national sample of 8000 elderly respondents that it was the change from married to unmarried status, rather than unmarried status per se, that led to a reported decline in health. Similarly, Seagraves (1980) in his extensive review of the research relating to marital status and mental health, indicated that the transitions from married to divorced or separated, or from marriage to widowhood were the critical points. A number of the widowhood studies also reinforce the idea of increased risk for both mortality and morbidity during the early months following widowhood (this is particularly true for men who are widowed).

This interesting observation that transitions are more stressful than a particular status itself can be understood in the context of the discussion of first and second order change in Chapter 1 of this volume. If marital transitions are perceived as first order changes, they are usually inherently less stressful and more predictable, while if they are considered to be major second order changes, then one would predict higher levels of stress. Thus, if marital change becomes more prevalent and more expectable, it shifts from second order to first order change and ultimately becomes less stressful.

Another factor that will affect the matter of increasing divorce rates vis-à-vis mortality and morbidity rates, is remarriage. As we pointed out in an earlier chapter, remarriage has been ignored until recently as an American phenomenon. It is now seen as one of the major factors in considering marriage in America. Unfortunately, national data do not reflect whether or not married individuals are in their first marriage or in a remarriage. Consequently we cannot develop a refined picture of the relative health of those in first marriages and remarriages. Therefore, the data that are available regarding the health of remarried individuals are survey data based upon self-report. In a large survey of individuals in California's Alameda County, Renne reported the following in regard to relative health of those who were happily married, and divorced and remarried:

> A large majority of people in our sample who are ever divorced had remarried, and while the remarried as a group tended to be less healthy than people in stable marriages, those who were satisfied with their current marriages reported better health than those who were still involved in unhappy first marriages. In other words, people who had divorced and remarried successfully were less susceptible to health problems than people who had remained in an unhappy marriage. If divorce itself were a symptom of illness signifying physical incapacity, or an inability to sustain close relationships with another person, for example, then people who had remarried after divorce would not only have been less satisfied with their marriages, as they were in our sample, but also less healthy in other respects, as they were not, to any significant degree. (1971, p. 347)

Renne also indicated that those who tended to remain in unhappy marriages were less healthy than those who had divorced and those who had not only divorced but had remarried. Using a national probability sample, Weingarten

(1980) also found that remarried individuals compared favorably with individuals in their first marriages on selected indicators of well-being, including a number of psychological and psychophysiological symptoms. Weingarten determined that one difference between the first married and those who were remarried was their relative utilization of professional help for problems. At some point in their lives, remarried individuals were much more likely to utilize mental health services and other professional services than were those who were first married. The remarried individuals tended to report higher levels of chronic stress than did those in first marriages.

Another factor that may affect the picture of the unmarried and their health in America is the predicted increase in divorce among the elderly in the United States. Relative to other age groups in the population the aged in America have a low divorce rate. However, over the past decade that situation has changed somewhat. As divorce becomes more acceptable and common in our society generally, there is an impact upon older individuals as well. Uhlenberg and Meyers (1981) indicate that for a number of reasons it should be expected that divorce will become much more prominent among the elderly. First, in subsequent decades it is more likely that there will be older individuals who have been affected by divorce earlier in their lives and these individuals will be in remarriages, which are more prone to end in divorce than are first marriages. The authors cite the increased acceptance of divorce among the aged and point to the increasing economic independence of women as affecting higher divorce rates because more women in subsequent decades will have their own retirement, social security, and other pension arrangements. Finally, Uhlenberg and Meyers point out that with the general reduction of mortality rates at earlier ages, there will be fewer marriages that will be terminated by death prior to old age. So, there will be an increased proportion of intact couples who will be subject to divorce. It is easy to extrapolate from this that individuals experiencing divorce in their later years will be particularly at risk because of the double status of (1) going into a transition, and (2) being more subject to physical and organic problems generally.

Jessie Bernard points out that there are gender differences in the process of remarriage as well as in marriage:

> Remarriage seems to be a kind of safe conduct voucher for men carrying them through many life stresses. There seems little doubt that having a wife—usually younger and healthier—to take care of the disabilities of aging is a positive factor not only in male survival but also in mental health. Equally good health-maintaining care may be available for the never married and non-remarried only among the fairly affluent. . . . Remarriage does not seem to do as much for women as it does for men; does not seem to have as great survival or mental health significance for them. (1980, p. 566)

It seems likely that with the substantial changes occurring in regard to sex roles and the large and increasing number of working women, this pattern will affect the differential between men and women with regard to the amount of health protection that marriage seems to afford. As reported earlier, it is anticipated that eventually the majority of women will be in the labor force. Other indications point to a greater sharing of work activities at home as well. Interestingly, these changes point out one of the ironies of contemporary changes in women's lives: the progress that has been made on a social, economic, and occupational front will probably be at the expense of increased risk for particular health problems. In other words, the differential between men and women will probably become less of a factor. There are indications that this is occurring. Men's life-styles have most often been cited as the major difference between mortality rates for men and women: Men tend to smoke more, they drive cars more, they are more likely to be employed and exposed to occupational risks and the general stresses of working, they tend to have more accidents, and seem to lead riskier lives. As the working habits of men and women tend to converge, it seems likely that the differences in life-styles will converge as well, and that women will also develop riskier and less healthy work and life habits. Contemporary data indicate that about one in three Americans today with a drinking problem is a female, while a decade before, women only accounted for one in six in this category. Heart disease death rates are now declining faster for men than for women. In 1963, men were four times as likely to be involved in automobile accidents; by 1977 the number of women drivers had doubled and women were half as likely as men to have automobile accidents. Similarly, the smoking patterns of contemporary women are quite different from those of older cohorts in that smoking has been more acceptable and common among women who entered adulthood during the 1950s, 1960s, and 1970s. It is estimated that in the late 1980s, if current trends continue, there will be an equal number of men and women smoking.

Northcott (1980) has pointed out that women have reported more depressive symptomatology and psychophysiological problems than men. However, in comparing Edmonton, Alberta area women who remained at home with those who worked, he found that working women were much less likely to report psychosomatic symptoms or indicators of depression. Northcott concluded that working women seemed to be able to balance the responsibilities of home and the workplace without suffering a great deal, and that the homemaker's role continued to be a demanding one that offered few social, economic, or emotional compensations. However, what Northcott did not indicate was that the working women were probably developing profiles that were more similar to those of working men, that is, they would report fewer illness episodes, fewer psychiatric symptoms, but become more subject to problems such as coronary heart disease.

CLINICAL IMPLICATIONS

These data suggest a number of implications for a practicing clinician. First, the marital status itself is a significant factor in assessing risk of physical morbidity and mortality as well as psychological health. This is particularly true of separated and divorced individuals, especially with respect to chronic conditions. It is possible that morbidity and mortality changes may be mediated not only by a loss of social support, but also by the direct consequences of loss of attachment bonds. This suggests careful scrutiny by the physician for signs of depression and also implies the benefits of re-establishing a coherent social support system for patients.

Second, while it is generally felt to be unwise for divorced patients to remarry hastily, it probably is generally wise to support realistic decisions to remarry, since it appears that remarriage helps protect an individual's health status.

Third, as the social status of women continues to improve, it might be expected that the differential in the health expectations of women in marriage will be attenuated and will ultimately become more similar to those of men.

Finally, we suspect that as changes in marital status become increasingly more acceptable in our society, they will be associated with lower degrees of stress, which, hopefully, will have a positive effect on the relatively higher morbidity seen in divorced and separated individuals.

REFERENCES

Antonovsky, A. *Health stress and coping*. Washington, D.C.: Jossey-Bass, 1979.

Bernard, J. Afterword. *Journal of Family Issues*, 1980, *1*, 561-571.

Bowlby, J. Grief and mourning in infancy and early childhood. *Psychoanalytic Study of the Child*, 1960, *15*, 9-15.

Carter, H., & Glick, P. *Marriage and divorce: A social and economic study*. Cambridge, Mass.: Harvard University Press, 1970.

Cox, P. R., & Ford, J. R. The mortality of widows shortly after widowhood. *Lancet*, 1964, *1*, 163-164.

Durkheim, E. *Suicide: A study in sociology*. New York: Free Press, 1951.

Fenwick, R., & Barresi, C. M. Health consequences of marital status change among the elderly. *Journal of Health and Social Behavior*, 1981, *22*, 106-116.

Gruenberg, E. The failures of success. *Health and Society*, 1977, *55*, 3-24.

Harlow, H. F., & Zimmerman, R. R. Affectional responses in the infant monkey. *Science,* 1959, *130*, 421-432.

Helsing, K. J., Szklo, M., & Comstock, G. W. Factors associated with mortality after widowhood. *American Journal of Public Health*, 1981, *71*, 802-809.

Jones, L. *Great expectations*. New York: Ballantine, 1980.

Kobrin, F. E., & Hendershot, G. E. Do family ties reduce mortality? Evidence from the United States, 1966-68. *Journal of Marriage and the Family*, 1977, *39*, 737-745.

Lynch, J. *Broken heart: The medical consequences of loneliness*. New York: Basic Books, 1977.

Northcott, H. C. Women, work and health. *Pacific Sociological Review*, 1980, *23*, 393–404.

Ortmeyer, C. E. Marital status. In C. L. Erhardt & J. E. Berlin (Eds.), *Mortality and morbidity in the United States*. Cambridge, Mass.: Harvard University Press, 1974.

Parkes, C. M., Benjamin, B., & Fitzgerald, R. G. Broken heart: A statistical study of increased mortality among widowers. *British Medical Journal*, 1969, *1*, 740–743.

Renne, K. Health and marital experience in an urban population. *Journal of Marriage and the Family*, 1971, *33*, 338–348.

Seagraves, R. T. Marriage and mental health. *Journal of Sex and Marital Therapy*, 1980, *6*, 187–198.

Spitz, R. Hospitalism. *Psychoanalytic Study of the Child*, 1945, *1*, 53–74.

Uhlenberg, P., & Meyers, M. A. Divorce and the elderly. *The Gerontologist*, 1981, *21*, 276–282.

Veevers, J. E. Parenthood and suicide: An examination of a neglected variable. *Social Science and Medicine*, 1973, *7*, 135–144.

Verbrugge, L. M. Marital status and health. *Journal of Marriage and the Family*, 1979, *41*, 267–286.

Weingarten, H. Remarriage and well-being. *Journal of Family Issues*, 1980, *1*, 533–560.

Young, M., Benjamin, B., & Wallis, C. The mortality of widowers. *Lancet*, 1963, *2*, 454–456.

CHAPTER THREE

Social Change and Couples Therapy: A Troubled Marriage

SHARON W. FOSTER
ALAN S. GURMAN

Patterns of marital social behavior have changed considerably since the rise of marital therapy in the 1950s. Age at first marriage has risen from 22.5 for men and 20.1 for women in 1956, to 23.8 for men and 21.3 for women in 1976 (U.S. Department of Commerce, 1977). That this trend toward later marriage is likely to continue is suggested by an increase in the proportion of single adults in the 25–39 age range: 24.9% of males and 14.8% of females in this group were single in 1976, as contrasted with 20.8% and 10.5%, respectively, in 1960 (U.S. Department of Commerce, 1977). These changes may be due in part to increasing trends for both sexes, but especially women, to complete their higher education and/or to obtain full-time employment prior to marriage. An increase in visibility, if not prevalence, of nonmarried cohabiting couples has also occured, with an estimated 1.9 million persons involved in this alternative to the traditional pattern (U.S. Department of Commerce, 1977). Married women are increasingly likely to be employed full time outside the home, with such employment regarded often as a primary source of self-involvement and satisfaction, and not simply as "just a job" (Carter & Glick, 1970). Couples are also increasingly likely to both delay and reduce child bearing: The total fertility rate at one point (1973) was one-half that of a decade and a half earlier.

Education, later marriage, and employment notwithstanding, divorces have risen markedly over the past two decades. The divorce rate in 1975 was double that of just a dozen years earlier, and more recent data suggest that

Sharon W. Foster. Eating Disorders Program, University of Wisconsin Center for the Health Sciences, Madison, Wisconsin.

Alan S. Gurman. Department of Psychiatry and Psychiatric Outpatient Clinic, University of Wisconsin Medical School, Madison, Wisconsin.

the rate of this change has continued to increase (U.S. Department of Commerce, 1977). Divorce rates are higher and have been increasing at a proportionately higher rate, in couples with higher socioeconomics status as measured by education and income levels. In spite of such marked trends, most (approximately four-fifths) divorced persons eventually remarry.

In spite of what appear to be increasingly prevalent, if not always socially sanctioned, options before, during, and subsequent to a marriage, epidemiological data suggest that married women experience more stress than either married men or single women. Married women, for example, report with greater than expected frequency such symptoms of psychological distress as nervousness, inertia, headaches, and insomnia (Bernard, 1972). Such data should be interpreted with care, however, as other data suggest that such symptoms may be more a function of the working/homemaker status than of marital status per se. Married women also appear to be at higher risk for depression than either single women or married or unmarried men (Knupfer, Clark, & Room, 1966; Weissman & Klerman, 1977). While any data reporting increases in such symptoms are prey to confounding by the greater acceptance of reporting psychological distress, it can be stated that changing demographic patterns with regard to marriage do not appear to have markedly decreased psychological distress for women in marriage.

The above data do not constitute all of the social changes germane to marital researchers and therapists.[1] Marriage has been the major social institution in which the vicissitudes of relationships and differences between men and women have been played out. Increasingly, women have been questioning long-held assumptions about their shaping of history, their economic contributions, and the degree to which putative differences between the sexes could be argued to be biologically predetermined. As such, it is not surprising that the nature of the institution of marriage, the roles of men and women within marriages, and the purposes and practices of marital therapy would also come under critical scrutiny. Revealed in the divorce statistics, it may be argued, is an unwillingness of couples to work out their problems. "Their problems," on the other hand, may well be at least as much social as dyadic, and result in part because in traditional marriages "for better or worse" applies in the former case to men and in the latter to women (Bernard, 1972). Bernard's thesis is that the institution of marriage, in traditional form, is pathogenic with respect to women. While this is an extreme view, the epidemiological data reported above at least do not refute this.[2] Whether the institution of marriage will continue to exist is probably

1. Throughout this chapter, "marital" and "couples" will be used interchangeably except where the context suggests otherwise, in which case "nonmarried," "cohabiting," or other terms will modify the term "couples."

2. Admittedly, such data only begin to address the relationship between marital status and psychological dysfunction. Clearly indicated is research partialing out the components of these correlations. Averaging, for example, may obscure what may be a relationship not between

less relevant a question than in what form it will exist. Projections based on current changes suggest that (1) women will increasingly tend to marry later; (2) there will be an increase in the proportion of nonaged adults living alone; (3) there will be a decrease in the relative frequency of divorce and separation; (4) there will be a decrease in the number of children per women of child-bearing age; and (5) there will be a decrease in the proportion of women's life span devoted to bearing and raising children (Glick & Parke, 1965). Thus, change in some salient aspects of marriage does appear highly probable.

Many sex-role differences between men and women are indisputably changing. Increasing numbers of women are not only entering the work force, but are seeking careers (Norton & Glick, 1976), and an increasing proportion of family income is contributed by women. There is also an increased use of child-care (especially preschool) facilities, suggesting that women no longer have sole, full-time responsibility for child rearing. The data on actual changes in stereotypic sex-role personality characterists, however, are more equivocal. While in both the popular and professional literatures there is an increased tendency to endorse personality trait and behavioral "androgyny," especially among college-educated, more "mature," or creative persons (Bem, 1974, Spence, Helmreich, & Stapp, 1975), there is also evidence to suggest that both self-descriptions and observed parental sex-role behavior may not have changed significantly in the last two decades. Some tentative projections suggest that changing sex-role attitudes (toward an ideal of increasing androgyny) may in the near future increasingly obtain in self-report and actual behavior (Donelson & Gullahorn, 1977). As such, the potential for increased resistance to sex-role bias, especially in so cardinal an area as marital therapy, should be anticipated. Social policy, and the self-monitoring of professional organizations (e.g., APA Task Force, 1978) may be anticipated to support these changes in concrete ways for women as psychotherapy consumers.

The consumer movement may also be an area of social change auguring examination not only of potential sex-role bias, but also of therapeutic effectiveness, deterioration, training standards, and other critical dimensions of marital therapy. The rise in litigation against the medical branch of the health-care profession and the potential for its extension to mental health professionals, is only the negative impetus to a review of consumer issues in marital psychotherapy. The right of the consumer to make decisions about when and whether treatment is called for, and the type of treatment that is accepted on the basis of informed expectations may be seen as eminently

---

marital status and psychological dysfunction, but between the nature of "health" of the marital relationship and psychological dysfunction. Variables that often covary with, but are distinguished from marriage, such as low or no nonhomemaker occupation, reduced opportunities for socializing, or constricted leisure-time activities, and in concert with other factors, may account for the epidemiological data better than marital status per se.

reasonable. Moreover, continued legislative effects with regard to national health insurance have already prompted some within the field to call for attention to be paid not only to direct (actual psychotherapy consumer) but also to indirect, third-party consumer issues.

Both current projected social changes require review of the way issues they raise bear upon marital therapy. While the actual practice of such therapy is of paramount concern, the intimate relationship among theory, practice, and evaluation requires a critical evaluation.

THREE MAJOR MODELS OF MARITAL DYSFUNCTION

Numerous authors have characterized the history of marital therapy as a practice bereft of theory (Haley, 1962; Manus, 1966; Olson, 1970). In the last decade, however, the psychoanalytic–object relations, systems theory, and behavioral frameworks have increasingly been adopted as bases for the organization and elaboration of marital theory, assessment, treatment, and research (Gurman & Kniskern, 1981a; Paolino & McCrady, 1978). These models are not mutually exclusive nor are they exhaustive of the domain of perspectives on marital dysfunction (Gurman, 1978, 1980b, 1981). They do, however, represent the prevailing orientations among marital therapists (Prochaska & Prochaska, 1978). A brief characterization of the distinctive features of each of these frameworks for understanding marital dysfunction will serve to highlight points germane to our subsequent discussion.

Psychodynamic Models

Psychoanalytic–object relations views generally hold that problems in relationships are a function of a twofold deficiency, the failure of the persons involved to separate psychologically from their families of origin, and concomitantly, their lack of the presence and integration of varied and flexible representations of self in relation to others. Consequently, the individual is prompted to seek a relationship based on mutual projective identification, that is, the fulfillment of needs previously frustrated, repressed, and split off in the person's family of origin. One thus attempts to achieve an integration of the self by idealizing and identifying with the mate. Collusion is required to maintain this false integration, with neither partner consciously recognizing the ways in which the mate serves as the ambivalently experienced object from the family of origin. This process by which the couple, despite experiencing considerable pain, continues to attempt to maintain their relationship has been best summarized by Dicks (1967):

One could glimpse something of the deeper unconscious bonds, which could best be understood if we assumed that they were *making such couples into a unit around which some sort of joint ego-boundaries were drawn*. These attributions to each other of unconsciously shared feelings constitute the essential "symbiotic" or collusive process. It now looked possible to answer the question as to what kept couples together despite every appearance and reality of suffering and mutual destructiveness in their relationship. . . . This stressed the need for unconscious *complementariness*, a kind of division of function by which each partner supplied part of a set of qualities, the sum of which created a complete dyadic unit. This joint personality or integrate enabled each half to rediscover lost aspects of their primary object relations, which they had split off or repressed, and which they were, in their involvement with the spouse, re-experiencing by projective identification. The sense of belonging can be understood on the hypothesis that at a deeper level there are perceptions of the partner and consequent attitudes towards him or her *as if* the other was part of oneself. The partner is then treated according to how this aspect of oneself was valued: spoilt and cherished, or denigrated and persecuted. (pp. 68–69)

Systems Theory Models

Systems theories share the assumption that "the whole is greater than the juxtaposition of its component parts." The relationship between the spouses is what is critical in family systems views. Processes internal or idiosyncratic to individuals, while not denied to exist, are generally downplayed (Gurman & Kniskern, 1981a). The two major systems theory approaches most applicable to marital dysfunction are the Bowenite (Kerr, 1981) and communications views (Bodin, 1981). The central concern of the Bowenite view is "differentiation of self" (Bowen, 1978) from the family of origin. Bowen uses the concepts of "family projection process" and "fusion" to describe the ways in which anxiety associated with parental conflicts is reduced by involving a child (or children). This may occur through redirecting attention toward problems of offspring (in which the symptom is usually admirably suited to incorporating the anxiety-arousing component(s) of the parental conflict) or by fostering the offspring's taking sides with or protecting one of the spouses. Attempts of such second-generation members to extricate themselves from the "stuck-togetherness" of this situation threaten the parental pseudoresolution of their conflicts, and are usually resisted. When such offspring marry, they are highly disposed to repeating a similar pattern. "Fusion" of spouses is seen in their high levels of emotional reactivity to and intrusive involvement in the psychological processes of the other. Bowen credits the differentiation between emotional and intellective functions in the individual, and the resulting ability to better define boundaries between oneself and the other, as necessary for separation from fusion in the family of origin and subsequently from the spouse.

Communications models emphasize the nature of marriage as a system of communicative transactions. Assuming the impossibility of not communicating, they point to discrepancies between verbal and nonverbal messages and sequences of dysfunctional communication (e.g., symmetrical and complementary) as responsible for marital dysfunction. Over time, these dysfunctions become rigidified into implicit "rules" governing the spouses' behavior toward each other. Communications models assert that by breaking such dysfunctional patterns, new and more constructive, flexible patterns will emerge.

Behavioral Models

Behavioral views emphasize the current, overt behavioral sources of marital dysfunction, particularly the high rates of reciprocated coercion (aversive control) exhibited by couples in conflict. These patterns are viewed as resulting from inadequate learning and/or implementation of observational, communicational, and problem-solving skills (Jacobson, 1981; Jacobson & Margolin, 1979). Increasingly, behavioral perspectives have incorporated cognitive and affective components in the conceptualization of marital dysfunction (Jacobson, 1981; Weiss, 1981). Weiss (1975), for example, has distinguished between response-controlled (short-term, discrete, "tit-for-tat") and stimulus-controlled (situation or rule governed) transactions. In so doing he has suggested that at times, focus on higher-order cognitive agreement on and as a basis for control of patterns of marital behavior may provide a framework for producing more positive and generalizable therapy outcomes. In addition to functional analytic principles, behavioral models have incorporated concepts from social–psychological exchange theory (Homans, 1961; Thibaut & Kelley, 1959), especially those emphasizing reciprocity of relationship exchanges.

In spite of numerous differences in the origin, focus, and range of phenomena for which they attempt to account, scholars, researchers and therapists in the field of marital dysfunction may at many junctures find their differences more apparent than real. Sager (1976, 1981), for example, has provided a highly original framework for conceptualizing and treating marital conflict that contains elements related to and potentially usefully adapted by persons of any of the above theoretical persuasions. We predict that marital therapists will increasingly develop more integrated conceptual frameworks, and become more eclectic in their treatment strategies (Gurman, 1978, 1980b, 1981). These caveats notwithstanding, current differences among workers from these varied orientations result in important divergences in their implications for consumers of marital therapy, and especially women.

CONSUMER ISSUES: MORE THAN MEETS THE "AYE"

Informed Choice

A major objective of recent publications devoted to the description of psychotherapies and the therapeutic process is to enable the consumer to make an informed choice about the treatment alternatives available. While marital therapists usually discuss with clients general procedural issues such as frequency of sessions, who will be seen, at least a general problem focus, and the financial cost of their services, it is probably true that few educate potential clients about various approaches available for the treatment of marital dysfunctions in general and those relevant to the problems presented by any one couple in particular. To some degree, clinical assessment and treatment approaches of choice are matters of professional judgment. To the extent, however, that the client is not informed of the alternatives to the one the therapist is recommending and willing or capable of offering, the therapist runs the risk of taking a "father (or mother) knows best" position. Certainly, there are times when full disclosure might be countertherapeutic (such as a plan to implement some form of paradoxical or strategic technique). On the other hand, the "countertherapeutic" rationale can too easily become generalized to situations where it does not apply. Another rationale sometimes given for not engaging in patient education functions is that status as an "authority" may be beneficial to the therapeutic process. However, one's status as an authority is not antagonistic to providing clients with a description of alternative available treatments. Indeed, such a presentation might serve to increase the therapist's perceived expertness by virtue of his or her knowledge of the range, currentness, and efficacy of various therapeutic approaches. Unfortunately, for at least some couples, such a presentation may actually interfere with establishing an early working alliance by suggesting that the therapist's confidence in his or her own method of therapy is uncertain. Indeed, too great an emphasis on available treatments *qua* "treatments" may actually be quite misleading, in that a good deal of the variance in marital therapy outcome is attributable to factors other than treatment "methods," such as the therapist's relationship skills (Gurman & Kniskern, 1978a, 1978b) and the "fit" between both patient types and treatment methods, and patients and therapists as persons (Kniskern & Gurman, 1981).

Consent to Treatment

A related, and perhaps more important, set of issues centers around providing the couple entering treatment a fairly detailed overview of the treatment recommendations and establishing a more or less specific contract with them. That is, once a couple has been offered a choice of treatment orientation, the issue of whether the therapist should obtain from them a more or less formal consent to entering treatment arises. Here, there is some variation among the three major orientations to marital therapy. Behavioral marital therapists often incorporate as a part of the assessment a specific, written contract outlining the responsibilities and tasks to be carried out by both the couple and the therapist (e.g., Gottman & Leiblum, 1974; Stuart, 1981; Jacobson & Margolin, 1979). The use of such contracts has been advocated on grounds that it (1) is a useful predictor of willingness to comply with intervention tasks; (2) emphasizes the joint nature of the therapy and discourages one spouse from attempting to form a coalition with the therapist against the other spouse; (3) reinforces the couple's working together for their mutual benefit; and (4) provides clarification of the treatment focus and treatment plan, and presents a structure within which such aims will be fostered. Generally, the aim is to lessen the likelihood that "clients will fruitlessly use the time to engage in the negative practice of prolonged fighting and it also facilitates the therapist's efforts to mobilize the clients' problem-solving efforts" (Stuart, 1975, p. 246). As a *desideratum* from the consumer's point of view, it both informs the couple of the treatment plan and provides grounds for a more active, collaborative relationship between consumer and therapist.

Systems-oriented marital therapists are more variable in the explictness of obtaining client consent to the treatment. Whitaker, for example, considers the "battle for structure," that is, whether the clients will accept the therapist's requirement that they "capitulate to the therapist's mode of operating," to be the first stage of the therapeutic process (Whitaker & Keith, 1981). Agreement to bring in additional (especially multigenerational) family members is a major component of this battle. Once the therapists have established control, their questions are directed toward mobilizing the couple's (or a family's) own initiative to become whole-oriented and disclosive in an experiential manner. The failure of the couple or family to agree at either of these stages to the therapist's structuring efforts may be seen in a rough-and-ready way as a rejection of the therapeutic contract. Bowen therapists also emphasize family initiative as necessary to beginning therapy, although the substance of initiative is different from that of the experiential systems therapists such as Whitaker. Here the "contract" can best be described as occurring when at least one member of the couple or family responds to the therapist's questions about the undercurrents of the tension of the whole by becoming more objective (Kerr, 1981). The assumption of the Bowen therapist is that, in a sort of domino fashion, such objectivity provides the means for the differentiation of one part of the system, which in turn will provoke differentiation in the rest of the system. In contrast, communications therapists (e.g., Bodin, 1981; Stanton, 1981a, 1981b) are highly directive from the outset, delivering interactionally based formulations about the rules governing the marital system and prescribing changes in the couple's interactional behavior. Consumers of the communications wing of systems-oriented marital therapies may be said to consent to the treatment when they accept the interactional formulation and carry out the behavioral prescriptions. In sum, among systems-oriented marital therapies consent to the type of treatment offered is in large part co-occurrent with initial therapeutic change, that is, acceptance that the symptom is a problem of a dysfunctional family system. While this strategy may be highly effective therapeutically, the consumer's understanding of the nature of the treatment and its relation to the presenting problems is more likely to occur during or subsequent to the therapy than at a postassessment, pretreatment point (Gurman, 1978).

Psychoanalytic–object relations marital therapists are intermediate to the above two orientations in their specificity of obtaining consent to treatment. As described by Nadelson (1978), a recommendation of (conjoint) marital therapy is preceded by interviews of both spouses individually and then together, and completion of a couple's evaluation questionnaire. Individual sessions permit both an assessment of individual problems contraindicating marital therapy, the development of an initial therapeutic alliance, and the disclosure of "secrets" (such as an affair) that might otherwise be manifested as resistance. A significant portion of both interview and questionnaire assessment is devoted to the clarification of the spouses' motivation and self-reported goals. Negotiation of the therapeutic contract occurs in a conjoint session (or sessions) in which the couple's own motivations and goals are reflected. Inclusion of a cotherapist is also negotiated at this point. Although Nadelson does not offer specific information about whether and in what manner anticipated phases and the nature of treatment as viewed by the therapist are communicated to clients, she does suggest that at numerous points in the therapy the couple be given the opportunity to reevaluate their motivations and goals, and decide whether goal refocusing, termination, or agreement to enter a new phase of therapy (e.g., movement from a communication and problem-solving focus to insight-oriented work) is called for. It is after the initial phase of treatment that the therapist's assessment about the couple's need to work through transference issues and the adequacy of the therapeutic alliance can better provide the basis for judgment about the need for such in-depth therapy.

Marital therapists are thus quite divergent in the specificity with which they develop and present their assessment of the couple's dysfunction, the nature and duration of treatment, and the degree to which the couple's consent to the contract is formally obtained. As has been noted, these differences in a number of respects reflect differences in orientation to marital dysfunction and therapeutic technique. As has also been noted, full disclosure of the treatment plan often may be either countertherapeutic or simply not possible in advance of evaluation of the couple's initial change efforts. At the same time, it should also be recognized that there are good therapeutic reasons for presenting and obtaining consent to treatment, such as those described in conjunction with behavioral approaches. Furthermore, the couple's willingness to seek further therapy at some future time when additional issues or problems become focal (a not uncommon situation) may depend on their sense of the satisfactoriness of earlier therapy experiences. Finally, even for couples with good insurance coverage, any long-term therapy represents a considerable investment of time and finances. On these grounds negotiation of obtaining consent to treatment should be considered an important response of the therapist to the couple both as consumers and as therapy clients. Written contracts have the advantage of reducing, although not eliminating, subsequent equivocation as to what was understood to be the agreement. They also may bring into sharper focus the dyadic (or familial) nature of the problem. Negotiation, formulation, and agreement to a written contract, however, should not adumbrate or in any manner detract from the interpersonal nature of the therapeutic relationship, and should not be employed as a substitute for careful attention to the development of a therapeutic alliance (Gurman, 1981). It is probably true that in many cases an oral contract will suffice. Whether written or oral, the therapeutic contract should at minimum include the following components, presented in language that can be readily understood by the couple: (1) assessment of the couple's dysfunction; (2) areas to be the focus of therapeutic efforts; (3) who will be seen by whom (format); (4) type of treatment to be offered; (5) anticipated length of treatment; and (6) administrative matters (e.g., frequency of sessions, cost). It should be explicit at the time of consent which of the components of the contract are subject to future renegotiation. Exploration of the couple's response, both affective and behavioral, to the contract negotiation and consent process may serve well as a transition to the initial stages of therapy.

Therapy Effectiveness

A third major area pertinent to consumer interest is therapy effectiveness. Demonstration of the comparative effectiveness of various types of marital therapy is not only necessary to providing the sort of information discussed in the first part of this section, but is also a crucial concern in its own right. With increased national and professional organizational attention to the possible passage of some form of national health insurance, this issue can only become one of increased importance, especially for innovative and rapidly proliferating treatment approaches such as marital therapy.

One particularly thorny issue is that of aiding consumers in identifying qualified marital therapists. At present, persons of widely divergent training and experience engage in the practice of some form of marital counseling or therapy. In addition, there are numerous programs or workshops (such as Marriage Encounter weekends; Doherty, McCabe, & Ryder, 1978) that are not presented as therapy per se. There is no single organization that is responsible for the certification of therapists, whatever their training, as skilled in marital therapy. While the American Association for Marriage and Family Therapy, through its Commission on Accreditation for Marriage and Family Therapy Education, has been granted governmental power to accredit training programs in the field, the scope of that commission does not include the accreditation, licensing or certification of individual practitioners. This is especially troublesome given that graduation from a psychiatric, clinical psychology, social work, pastoral counseling or other mental health degree program does not guarantee competence or even experience with marital therapy. Even among more educated segments of the population, confusion still exists as to differences in the background of mental health professionals, and so therapists cannot and should not assume that potential clients have selected the professional most suited to their needs. While data on therapist factors (including type of training, level and type of experience, as well as interpersonal factors) associated with various degrees of positive outcome are still sparse (Gurman & Kniskern, 1978a; 1981b), data do suggest that therapist interpersonal skills, particularly those associated with the "client-centered triad" (Gurman, 1977) are keenly important. In a recent extensive review of this literature, Gurman and Kniskern (1978a) concluded that

> a reasonable mastery of technical skills may be sufficient to prevent worsening or maintain pretreatment functioning, but more refined therapist relationship skills seem necessary to yield truly positive outcomes in marital–family therapy. Moreover, a minimal level of empathic ability is probably needed just to complete therapeutic tasks in the most behavioral of such therapies. (p. 875)

While the need for further well-designed research in this area cannot be overemphasized, the important consideration here is how such information can be conveyed to potential recipients of marital therapy. At present, perhaps the two major means by which clients come to any one particular therapist are through recommendations from acquaintances who have been previous clients of that therapist, and referrals from other mental health personnel. While nonprofessional "grapevine referrals" can and probably do function to effect an initially positive interpersonal stance of clients toward the therapist, the danger is that the "halo" component of this attitude may be generalized negatively to other therapists if for any of a variety of reasons the therapy contact results in either no change or negative outcome, both of which, of course, occur in marital therapy (Gurman & Kniskern, 1978b). Referrals from other mental health professionals will probably continue to be a predominant means by which couples enter therapy with a qualified couples therapist, and such referring persons may also function so as to orient consumers to the range of treatments available, consider the rationale for seeking couples therapy, and clarify the qualifications of the person to whom they are being referred. Even these referrals, however, are subject to the referring person's own expertise, judgment, and knowledge of the work of therapists in the community. While some of the responsibility for qualified therapist selection rests with the consumer, and while both popular literature and consultation to, for example, a community mental health center, are available to them, we can hardly expect consumers to be expert judges of a qualified marital therapist. As such, a foremost responsibility of the marital therapist is to present the client with an opportunity to ask questions about his or her training, experience, and orientation. Questions about the therapist's competence, especially at the first interview or in the early phase of treatment, should not automatically be treated as grist for the transference or resistance mill (by therapists of any theoretical persuasion). While persistent questions of this type continuing over a number of sessions, or occurring, for example, after a major disclosure on the part of the client(s), may reflect such processes, they may also be fairly straightforwardly expressive of a desire on the client's part for cognitive clarification and structuring of their expectations. A relatively simple strategy would be to rule out such hypotheses by responding directly to the inquiry, then evaluating whether other issues are involved. The point here is that such questions, in the proper context, are perfectly reasonable requests.

A second issue is that of the effectiveness of various formats for the treatment of marital problems, primarily differentiating among individual, concurrent, conjoint, or couple group approaches. Here, data provide relatively unequivocal support for the superiority of conjoint marital and conjoint group marital over individual treatment for couples problems. Gurman and Kniskern (1978a, 1981b) note that concurrent or collaborative therapies, to the extent that these methods have received research attention, do not appear to be strong competitors. Still, there may be conditions under which therapeutic effectiveness may be augmented by conducting a number of individual sessions with one or both of the spouses (Gurman & Kniskern, 1978a). Such practices clearly merit future research attention.

A third area of importance is, generally speaking, that of the comparative effectiveness of marital therapies conducted within each of the three major frameworks of marital therapy (Gurman, 1978; Gurman & Kniskern, 1981a; Paolino & McCrady, 1978). For most researchers and clinicians, the impulse (and rightly so) is to regard such a question as at best misleading and at the extreme meaningless. Not only is there wide variation within each of these broad orientations in terms of both fundamental assumptions and specific techniques employed, but also the investigation of therapeutic efficacy should be focused more analytically on describing just what variables are productive of positive therapeutic outcome. At the same time, our knee-jerk critical responses should not keep us from overlooking the fact that even so general a question would be regarded as fairly sophisticated if it came from any one prospective couple. Furthermore, even if one were able to provide empirically based information to consumers on all possible therapist × problem × technique × client × setting interactions, the couple is likely to be unimpressed. The relevant concern for any couple is the relatively circumscribed one of whether any proposed therapy "will work for them." At the present state of the art such questions are, of course, unanswerable even in probabilistic fashion.

Given the above constraints, however, a number of comments may be made about the evaluation of the comparative efficacy of these three major types of marital therapy, recognizing that the benefit to consumers may in this case come more indirectly, through the therapist's awareness of, and further training in, demonstrably effective therapy.

First, it is still true, as noted in earlier reviews (Jacobson, 1978; Gurman & Kniskern, 1978a) that there is almost no relatively "pure" outcome research on systems-oriented or psychoanalytic–object relations-oriented marital therapy. In part, this may be due to historical factors. Behavioral marital therapies have been psychologist born and bred, and that discipline in general, and behaviorally oriented psychologists in particular, have always been highly empirically based. Systems-oriented marital therapists have been remarkably productive and innovative spurs to the study of family systems, but as noted by Jacobson (1978), this family orientation has predominated over concern with the marital dyad alone. It is also true that at least among some systems-oriented therapists, serious questions have been raised about whether the therapeutic phenomena of interest can be subjected to objective study. An oft-repeated aphorism of Whitaker (1980) is "the problem with researchers is that they don't realize you can't get mother's milk from data." True, but postweaning psychologists need something more substantial to feed on. The psychoanalytic tradition has also found it notoriously difficult to reconcile theoretically central phenomena with the empiricist demands of research. What little can be drawn from the existing research literature suggests that marital therapists would do well to be technically heterogeneous. Although Jacobson (1978) has argued that among components of the behavioral approach "those aspects of the approach which emphasize communication training are necessary and probably sufficient," it is also clear that an at least equally necessary set of variables involve therapist relationship skills (Gurman & Kniskern, 1978a, 1978b, 1981b). Advocates of time-limitedness as a component of an effective therapeutic program have not yet demonstrated that this component leads to superior outcomes in comparison to open-ended treatment. Here marital therapists might do well to follow the psychoanalytic–object relations therapists in evaluating the couple's needs and motivations for more intensive insight-oriented therapy subsequent to the initial communication (and contracting) training. Consumers, clinicians, and researchers alike need comparative studies aimed at isolating the specific components of treatment interventions from a variety of frameworks which are most effective for specific marital dysfunctions.

PROFESSIONAL ACCOUNTABILITY FOR THE RESULTS OF THERAPY: THE CROSSROADS OF INCOME AND OUTCOME?

In addition to the usual variety of clinical criteria on which the outcomes of marital therapy may be assessed, there are a number of additional criteria involving treatment efficiency that must be considered in order to gauge meaningfully the impact of the various marital therapies. In a time when consumers of psychotherapy are becoming increasingly sophisticated about treatment services, and increasingly cost conscious, marital therapists must be accountable not only for demonstrating their efficacy in symptomatic and other clinical terms, but also in terms of a number of metadimensions of effectiveness (Gurman & Kniskern, 1981b).

Treatment Length

While some courses of marital therapy last a year or more, it is clear that, by traditional individual psychotherapy standards, the most marital therapy is of short duration, whether by design or by default (Gurman, 1980a, 1981).

Treatment length may involve three dimensions. First, there is the obviously important question of the effects of length as measured by total number of treatment sessions. The second dimension involves the frequency of treatment sessions (e.g., once a week vs. biweekly). Finally, the total elapsed time of therapy must be considered. Given the current lack of evidence that lengthier treatments (measured by number of sessions) are generally superior to briefer or to time-limited treatments (Gurman & Kniskern, 1978a) the practical clinical question should be whether the temporal distribution of sessions has particular impact on treatment outcome, and in what specific clinical situations. Thus, the length of marital treatment, whether measured in terms of total treatment hours and/or total elapsed time of treatment, is an obvious efficiency-related criterion to be considered in the complex matrix of factors leading to judgments about the outcomes of the marital therapies. Given equivalent therapeutic outcomes, generalizability of treatment effects, and durability of those effects, briefer therapies should be judged superior to longer-term methods.

System Involvement

The degree of family involvement required to achieve particular therapeutic ends also needs to be incorporated into a far-reaching assessment of marital therapy outcome. Thus, for example, equivalent therapeutic outcomes achieved for the treatment of a given clinical problem would demonstrate quite different efficiencies if Treatment X required the active involvement of both spouses, while Treatment Y required only one spouse's involvement.

Thus far, there is rather persuasive evidence (Gurman & Kniskern, 1978a, 1978b) that the treatment of marital problems is most effective when both spouses are involved in therapy. While each spouse may be involved in therapy under collaborative or concurrent treatment formats, conjoint treatment is especially powerful. Moreover, existing evidence (Gurman & Kniskern, 1978b) suggests that, in general, the treatment of only one spouse for marital difficulties (i.e., in individual therapy) is twice as likely as conjoint treatment to lead to deterioration (i.e., negative effects) of the marital relationship or of either the treated or the untreated partner. Still, even these data, provocative as they are, are rather unspecific with regard, for example, to the clinical disorder being treated. There is little reason to believe that marital or family therapy of any sort is always the treatment of choice for psychological problems (cf. Garfield & Bergin, 1978). Indeed, comparative studies of individual versus marital treatment methods are rare, especially in terms of their relative efficacy with well-defined disorders. Thus, comparative studies of marital therapies with individual therapies that have already received encouraging empirical support in the treatment of specific disorders are sorely needed. Since successful treatments have already been developed for a small number of important, common, and specific clinical syndromes, the issue at hand is whether any currently available marital therapy methods can, while at least matching effectiveness with these individual methods, demonstrate reliably positive impact on psychological dimensions and criteria not addressed directly by individual therapy methods. For example, why should any marital therapy be used to treat mild to moderate depression since there already exists a frequently effective treatment for this disorder, unless such a therapy can be shown to be equally effective on, say, symptomatic criteria, and superior on other criteria, for example, prevention of relapse, lowered incidence of depression in other family members, etc.? If a given method of marital therapy were shown to be equally effective on symptomatic criteria, but not on other dimensions, that marital therapy method's applicability to the treatment of depression would need to be seriously questioned, since treating a marital dyad is significantly less cost-effective than treating the identified patient alone.

Treatment Compliance

Closely related to the issue of the amount of system involvement required to achieve particular therapeutic effects, is the efficiency criterion of treatment compliance. If, for example, Marital Treatment A achieves consistently superior outcomes to Marital Treatment B in the therapy of Problem X, yet accumulates a dropout rate or a rate of premature termination several times greater than that accruing to B, arguments favoring the superiority of A would need careful qualification and re-evaluation. Thus, if the rate of couples remaining in Treatment A were sufficiently low, the general value of offering this treatment could be questioned on the basis of its limited applicability to large numbers of distressed families. Gurman & Kniskern (1978a, 1978b) have identified several factors that seem to increase the probability of early, that is, premature, withdrawal from marital treatment in general, but little is currently known about the factors influencing this phenomenon within different marital treatment methods. While patient (i.e., couple) factors such as low motivation for therapy in one spouse, ambivalent motivation in both spouses, inability to arrive at a treatment contract, etc., obviously influence early withdrawal from couples therapy, the existing evidence suggests that a disproportionate amount of the variance in early therapy withdrawal is due to therapist variables. Indeed, the evidence to date (Gurman & Kniskern, 1978b) suggests that the dropout-inducing marital therapist is probably the same composite person as the deterioration-inducing marital therapist.

Thus, a particularly provocative issue is whether different approaches to marital therapy are especially likely to encourage (or even require) the kinds of therapist behavior that seems to lead to both early withdrawal and to negative outcomes. In a time of heightened professional accountability for its' pratitioners' outcome, treatment methods must be as carefully scrutinized as are practitioners themselves.

Patient Costs

Patient costs, both financial and psychological, also need to be considered in determining treatment efficiency. Direct monetary costs, of course, are influenced enormously by the cost of therapist training and the disseminability of the method; for example, MA-level therapist will charge lower fees than their MD or PhD colleagues, and group therapies almost always cost patients less (per session) than treatment given to one couple at a time. Moreover, treatments of equal clinical outcome are probably not of equivalent general value if one extracts a much higher emotional toll (to achieve the same outcome) from patients than the other.

Costs of Therapist Training

As just noted, the costs of therapist training constitute a significant contribution to direct patient costs. To date we are aware of no empirical evidence that nonprofessional marital therapists, either as a group or under special circumstances, are able to achieve clinical outcomes that match those of professionally trained therapists. Were this outcome equivalence to obtain, even for a restricted number and range of clinical problems, nonprofessionally delivered treatments for those specific difficulties would be preferred.

There is an additional, and enormously obvious, potential factor that can (and usually does) increase patient financial costs: It is called cotherapy. Cotherapy is an area loaded with controversy and mostly devoid of data (Gurman & Kniskern, 1978a). For example, Haley (1976) asserts with passion his uncompromising belief in the wastefulness and irrelevance of the practice, while Whitaker (Whitaker & Keith, 1981), with equal fervor, argues that cotherapy is almost always a necessity. Obviously, it is absolutely clear that the issue is not so absolute! The necessity of using cotherapists clearly varies as a function of factors about which we can only now speculate (e.g., severity of the presenting problem, felt therapist comfort), but about which we need unambiguous data. For example, the working style of a highly directive therapist (e.g., Haley) might well be compromised by the presence of a cotherapist, while the therapeutic power of self-disclosure of other therapists (e.g., Whitaker) might render them too personally vulnerable to be effective in the absence of a cotherapist.

The question that needs to be answered, then, is, under what conditions of practice within any marital treatment method does cotherapy yield clinical outcomes that are superior to therapy done by solo therapists, and, does even this superiority (if found) justify the continued practice of cotherapy in terms of broader extratherapeutic considerations, such as treatment efficiency and financial cost (to both patient and service provider)?

Treatment Disseminability

The disseminability of a treatment method is another important index of therapeutic efficiency. For example, if Marital Treatments X and Y are of equal power in terms of patient-related change criteria, yet X can be administered (with no loss of therapeutic effectiveness) to groups of couples, then X would have an important leg up over Y in terms of this dimension of efficiency. Disseminability is also influenced, as noted earlier, by the degree to which a marital treatment method is teachable to clinicians lacking a doctorate, including paraprofessionals.

FEMINIST ISSUES: "WILL THE FALL NEVER COME TO AN END?"

In Lewis Carroll's *Alice in Wonderland*, Alice, spying a most unusual and intriguing rabbit, jumps in after it down its rabbit hole. As she tumbles through the unexpected length of the tunnel, she wonders, "Down, down, down. Would the fall never come to an end?" Feminists seeking nonsexist treatment for couples dysfunctions too often find themselves in an analogous position. Seeking to find relief from depression that may well have its roots in a marital relationship, hoping to improve a troubled marital relationship, or striving to enrich a relationship, they may find their aims as elusive as the rabbit. Therapy *techniques*, as well of much of marital theory, deserves of careful critique with respect to the ways in which they may preserve role-stereotypic intrapsychic and interpersonal aspects of women's functioning.

Sexism and Models of Marital Health/Dysfunction

Of fundamental concern to feminists have been the models of adequate or healthy functioning toward which the marital therapist seeks to effect change in distressed couples. Such models are implicit, if not explicit, in all marital psychotherapies, attempts to develop assessment and treatment that are value-free notwithstanding (Gurman & Klein, 1980, 1984). To the extent that models of healthy relationship functioning are based on normative, that is, socially "engendered" conceptions, there is compelling reason to examine the effects of sexist social conditioning on the theories and techniques employed by marital therapists.

PSYCHOANALYTIC MODELS

Psychoanalytic models have received intense criticism from feminists as repressive of women sexually, intrapsychically, and interpersonally (Chesler, 1972; Hare-Mustin, 1978). The question here is whether more recent applications of and developments in this view in the field of marital therapy are deserving of a similar critique. In some respects, unfortunately, the response is affirmative. Dicks (1967), an enormously influential marital therapist, writing less than a decade and a half ago, introduces among his basic object relations concepts the following view:

> For success in marriage there must be present in each partner a clear and definite sense of sexual identification. This is an essential personal quality for acceptance of the different roles each has to play along broadly masculine and feminine lines. Endocrinology offers a biological link between constitution, body-image, and sexual self-identification . . . the man's sexual identity is linked as a rule to his implicit readiness for action, by which he achieves.
>
> Economic security and social–occupational status ("has standing"), is something to be reckoned with outside. The woman's identity is typically linked with cherishing, nourishing, maternal functions towards *his* children *for* him. Few marriages can endure when these primary biological tasks are completely denied, or even if some of the secondary roles deriving from them are too flagrantly reversed. (p. 33; emphasis in original)

For those who appreciate the positive contributions of object relations theory, the sexist implications of these fundamental presumptions are disquieting indeed: Biology is destiny? Male equals active; female equals passive? Women receive their identity through that of their husbands? Achievement and cherishing are somehow incompatible in the same person? While

Dicks makes these comments in the context of discussing the social norms and values bearing upon individual identity, it is apparent that a biological component is also viewed by him as exerting a determining influence on individual and marital identity. On the other side of the coin, his view of the nature of marital dysfunction contains elements supportive of the potential for women's functioning as individuated persons:

> We see this very high need for a total relationship as a demand that the mate should contain all the role potentials of a large ideal group norm, tolerant of and responsive to all the partial identities and facets of personality one would wish to express towards them. (p. 17)

The intense "emotional overdependence" arises from lack of satisfaction in the workaday world and the isolation of the marital/family nuclear unit as well as from the psychological processes of idealization, splitting, projective identification, and collusion. In contrast, in the healthy marital relationship, the self does not require the other to be seen in rigid fashion in order for the self to attempt to be whole.

> The successful adaptation to modern marriage seems to require a blend of autonomy of the individual—an established sense of personal identity and ego strength—with a preservation of the capacity for dependence . . . the "ultimate" mutual commitment [is] two integrated persons finding in each other the security to "be themselves" in flexible role changes, which allows freedom of expression to all levels of the ego or self, implying also equal acceptance of the partner's variance and otherness. (Dicks, 1967, p. 29)

The inclusion of gender identity in the description of a healthy dyadic relationship is found among other psychoanalytic–object relations theorists, such as Meissner (1978), although, significantly, he views the integration of opposite-gender qualities as desirable to an individual's functioning:

> The quality of gender identity for both sexes is enhanced and embellished through mutual identifications. Thus, the capacities in the male for tender affection and nuturance can be significantly enhanced by his identifications with his wife, insofar as they become meaningfully integrated with the securely established and supportive pattern of his own masculine identity. Correspondingly, the woman can become more secure and confident of her own capacities for meaningful endeavor and self-assertion in a variety of intellectual and work pursuits by identification with her husband. (Meissner, 1978, p. 45)

For Meissner, in contrast to Dicks, the instrumental–expressive and associated role-theoretic concepts (Parsons & Bales, 1955) do not figure importantly, and, in fact, are expressly distinguished from the theoretical focus:

> The concept of role does not play a significant part in the present construction. The organization of the family can certainly be described in terms of

roles and their related concepts, but these remain essentially sociological and non-psychoanalytic. While the concept of role provides a bridge between the level of individual personality and the functioning of the group, it does not specifically base itself on nor reflect dynamic issues related to the psychoanalytic structure and integration of personality. (Meissner, 1978, p. 54)

The influential work of Sager (1976, 1981) represents a third variation on the psychoanalytic–object relations perspective. He not only regards such issues as independence–dependence, dominance–submission, activity-passivity, and task responsibility expectations as elements of the couple's own contracts (in which there is considerable cross-couple variation), but also explicitly acknowledges the potential for influence of his own acknowledged "male supremicist" biases.

Finally, Skynner (1981) offers the most sanguinely open view on gender roles from an object-theoretical position:

Perhaps our main mistake lies in the very attempt to define these roles in some stable, permanent way rather than, as in a healthy marriage and family, to remain permanently (and uncomfortably!) open to the developmental experience and expansion of consciousness that these relationships automatically make available to us, if we can bear to accept them. (p. 51)

In contrast to classical psychoanalytic theory, then, there exists wide variation in current psychoanalytic–object relations marital theories as to the impact of biological and social components of sex bias. One feature of this perspective, especially as embodied in Dicks, should be regarded as a qualifier of sexist charges against this orientation. While sexist biases do exist, dispassionate examination reveals that excessive rigidity and/or dependence on the other to "complete" the integration of the self is a mark of pathology in the relationship. Personality integration and flexibility at both individual and dyadic levels are hallmarks, in this view, of healthy marital interaction.

SYSTEMS MODELS

At first glance, systems models might not be faulted at a theoretical level on sexist grounds. The salient parameters in this perspective are those of, for example, clarity and extent of communication, commonality in the understanding of the rules inherent in the couple's interaction, flexibility and change, and the effectiveness of the system in accomplishing tasks both internal and external to the system. As such, the lack of attention to the substantive content of these system properties would seem to render systems theories mute on sexist grounds. Closer inspection, however, discloses that biases do exist in at least two influential systems theory models. Bowen (1978) distinguishes between objectivity or intellectuality and emotionality and gives the nod to the former as characteristic of healthy differentiation. Given that objectivity and the ability to remove or distance oneself from involvement in interpersonal situations has been prototypic of culturally valued male behavior, this strand of the model is sexist, both in terms of valuing objectivity and in obscuring the fact that being able to discriminate those situations in which emotional experience and expression should be encouraged. It is the very silence on the substantive nature of systems properties that warrants concern for potentially sexist implications of communications approaches (e.g., Stanton, 1981b) to marital systems. One could easily envision, for example, a system in which a rule was clear and agreed upon (e.g., wife gets to complain about the lack of meaning or importance of her actions, husband reassures her that she is quite important to him) yet flexible (wife takes a night course, husband states delight that she is finding what she wants), yet in which basic developmental issues (wife stays in the marriage because she has learned to respond positively to "being needed") are not explored. Attention primarily to the topography of the marital system in some ways may thus serve to perpetuate the status quo by not offering spouses the opportunity to explore the range of choices open to them, both dyadically and individually.

BEHAVIORAL MODELS

Behavioral models suffer from a similar "restriction of range," underlying which is the failure to take into account intrapsychic/interpersonal dysfunctions that may provide the context for, or exist in addition to, the couple's presenting problems. A situation may occur for example, in which the wife seeks an increased frequency of approval from her husband. The adequacy of the woman's own self-esteem, and/or the availability to her of other sources of positive valuation, would not be signaled as important further areas of evaluation within behavioral models. Relatedly, the exchange-theoretic assumptions of behavioral models do not in themselves mandate the assessment of the developmental quality of what is or what is desired by the couple to be exchanged. What is, in general, omitted from these models is cognizance of the very real possibility that the woman's repertoire, both behaviorally and cognitively, may be circumscribed due to culturally normative sexist conditioning. This is all the more ironic given that the dynamic deficits at issue themselves are in large part a result of social learning.

Finally, theoretical disagreements among proponents of various marital therapies may at times function to obscure more immediate social and political realities for women. Consider the following:

> The motives for a particular relationship are somewhat less important to an understanding of that relationship than are the means available to the partners for accomplishing goals within that relationship . . . [yet]

99

couples stay together for reasons not readily apparent to a behavioral exchange model, and without invoking motivational constructs such relationship stability is not well explained within such models. (Weiss, 1981)

The answer for many patients may lie not with collusion, projective identification, etc., but with something much more immediate—money. Lack of training or recent work experience, lack of independent financial resources to pay for attorney and court costs for a contested divorce, anticipated problems in establishing and maintaining an independent household (especially if children are involved) may well function to restrict women to unhappy marriages. While the modification of such contingencies is not within the domain of the marital therapist's professional activity, their assessment should not be overlooked in models of marital dysfunction.

Potential Bias in the Application of Marital Therapy Techniques

In this section, the potential for sex-role bias will be assessed with respect to the conduct of therapy within each of the three major orientations considered above. Such biases, in all fairness, are probably usually unwitting, and not reflective of any explicit attempts to shape or perpetuate any potentially negative impact on either women's behavior or their own or their spouses' construal of them. Marriage, however, has traditionally been the relationship *sui generis* in which sex-role biases are socially inculcated, or become operative even in previously "liberated" persons. The challenge of conducting "bias-free" therapy in such a context is indeed demanding. Bias certainly may be exerted independent of technique by the therapist's conveying his or her values by voice inflection, posture, relative amount of attention to each of the spouses (especially content-dependent), seating arrangements, and so on. These all may provide subtle cues to the couple about the therapist's view of their problem, lead one member of the couple to feel "more understood," and suggest therapist-valued change directions irrespective of the major techniques or tasks applied. Sex of therapist and presence/absence, status, and type and degree of activity of an opposite-sex cotherapist may also suggest important sex-role related values to the couple (Rice & Rice, 1975). Furthermore, the potential exists for bias at the point of entry of the couple into therapy along such lines as, at whose initiative and with what history they have come, who is seen as having what involvement in and what responsibility for the problem, any familial or friendship–group pressures on the couple vis-à-vis the nature of the problem and/or the objective of the therapy, and even so simple a detail as who is paying for the therapy. Such issues are matters for assessment and "defusing" early in the assessment, and are not matters of model-related techniques per se. There are, however, aspects of frequently employed techniques that deserve serious consideration for their implications for women in marital treatment.

A hallmark of these techniques is the historical–developmental focus on (largely individual) factors that have contributed to current marital dysfunction. Such a focus may have significant profeminist benefit in terms of aiding women in discovering and confronting fundamental and pervasive familial and social sexist conditioning. This strategy may also serve reconstructively to change basic intrapsychic/interpersonal patterns on the basis of which intensely dependent collusions were or might subsequently be formed. On the other hand, such a focus may also operate so as to diminish women's affect about and active attempts to respond constructively to present sources of dissatisfaction. It may also function so as to divert attention from the patterns of interaction and unresolved issues in the present marital relationship as sources of relationship dissatisfaction. Pathology-imputing features of this approach, especially within a psychiatric context, may also detract from more concrete interactional dysfunctions and increase the feelings of helplessness to which women are already all too subject (Gurman & Klein, 1980).

In addition to these general considerations, there are a number of factors more specifically associated with the application of particular techniques that may foster, by fiat, negative implications for women. One such example is the context in which the ascription of resistances may occur. The attribution and analysis of resistances may not only reflect to the patient the nature of the focus of the treatment (as characterized above) but may also discourage what may be attempts to consolidate any gains that might have been made to the point at which the construed resistance occurs. A case in point is the following:

> Other manifestations of resistance . . . [are] the perpetual creation of one crisis after another to generate affect via displacement from the real issues—for example, discussions of money when the major concerns are in other areas. (Nadelson, 1978, p. 141)

Every therapist has experienced such "crisis-oriented" couples, and such crisis-oriented points in marital therapy, which often reflect just those resistances suggested. It is also the case, however, that at times such situations may call for the therapist's direction of more active problem-solving efforts on the part of the couple. This is an especially unfortunate choice of example from the present vantage point, as men, on the average, still contribute either the whole or the greater part of the family income (Carter & Glick, 1970) and usually also hold primary responsibility for household financial management. One fairly straightforward tack would be to treat such occurrences as legitimate at first, using a problem-solving approach, and subsequently to explore resistances if crisis clarification reveals no major conflict or if one or both of the spouses sabotage problem-solving efforts.

A potentially deleterious effect may accrue to women in the implementation of another psychoanalytic technique, that of encouraging the development of a therapeutic regression. This is especially deserving of concern in cases in which dependency needs would be anticipated to come to the fore in women. For couples who stay in treatment, this is problematic primarily only where deficiencies in the transference (see below) ensue in hopelessness about change and/or lack of confidence in, or not feeling understood by, or trusting in, the therapist. Recognizing that such issues are themselves subject to further therapeutic work, regression becomes a problem primarily (although significantly) in premature termination. Such termination is, of course, far from readily predictable. Termination in the middle phase of therapy, however, may exacerbate psychological patterns that are regressive as well as characterological for some women.

A third potential source of bias exists in relation to transference and countertransference phenomena. The relatively less active (as contrasted, e.g., with behavior therapists) stance of the psychodynamic marital therapist, especially in cases where the therapist is male, may evoke feelings in women about the inaccessibility or lack of emotional expressiveness in men. This may at times reflect the actual therapeutic relationship as much as the patient's transference to, for example, her husband or father. Further, as Nadelson (1978) aptly points out:

> Another issue at this early phase of treatment, noted earlier, is the attempt of one partner to engage the therapist so that he or she takes sides. This is often seen around the issue of role-based expectations. The therapist must be aware that this polarization is occurring and be able to define what is expected of him or her. This behavior is an early manifestation of transference and may evoke countertransference feelings on the part of the therapist. (p. 141)

SYSTEMS APPROACHES

Here, as with systems models of the marital relationships, Bowenite and communications techniques require separate consideration. Bowenite techniques, especially the emphasis on examination of the family of origin of each spouse, are subject to some of the general charges related to historical focus that were applied earlier to psychodynamic approaches. In addition, the Bowenites contend that "the therapeutic method . . . is based on the assumptions that reduction of anxiety in the emotional field will improve the functional level of differentiation of self and reduce symptoms and, secondly, improvement in basic level of differentiation will increase the adaptability of the person to intense emotional fields" (Kerr, 1981). A major psychotherapeutic technique is to direct questions to each of the spouses, phrased in such a manner as to elicit more objective construals with respect to marital and familial relationships. The problem here is twofold. First, for some couples, a primary problem may not be too much emotionality or overt anxiety per se, but suppression of difficulties in the direct expression of feelings. For the significant proportion of married women in whom depressive symptomatology is prominent, the expression of anger may be an important therapeutic goal. Second, the assumption that intellectual distance "will increase the *adaptability* of the person to intense emotional fields" (emphasis added) may compound such depressive positions by not recognizing the need and providing training for communication and active problem-solving skills deficits. The second potentially biasing feature of this approach is the increasing tendency to see the spouses separately for at least some portion of the treatment (Kerr, 1981). While not so much a bias toward women per se, this strategy may overshadow the importance of couple's working together on the concrete issues or interactional patterns existing in the current relationship, and for nonworking women, may increase feelings of isolation and reinforce existing fears that this is "her problem."

Perhaps the major criticism of communications approaches should be directed more at inappropriately applied techniques than at potential biases reflected in the design or nature of the techniques per se. One arm of the communications orientation advocates the use of paradoxical or "strategic" techniques (Haley, 1976; Stanton, 1981a). These techniques depend in part for their efficacy on formulations delivered in a highly structured, directive manner. Moreover, these directives are usually counterintuitive in content, and are often offered with little attendant straightforward rationale. A woman responding to these directives, especially if the therapist is male, may well find those aspects of the experience distasteful or even discouraging of attempts she may have made or may seek to make to form a more collaborative therapeutic relationship. This issue may also be stated the other way around, in terms of what, from a feminist view, is often missing in such strategic therapies. As Gurman (1978) has pointed out, marital therapy that relies heavily on paradoxical interventions to produce change rarely include concomitant skill-training components (e.g., problem solving, communication, assertiveness) that are likely to enhance the posttreatment generalization and durability of therapeutic effects. Providing spouses, especially women, with concrete coping skills may be an important way of helping to give "power to the person" (Mahoney & Thoresen, 1974).

BEHAVIORAL APPROACHES

It has been a mainstay of behavioral approaches to develop treatment techniques and modes of implementation that would be value-free. Paradoxically enough, the very components of behavioral techniques that minimize judgmental aspects of the therapist's activities are those most prey to resulting in potentially biased effects on women (Gurman & Klein, 1984).

Potentially biasing consequences of behavioral treatment are often not very obvious. The first potential for bias occurs even before treatment per se is initiated, in the nature of behavioral inventories used for assessment purposes. The Spouse Observation Checklist (SOC) (Weiss, 1975) and the Marital Pre-Counseling Inventory (Stuart, 1981), for example, are two assessment devices that, while differing in scope, both have as an objective aiding couples to define sources of marital satisfaction and dissatisfaction in a concrete, observable manner. At first glance, the observational specificity of such instruments would appear to make them perfect antidotes to the role-expectation coloring of the therapist's assessment and interventions. On the other hand, women are becoming increasingly aware of the ways in which they have learned to see themselves as "objects," and of ways in which they have been socialized precisely in this tendency to define and evaluate their self-worth in terms of their ability to please significant others, especially a mate. In this context, then, the use of "P's" ("Pleases") and "D's" ("Displeases") (Wills, Weiss, & Patterson, 1974) in the assessment and treatment of marital dysfunction may have the effect of hypostasizing and exacerbating such socialized psychopathology. Furthermore, it is also important to assess the idiosyncratic meanings that the particular behaviors on such devices have for the couple, both dyadically and individually. Such "behaviors" as "nags," "argues," or "interrupts," for example, may have important contextual meaning for the couple, and a topographic interest in such "behaviors" may be misleading. A behavior that is described by husband as "argues," for example, might well be described as "assertive" by the wife, and such differences may reflect an underlying struggle over power or autonomy. Failure to take into account the ways in which both the inventory completion task itself as well as the encoding of events into so-called behavioral description thus suffers from the "fallacy of misplaced concreteness." In spite of behavioral marital therapists' best attempts to be empirical, construal of and affective associations to such behavioral descriptions do exist, and cannot be dismissed or reduced in their psychological significance by reference to their "inferential" nature. In addition, it is also possible that such inventories may be used implicitly as a sort of checklist by which one spouse assesses the other in terms of a role-based model. In some such cases, such ratings may be a function of the degree to which the couple has had exposure to alternatives to such "model" expectations. Whether one or both of the spouses have an interest in, or may benefit from, learning to experience a formerly displeasing (role valued) behavior as pleasing may be an important consideration in the formulation of therapeutic goals. For example, husband may find wife's agreement (e.g., with his opinions on finances or sexual expression) pleasing, and wife may not rate those areas (or her not contesting his opinions) as problematic. Whether the woman might derive satisfaction from increased participation in financial decisions or taking more initiative in sexual activities deserves appraisal by the therapist. In other words, there may be components of such ratings that are based on skills deficits related to, but distinguishable from, psychodynamic factors suggested earlier. This is not meant to imply that marital therapists should teach all women to be "liberated" (where the quotation marks imply discouraging them from any or all traditional role behaviors). What is advocated is the opportunity for choice. Blindly proceeding with interventions based on these inventories may, in a number of ways, do a serious disservice to women (Gurman & Klein, 1984).

Communication training in one form or another is almost universally a component of behavioral marital therapies. Not so universal is the appropriateness of its application. Broadly conceptualized, communication deficits are one of the most common problems in marriage. The question is the degree to which various types of deficits are amenable to the same or similar treatment packages. As has been previously suggested (Gurman & Knudson, 1978; Gurman, Knudson, & Kniskern, 1978; Gurman & Klein, 1984; Knudson, Gurman, & Kniskern, 1979) communication training techniques typically give greater weight to rational modes of communication than to highly affectively toned modes. Yet for many women the expression of powerful affect, especially anger, may be appropriate. For the same "reason," so to speak, such techniques are not particularly responsive to the complaint on the part of women heard by almost every marital therapist, that their husbands do not let them in on their feelings. (In all fairness, this is increasingly said by men about themselves.) Aiding a couple in pinpointing or increasing the frequency of communication is a very different task from shaping experience-congruent communication.

Finally, all the problem-solving exercises extant are powerless to effect change unless the problems at issue are those at the heart of the marital conflicts. Underlying the dissatisfactions of many couples are what Gottman, Notarius, Gonso, and Markman (1976) have termed "hidden agendas." For the many women for whom power is a concern, "getting to" make decisions (e.g., about how the couple will spend money) is not equivalent to addressing the problem of why in that relationship she had not previously been doing so.

Critique of Research on Marital Conflict and Therapy Outcome

A third area of concern to feminists has been the degree to, and manner in which, sexist assumptions enter into the selection of research problems, questions of design and measurement, and the conclusions drawn. As extensive reviews of these issues already exist (cf. Hicks & Platt, 1970; Laws, 1975; Gurman & Klein, 1980, 1984), our comments here will serve only to highlight the major issues.

Research on marital conflict, at least from the time of the "schizophrenogenic mother," has tended to be relatively insular, focusing more on intrafamilial (and, then, largely noninteractive) phenomena. As such, it has largely ignored political, social, and (hence) psychological realities for women. Psychological events are, we believe, multiply determined, and the causal chain extends further than, for example, "husband's withdrawing–

wife's nagging." Rausch, Barry, Hertel, and Swain (1974), for example, offer data suggesting that "husbands engaged in more acts directed toward resolving the conflict and reconciling with their partners than did wives. The wives, on the other hand, engaged in more appeals and more acts of coercion or personal attack." Rausch *et al.* go on, rightly, to suggest that variables underlying such differences may largely have to do with power (cf. Deutsch, 1969) and cite studies documenting the greater adjustments in marriage required of women than of men (e.g., Burgess & Cottrell, 1939; Landis, 1946; Burgess & Wallin, 1953; Bernard, 1964). Subsequently, however, they note findings suggesting that "factors pertaining to the husband appear to be crucial to marital success" (cf. Barry, 1970), and then offer the following:

> The use of words as strategic devices for gaining an end have, it seems, been employed by women throughout history. A female's reputation as a scold, a shrew, a nag attest to the costs incurred from crossing her desires. We are not suggesting that the wives in our sample are nags, but we are pointing to the possibility that women, as a low power group, may learn a diplomacy of psychological pressure to influence male partner's behaviors. Men—more powerful because they have more readily available outlets other than marriage for growth, development, and satisfaction—can from their strength support and care for others dependent on them [women and children]. Women and women's needs are given less legitimacy, since they are in a weaker position. To attain gratification they have mastered techniques of manipulating emotional communication. (Rausch *et al.*, 1974, pp. 152–153)

Missing entirely from these accounts of "husband factors" and women's "manipulation" are concrete suggestions for questions and/or variables that might be addressed in future research. Of interest, for example, might be the effect on "marital success" of women beginning or returning to work, women's developing more varied support/friendship networks, and the effect of change to more androgynous task division. Also of interest would be research directed to studying sources of personal and dyadic satisfaction in couples with alternative lifestyles, such as nonmarried cohabiting couples or couples in which traditional sex roles have been reversed (i.e., woman works, man stays at home). Moreover, stereotype-reinforcing language, as in the above, is neither necessary nor desirable, and is reminiscent of "blaming the victim" (Ryan, 1971). Research on marital conflict must begin to address women's behavior and experience in the marital dyad as an open system. Variables external to the marriage per se increasingly should be examined as important determinants of marital distress and conflict.

The latter phrase points to another area of concern to feminists in studies of both marriage and marital therapy outcome. Constructs related to the nature of marital dysfunction are rarely carefully distinguished and are sorely in need of conceptual and empirical clarification. This is especially important since current usage strongly tends to rely on definitions in which tacit sanction is given to women's accommodation as a condition of marital functioning. Marital distress and marital conflict are not synonymous, marital stability (defined as absence of divorce or separation) is not equivalent to marital satisfaction, nor can marital dysfunction properly be discussed without reference to what is being construed as a functional marital relationship (Gurman *et al.*, 1978; Knudson *et al.*, 1979). Lacking adequate conceptual refinement of these constructs, marital researchers and therapists, by fiat, run the real risk of preserving the status quo. Moreover, obscurantism at the conceptual level may be compounded by attempts to apply these constructs as bases for work at an empirical level. Global ratings of marital satisfaction, for example, while able to differentiate clinic and nonclinic couples, have not proved particularly meaningful. Such ratings are notoriously subject to socially desirable responding on the part of both couples and "objective" third parties (Laws, 1975). "Agreements" (as measured, for example, in the widely employed Locke–Wallace Marital Relationship Inventory), whether assessed directly or through spouse–spouse correlations, are subject to a host of response biases and potential statistical artifacts (Cronbach & Gleser, 1953; Cronbach, 1955; Klein, 1976). Such instruments are thus of questionable validity with respect to the constructs of interest above, even granting claims for their power to discriminate between distressed and nondistressed couples (Navran, 1967; Terman & Wallin, 1949). The study of actual behavior in relation to normatively biased self-report in itself, of course, may be interesting. A number of suggestions have been offered by Laws (1975) for avoiding these problems, among which are scales constructed with positively and negatively keyed social-desirability-matched items, and the use of ecologically realistic conflict-engaging tasks. The use of forced-choice or multidimensional scaling procedures may also at least reduce problems of statistical artifacts. The assessment of agreement/distress/satisfaction with respect to a variety of particular content or interactional domains should also be encouraged. Attention to such methodological problems may go far in aiding researchers in discovering those variables associated with women's sources of marital satisfaction.

A fourth issue for feminists in marital therapy outcome research is the vantage points from which change is assessed. All too frequently change ratings have been solely those of the therapist (Gurman & Kniskern, 1978a). The couple's joint and/or individual judgments are too infrequently considered. Moreover, the therapist making such ratings is often male, and not infrequently subscribes to socially valued sex-role biased beliefs (APA Task Force, 1975). There is also the potential for positive "halo" effects to become incorporated in such ratings. This is certainly an endemic issue in therapy outcome research generally. What makes it especially troublesome in the evaluation of marital therapy outcome is the potential for capitulation or adaptation on the part of the wife to reduce the level of reported marital distress and thus yield (perhaps small) positive change ratings. From a feminist perspective, such change could hardly be construed as desirable. While assessment of the degree and direction of change from the woman's perspective will not necessarily obviate this problem, not including spouses' individual assessments will guarantee the potential for such problems. A straightforward answer to Freud's question, "What do women want?" will be not obtained unless we ask them!

A related problem in the assessment of change occurs in the use of behavioral observation coding systems. Paradoxically, the objectives in the development and application of such systems included that of avoiding the evaluational as well as methodological problems of global satisfaction ratings. The "objectivity" claimed for the use of at least one such coding system, however, should be seriously questioned. The Marital Interaction Coding System (MICS) (Hops, Wills, Patterson, & Weiss, 1972) provides a means for coding discrete spouse behaviors as "positive" or "negative." "Compromise," for example, would be universally coded as positive, whereas "Disagreement" would be coded as negative. Such coding rules ignore (1) the idiosyncratic meaning that particular behaviors may have for the couple (e.g., in the proper context, "criticism" could be regarded as constructive), and (2) the fact that, from a therapeutic perspective, "failure to attach the clinically appropriate meaning to the appearance of these "negative" behaviors may obscure the *positive* value of purportedly negative verbal behaviors, and the *negative* value of purportedly "positive" behaviors" (Gurman & Klein, 1984, p. 179). It should be noted that such a criticism is not directed against the potential contribution of behavioral coding of marital interaction per se, or even against attempts to develop coding rules that could be universally applied by an outside observer. Rather, the point is that behavioral interaction coding systems do not provide the basis for adequately accounting for either the context or the idiosyncratic psychological meaning to the couple of particular behavioral events. As such, the potential for coding behavior as "negative" that may be constructive for a particular woman within a particular relationship is high.

The employment of such a template is part of a larger problematic framework employed by behavioral marital researchers, termed "Matching-to-Sample" (Alexander & Barton, 1976; Barton & Alexander, 1981; Parsons & Alexander, 1973). Eschewing development of theoretical formulations about the nature of healthy marital relationships, these authors offer the following views: "This philosophy asserts that there is not necessarily a theoretically derived ideal form of family process, but rather that remediating family problems might best be accomplished by helping disturbed families attain the same patterns of family interaction that are characteristic of nondistressed families" (Barton & Alexander, 1981). The assumptions here run aground on a problem noted earlier, that the construct of "nondistressed" is ipso facto meaningful and unambiguous. The difficulties with this assumption are that absence of reported distress does not imply the

108

converse, that is, that of felt marital satisfaction, and that clinic couples, while experiencing pain, might well be argued to be presently or potentially healthier than nonclinic couples by virtue of their acknowledgment of, and motivation to change, problems in the marital relationship. Moreover, so-called nondistressed families have been found not at all free of nonsymptomatic members (e.g., Manhattan Midtown Project). The potential for problems at the more complex interactional level is even greater. As such, to presume that normative marital interaction patterns are not only nondistressed but worthy as "patterns" toward which to shape clinic couples is not only tenuous but potentially dangerous. Explicitly preserving the status quo runs the twofold risk of regarding challenges or pain as inherently non-growth-promoting and of construing women's acquiesce, capitulation, or even chronic depression as sanctionable.

Finally, research that fails to include multiple targets (husband, wife, husband–wife interaction) as well as multiple domains (behavior, experience) runs the risk of tending to be self-perpetuating or self-validating. Neither, for example, "behavior counts" nor self-reports alone are sufficient to account for the range of phenomena salient in the study of couples relationships. This assertion cannot be waved away by pointing to multiple programs of research conducted with different orientations as being "complementary," as few research projects are so parallel in other respects as to provide points of comparison. Gurman and Kniskern (1978a, 1981b) have offered a comprehensive framework that provides a useful guide for researchers interested in designing studies that reveal more of the complexity of the nature of both healthy and dysfunctional marital relationships.

CONCLUSION

The focus of this discussion has been on a number of significant contemporary social changes and their implications for marital theory, therapy, and research. These are by no means the only social changes with such implications. Other trends with the potential for impact on marital therapy include increases in the number of stepfamilies, dual-career couples, and alternative relationship patterns (including "serial monogamy," communal life-styles, and homosexual couples). Particularly deserving comment is our consideration of feminist implications for marital therapy without equal time to the small but growing "male liberation" movement (Goldberg, 1977). Our rationale for this choice of emphasis is largely a reflection of the degree to which the feminist movement has gained social recognition and is credited more or less directly with having affected women's behavior and understanding of their experiences. Awareness of and scrupulous avoidance of potential sex-role bias called for by feminists should not, however, lead marital therapists into the opposite trap of promoting radical feminist goals without clearly labeling their activities as such (Gurman & Klein, 1984). Furthermore, while our own values are egalitarian, we recognize that there are couples who would not choose such values as fundamental to their own relationships. That the interplay among political orientation, social changes, and the activity of mental health professionals is intricate and omnipresent should not deter us from careful examination of the consequences of this interplay in our influence on the lives of others.

As research increasingly demonstrates the ways in which the marital dyad functions as a part of larger social, and economic and political systems, our models and therapeutic interventions will require revision accordingly. If, as predicted by Bernard (1972), for example, multi-unit or communal households increasingly become prevalent, marital therapy will likely become in even more ways than at present "a family affair." Cognizance of, and considered responsiveness to, social change cannot be merely an interesting diversion to the central tasks of advancing and applying psychology as a science; it is an integral part of such endeavors. Our ability to unravel the fabric of the multiple influences on, and consequences of, marital interactions is required if we are to enable patients to choose the threads they seek to weave.

REFERENCES

Alexander, J. F., & Barton, C. Behavioral systems therapy for families. In D. H. Olson (Ed.), *Treating relationships*. Lake Mills, Iowa: Graphic, 1976.

American Psychological Association Task Force. Report of the task force on sex bias and sex-role stereotyping in psychotherapeutic practice. *American Psychologist*, 1975, *30*, 1169–1175.

Barry, W. A. Marriage research conflict: An integrative review. *Psychological Bulletin*, 1970, *73*, 412–454.

Barton, C., & Alexander, J. F. Functional family therapy. In A. S. Gurman & D. P. Kniskern (Eds.), *Handbook of family therapy*. New York: Brunner/Mazel, 1981.

Bem, S. L. The measurement of psychological androgyny. *Journal of Consulting and Clinical Psychology*, 1974, *42*, 155–162.

Bernard, J. *The future of marriage*. New York: Bantam, 1964.

Bodin, A. The interactional view: Family therapy approaches of the Mental Research Institute. In A. S. Gurman & D. P. Kniskern (Eds.), *Handbook of family therapy*. New York: Brunner/Mazel, 1981.

Bowen, M. *Family therapy in clinical practice*. New York: Jason Aronson, 1978.

Burgess, E. W., & Cottrell, L. S. *Predicting success or failure in marriage*. New York: Prentice-Hall, 1939.

Burgess, E. W., & Wallin, P. *Engagement and marriage*. Chicago: Lippincott, 1953.

Carter, H., & Glick, P. *Marriage and divorce: A social and economic study*. Cambridge, Mass.: Harvard University Press, 1970.

Chesler, P. *Women and madness*. New York: Avon, 1972.

Cronbach, L. J. Processes affecting scores on "understanding of others" and "assured similarity." *Psychological Bulletin*, 1955, *52*, 177–193.

Cronbach, L. J., & Gleser, G. C. Assessing similarity between profiles. *Psychological Bulletin*, 1953, *50*, 456–473.

Deutsch, M. Conflicts: Productive and destructive. *Journal of Social Issues*, 1969, *25*, 7–41.

Dicks, H. V. *Marital tensions*. Boston and London: Routledge & Kegan Paul, 1967.

Doherty, W. J., McCabe, P., & Ryder, R. G. Marriage encounter: A critical appraisal. *Journal of Marriage and Family Counseling*, 1978, *4*, 99–106.

Donelson, E., & Gullahorn, J. E. *Women: A psychological perspective*. New York: Wiley, 1977.

Glick, P. C., & Parke, P. New approaches in studying the life cycle of the family. *Demography*, 1965, *2*, 190.

Goldberg, H. *The hazards of being male*. New York: Signet, 1977.

Garfield, S. L., & Bergin, A. E. (Eds.). *Handbook of psychotherapy and behavior change* (2nd ed.). New York: Wiley, 1978.

Gottman, J., & Leiblum, S. *How to do psychotherapy and how to evaluate it*. New York: Holt, Rinehart & Winston, 1974.

Gottman, J., Notarius, C., Gonso, J., & Markman, H. *A couple's guide to communication*. Champaign, Ill.: Research Press, 1976.

Gurman, A. S. The patient's perception of the therapeutic relationship. In A. S. Gurman & A. Razin (Eds.), *Effective psychotherapy: A handbook for research*. New York: Pergamon, 1977.

Gurman, A. S. Contemporary marital therapies: A critique and comparative analysis of psychoanalytic, behavioral and systems theory approaches. In T. J. Paolino & B. S. McCrady (Eds.), *Marriage and marital therapy: Psychoanalytic, behavioral, and systems theory perspectives*. New York: Brunner/Mazel, 1978.

Gurman, A. S. Dimensions of marital therapy: A comparative analysis. *Journal of Marital and Family Therapy*, 1979, *5*, 5–16.

Gurman, A. S. *Brief marital therapy: By design or default?* Keynote address to the Ontario Association for Marriage and Family Therapy, London, Ontario, April 1980. (a)

Gurman, A. S. Behavioral marital therapy in the 1980's: The challenge of integration. *American Journal of Family Therapy*, 1980, *8*, 86–96. (b)

Gurman, A. S. Integrative marital therapy: Toward the development of an interpersonal approach. In S. Budman (Ed.), *Forms of brief therapy*. New York: Guilford, 1981.

Gurman, A. S., & Klein, M. H. Marital and family conflicts. In A. Brodsky & R. Hare-Mustin (Eds.), *Women and psychotherapy*. New York: Guilford, 1980.

Gurman, A. S., & Klein, M. H. Marriage and the family: An unconscious male bias in behavioral treatment? In E. Blechman (Ed.), *Behavior modification with women*. New York: Guilford, 1984.

Gurman, A. S., & Kniskern, D. P. Research on marital and family therapy: Progress, prospect and perspective. In S. Garfield & A. Bergin (Eds.), *Handbook of psychotherapy and behavior change* (2nd ed.). New York: Wiley, 1978. (a)

Gurman, A. S., & Kniskern, D. P. Deterioration in marital and family therapy: Clinical, conceptual and empirical issues. *Family Process*, 1978, *17*, 3–20. (b)

Gurman, A. S., & Kniskern, D. P. (Eds.), *Handbook of family therapy*. New York: Brunner/Mazel, 1981. (a)

Gurman, A. S., & Kniskern, D. P. Family therapy outcome research: Knowns and unknowns. In A. S. Gurman & D. P. Kniskern (Eds.), *Handbook of family therapy*. New York: Brunner/Mazel, 1981. (b)

Gurman, A. S., & Knudson, R. Behavioral marriage therapy: A psychodynamic-systems analysis and critique. *Family Process*, 1978, *17*, 121–138.

Gurman, A. S., Knudson, R. M., & Kniskern, D. P. Behavioral marriage therapy: IV. Take two aspirin and call us in the morning. *Family Therapy*, 1978, *17*, 165–180.

Haley, J. Whither family therapy. *Family Process*, 1962, *1*, 69–100.

Haley, J. *Problem solving therapy*. San Francisco: Jossey-Bass, 1976.

Hare-Mustin, R. T. A feminist approach to family therapy. *Family Process*, 1978, *17*, 181–194.

Hicks, M. W., & Platt, M. Marital happiness and stability: A review of the research in the sixties. *Journal of Marriage and the Family*, 1970, *32*, 59–78.

Homans, G. C. *Social behavior: Its elementary forms*. New York: Harcourt, Brace & World, 1961.

Hops, H., Wills, T. A., Patterson, G. R., & Weiss, R. L. *Marital interaction coding system*. Unpublished manuscript, University of Oregon, 1972.

Jacobson, N. S. A review of research on the effectiveness of marital therapy. In T. J. Paolino & B. S. McCrady (Eds.), *Marriage and marital therapy: Psychoanalytic, behavioral, and systems theory perspectives*. New York: Brunner/Mazel, 1978.

Jacobson, N. S. Behavioral marital therapy: In A. S. Gurman & D. P. Kniskern (Eds.), *Handbook of family therapy*. New York: Brunner/Mazel, 1981.

Jacobson, N. S., & Margolin, G. *Marital therapy: Strategies based on social learning and behavior exchange principles*. New York: Brunner/Mazel, 1979.

Kerr, M. Family systems theory and therapy. In A. S. Gurman & D. P. Kniskern (Eds.), *Handbook of family therapy*. New York: Brunner/Mazel, 1981.

Klein, M. Feminist concepts of therapy outcome. *Psychotherapy: Theory, Research and Practice*, 1976, *13*, 89–95.

Kniskern, D. P., & Gurman, A. S. Advances and prospects in research in family therapy. In J. P. Vincent (Ed.), *Advances in family intervention, assessment and therapy* (Vol. II). Greenwich, Conn.: JAI Press, 1981.

Knudson, R. M., Gurman, A. S., & Kniskern, D. P. Behavioral marriage therapy: A treatment in transition. In C. Franks & G. T. Wilson (Eds.), *Annual review of behavior therapy* (Vol. 7). New York: Brunner/Mazel, 1979.

Knupfer, G., Clark, W., & Room, R. The mental health of the unmarried. *American Journal of Psychiatry*, 1966, *122*, 842.

Laws, J. L. A Feminist view of marital adjustment. In A. S. Gurman & D. G. Rice (Eds.), *Couples in conflict*. New York: Jason Aronson, 1975.

Landis, J. T. Length of time required to achieve adjustment in marriage. *American Sociological Review*, 1946, *11*, 666–667.

Mahoney, M. J., & Thoresen, C. E. *Self-control: Power to the person*. Monterey, Calif.: Brooks-Cole, 1974.

Manus, G. I. Marriage counseling: A technique in search of a theory. *Journal of Marriage and the Family*, 1966, *28*, 449–453.

Meissner, W. W. The conceptualization of marriage and family dynamics from a psychoanalytic perspective. In T. J. Paolino & B. S. McCrady (Eds.), *Marriage and marital therapy: Psychoanalytic, behavioral, and systems theory perspectives*. New York: Brunner/Mazel, 1978.

Nadelson, C. Marital therapy from a psychoanalytic perspective. In T. J. Paolino & B. S. McCrady (Eds.), *Marriage and marital therapy: Psychoanalytic, behavioral, and systems theory perspectives*. New York: Brunner/Mazel, 1978.

Navran, L. Communication and adjustment in marriage. *Family Process*, 1967, *6*, 173–184.

Norton, A. J., & Glick, P. C. Marital instability: Past, present and future. *Journal of Social Issues*, 1976, *32*, 5–20.

Olson. D. H. Marital and family therapy: Integrative review and critique. *Journal of Marriage and the Family*, 1970, *32*, 501–538.

Paolino, T. J., & McCrady, B. S. (Eds.). *Marriage and marital therapy: Psychoanalytic, behavioral, and systems theory perspectives*. New York: Brunner/Mazel, 1978.

Parsons, B., & Alexander, J. F. Short term family intervention: A therapy outcome study. *Journal of Consulting and Clinical Psychology*, 1973, *41*, 195–201.

Parsons, T., & Bales, R. F. *Family socialization and interaction process*. Glencoe, Ill.: Free Press, 1955.

Prochaska, J., & Prochaska, J. Twentieth century trends in marriage and marital therapy. In

T. J. Paolino & B. S. McCrady (Eds.), *Marriage and marital therapy: Psychoanalytic, behavioral, and systems theory perspectives.* New York: Brunner/Mazel, 1978.

Rausch, H. L., Barry, W. A., Hertel, R. K., & Swain, M. A. *Communication, conflict, and marriage.* San Francisco: Jossey-Bass, 1974.

Rice, J. K., & Rice, D. G. Status and sex-role issues in co-therapy. In A. S. Gurman & D. G. Rice (Eds.), *Couples in conflict.* New York: Jason Aronson, 1975.

Ryan, W. *Blaming the victim.* New York: Random House, 1971.

Sager, C. J. *Marriage therapy and couples contracts.* New York: Brunner/Mazel, 1976.

Sager, C. J. Couples contracts and marriage therapy. In A. S. Gurman & D. P. Kniskern (Eds.), *Handbook of family therapy.* New York: Brunner/Mazel, 1981.

Skynner, A. C. R. An open-systems, group-analytic approach to family therapy. In A. S. Gurman & D. P. Kniskern (Eds.), *Handbook of family therapy.* New York: Brunnzer/Mazel, 1981.

Spence, J. T., Helmreich, R., & Stapp, J. Ratings of self and peers on sex role attributes and their relation to self-esteem and conceptions of masculinity and feminity. *Journal of Personality and Social Psychology,* 1975, *32,* 29-39.

Stanton, M. D. Strategic approaches to family therapy. In A. S. Gurman & D. P. Kniskern (Eds.), *Handbook of family therapy.* New York: Brunner/Mazel, 1981. (a)

Stanton, M. D. Marital therapy from a structural/strategic viewpoint. In G. P. Sholevar (Ed.), *Marriage is a family affair: A textbook of marital and family therapy.* Jamaica, N.Y.: S.P. Medical and Scientific Books, Spectrum Publications, 1981. (b)

Stuart, R. B. *Helping couples change.* New York: Guilford, 1981.

Stuart, R. B. Behavioral remedies for marital ills: A guide to the use of operant-interpersonal techniques. In A. S. Gurman & D. G. Rice (Eds.), *Couples in conflict.* New York: Jason Aronson, 1975.

Terman, L., & Wallin, P. The validity of marriage prediction and marital adjustment tests. *American Sociological Review,* 1949, *14,* 497-504.

Thibaut, J. W., & Kelley, H. H. *The social psychology of groups.* New York: Wiley, 1959.

United States Department of Commerce. *Social indicators 1976: Selected data on trends and conditions in the United States.* Washington, D.C.: U.S. Government Printing Office, 1977.

Weiss, R. *Spouse observation checklist.* Unpublished manuscript, University of Oregon, 1975.

Weiss, R. Strategic behavioral marital therapy: Toward a model for assessment and intervention. In J. P. Vincent (Ed.), *Advances in family intervention, assessment and theory* (Vol. II). Greenwich, Conn.: JAI Press, 1981.

Weissman, M., & Klerman, G. L. Sex differences and the epidemiology of depression. *Archives of General Psychiatry,* 1977, *34,* 98-111.

Whitaker, C. A. Personal communication, May 1980.

Whitaker, C. A., & Keith, D. V. Symbolic-experiential family therapy. In A. S. Gurman & D. P. Kniskern (Eds.), *Handbook of family therapy.* New York: Brunner/Mazel, 1981.

Wills, T. A., Weiss, R. L., & Patterson, G. R. A behavioral analysis of the determinants of marital satisfaction. *Journal of Consulting and Clinical Psychology,* 1974, *42,* 802-811.

Marriage and Marital Therapy

CHAPTER FOUR

An Overview of the Psychodynamics of Couples: Bridging Concepts[1]

DAVID A. BERKOWITZ

Like parenthood (Benedek, 1959), marriage as a developmental process (Blanck & Blanck, 1968) can provide the opportunity either to rework earlier developmental difficulties in order to arrive at a new level of integration, or maladaptively—at a great expense to the character structure and development of each individual—to attempt to resolve these internal difficulties through externalization, that is, by seeking change in the spouse. In this latter situation, each member of the dyad seeks to feel better about himself or herself through changing the other. How frequent is the opening gambit of the patient in either individual or marital therapy that a change in the spouse who is being blamed for the difficulties would be the answer to his or her problems! As is well known, many marry precisely in an unconscious effort to resolve underlying intrapsychic difficulties (Dicks, 1963).

In this chapter, I focus on the understanding of how individuals choose and use objects in intimate interpersonal relationships, in attempts to resolve and master internal intrapsychic issues growing out of early significant relationships in their families of origin. I discuss and illustrate certain concepts that bridge the intrapsychic and the interpersonal, including forms of projection, the concept of transference in its broad sense, the defense mechanism of identification with the aggressor, and the recently described selfobject transference. Finally, some therapeutic considerations are briefly discussed.

Psychoanalytically oriented marital psychotherapy—both for purposes of dynamic understanding and for conceptualizing the treatment process—

1. An earlier version of this chapter was presented at the symposium "Marital and Sexual Therapy," June 18, 1982.

David A. Berkowitz. Department of Psychiatry, Tufts University School of Medicine, Boston, Massachusetts, and Faculty, Boston Psychoanalytic Society and Institute, Boston, Massachusetts.

has been steeped in a search for concepts that bridge the gap between the inner world of the individual and the external, social world of the couple. The focus has been on the interaction and reciprocal influences between the interpersonal and the intrapsychic. More specifically—since there is always an interplay between the individual and the couple or the family—the clinician's task is to try to assess and formulate *to what extent* external forces from the family or spouse are influencing, motivating, reinforcing, perpetuating, or contributing to the internal conflict, symptoms, or difficulty of the individual and the difficulty he or she presents in treatment (i.e., "resistance"). The task of the clinician is also to try to assess and formulate to what extent the internal problems and conflicts of the individual are being externalized in a way that has important ramifications for the marriage.

Conceptual bridges have been provided mainly from adapting ego mechanisms of defense which largely depend for their successful function on involving, in some major way, significant objects in one's environment. That is, much of this thinking has involved the application of intrapsychic mechanisms of defense to the interpersonal field (Avery, 1977; Dicks, 1963; Framo, 1970; Main, 1966; Zinner, 1977; Zinner & Shapiro, 1972). To some extent, these concepts have evolved via their being directly observed in the marital situation; to some extent, they have evolved indirectly via extrapolation from the patient–therapist field of observation to the marital situation.

Projective identification encompasses many of these defense mechanisms and despite certain problems with the concept, the basic idea can be quite useful. The individual attempts to perceive his or her own repudiated qualities or impulses in the other, and may experience these qualities or impulses in the other vicariously. This implies a loss of good differentiation and a blurring of boundaries between self and object. Viewing projective identification as an intrapsychic defense mechanism, Kernberg (1975) has stressed the lack of differentiation between self and object and the need to control the external object out of fear of projected aggressive impulses. Furthermore, the individual may attempt to induce in the other his or her own repudiated qualities. Projective identification has also been referred to as "projective transference distortion" or "irrational role assignment" (Framo, 1970), "externalization" (Brodey, 1965), "trading of dissociations" (Wynne, 1965), and a variety of other terms.

Via projective identification, members of the couple are said to split off disavowed aspects of themselves and project them onto the other; these projections then govern their perceptions of and behavior toward one another. Members of the couple relate toward significant others onto whom they project aspects of themselves in the same manner as they would were these projections internalized. Thus, internalized conflict *within* individuals is externalized, assuming the form of interpersonal conflict *between* spouses.

In projective identification, as opposed to simple projection, the person projecting identifies vicariously with the recipient of his or her projections and remains very involved with the recipient's activities which confirm the projection. Additionally, the projector may actually seek, through provocation, to induce certain behaviors in the other. "Identification" in "projective identification," according to Zinner and Shapiro (1972), refers to the relationship between a subject and his or her projected part as he or she experiences it within the object. As an example, Dicks (1963) described the "man's man" husband who projects his dependency onto his "little woman" wife and punishes her for that quality.

VICARIOUS EXPERIENCING OF EXTERNALLY LOCATED CONFLICT

A frequently encountered variety of projective identification is the process of locating in the spouse dissociated aspects of the self of which one is consciously unaware. Akin to Wynne's (1963) "trading of dissociations," this has been described by Framo (1970) as the collusive carrying of psychic functions by the partner. Such locating is implied in Dicks's (1963) concept of the marital pair working as if it were a "joint personality" and in Avery's (1977) reference to one partner of the sadomasochistic couple being "nominally" sadistic or "ostensibly" masochistic. It is also implicit in the notion of the "phobic companion or partner." In all of these cases, the covert needs of the less symptomatic appearing partner are thought to be gratified vicariously through identification with the overtly symptomatic member of the pair.

Case Examples

A couple came for therapy after the sudden, tragic death of their first-born infant. The wife brought in pictures of the baby, wept, and shared her grief openly with the therapist. The husband, who showed little emotion over the loss and avowed that he was there mainly for the sake of his bereaved wife, nevertheless faithfully attended the sessions. To the extent that he was able to grieve, he seemed to be doing so vicariously through the wife. He finally began to grieve openly after 5 months of treatment.

A manifestly independent, but covertly dependent man chauffered his agoraphobic wife everywhere, ostensibly because of her overwhelming anxious dependency. Professing that his attendance at the interview was for the sake of his "sick" wife, he acknowledged under questioning that they mutually depended on one another desperately, "like two people leaning against a sheet." The extent to which she was covertly required to remain fixed in a dependent and phobic position could then be explored.

Dicks (1963) ascribed the hypermasculine husband's intolerance of his wife's emotionality to rigid defenses against the man's own despised, repressed dependent yearnings which are projected onto his wife. Zinner

(1977) gave a similar example in which the wife, in reciprocal fashion, projected her aggressiveness onto the husband and accepted the projection of his helplessness onto her.

In a similar vein, Main (1966) described an interlocking system of mutual projections in a couple with an unconsummated marriage. In Main's case, a wife projected onto her husband a hated, despised part of herself felt as ignorant, helpless, and weak, while the husband projected onto his wife a hated and feared part of himself concerned with excellence, aggressive striving, potency, and strength. Main elegantly traced each of their respective genetic backgrounds and dynamic reasons necessitating the projections. He explained the husband's projection of his aggressiveness largely as a guilty and fearful retreat from Oedipal rivalry with his own weak father. He explained the wife's need to project her weakness as resulting from both an attempt at defensive identification with an idealized father and a wish to conceal an earlier identification with a despised, ignorant and weak father. In this interlocking system, the wife could then complain contemptuously about her husband's impotence, inadequacy, and defectiveness. The husband, in turn, experienced his wife as excessively demanding and aggressive.

In an oversimplified way, then, projective identification is one bridging concept that begins to address the dividing up and parceling out of various nonintegrated psychic structures in an interpersonal way. Zinner and Shapiro (1974) pointed out that the family or couple as a group acts, then, *as if* it were a "single psychic entity."

Zinner and Shapiro (1972) summarize the qualities of a relationship in which projective identification plays a determining role as follows:

> 1) The subject perceives the object as if the object contained elements of the subject's personality; 2) the subject can evoke behaviors or feelings in the object that conform with the subject's perceptions (i.e., the subject maneuvers the object into the requisite stance); 3) the subject can experience vicariously the activity and feelings of the object; 4) participants in close relationships are often in collusion with one another to sustain mutual projections, i.e., to support one another's defensive operations and to provide experiences through which the other can participate vicariously. (p. 525)

MOTIVATIONS FOR INTERPERSONALIZATION

The projected qualities derive from internal conflict that is the result, in part, of internalized unresolved conflictual significant relationships from one's earliest years in one's family of origin. Attempts are made to master and resolve through re-enactment or repetition—however unsuccessful these attempts may be—these early relationships and their effects. The mechanisms described thus serve a dual function. First, they mitigate intrapsychic conflict within the individual. Second, they serve to recapture and restore through reenactment important conflictual early relationships with significant figures from each partner's family of origin. In particular, past relationships or those aspects of past relationships which have not been grieved or put into perspective (Semrad, 1969; Paul, 1967; Skynner, 1976; Zinner & Shapiro, 1972) intrude into the present and are compelled to be repeated in the current marital relationship. The mechanisms being described are thus both defensive and restorative. They defend against internal conflict and are object-conserving at the same time.

THE CONCEPT OF TRANSFERENCE IN INTIMATE RELATIONSHIPS

The operation of projective identification in marital relationships thus is similar to the transference that forms in psychoanalytic therapy, where, however, there is not the collusive interplay of mutual projections one observes in the marital dyad (Zinner, 1977). Transference, used in its broadest sense, is one of the universal and ubiquitous determinants of every adult relationship (Sandler, Dare, & Holder, 1973; Brenner, 1976). As Sandler *et al.* (1973) note: "Transference elements enter to a varying degree into all relationships, and these (e.g., choice of spouse or employer) are often determined by some characteristic of the other person who (consciously or unconsciously) represents some attribute of an important figure of the past" (p. 48).

Sandler (1976) has advanced the notion of "unconscious cueing" as an alternative to the concept of projective identification for understanding the workings of transference. Although it focuses on the patient–therapist relationship, this notion seems especially applicable to couples. Sandler (1976) states further:

> In our conclusions about transference we took the step of extending the notion of the patient's projection or externalization of some aspect of the past or of a figure of the past, onto the person of the analyst, to all his attempts to manipulate or to provoke situations with the analyst. I believe such "manipulations" to be an important part of object relationships in general and to enter in "trial" form into the "scanning" of objects in the process of object choice. In the transference, in many subtle ways, the patient attempts to prod the analyst into behaving in a particular way and unconsciously scans and adapts to his perception of the analyst's reaction. (p. 44)

People thus not only project, but also unconsciously choose objects to conform to their perceptions. Sandler (1976) emphasizes that

> the role-relationship of the patient in analysis at any particular time consists of a role in which he casts himself, and a complementary role in which he casts the analyst at that particular time. The patient's transference would thus represent an attempt by him to impose an interaction, an interrelationship (in the broadest sense of the word) between himself and the analyst. (p. 44)

Sandler (1976) suggests that rather than the analyst regarding some aspect of his or her own behavior as deriving entirely from within, it might more usefully be viewed as "a compromise between his own tendencies or propensities and the role-relationship which the patient is unconsciously seeking to establish." Sandler does not find the terms "projection," "externalization," "projective identification," and "putting parts of oneself onto the analyst" sufficient to explain and to understand the processes of dynamic interaction which occur in the transference and countertransference. He suggests that a complicated system of "unconscious cues," both given and received, is involved. He points out that this is the same sort of process that occurs in normal object relationships and in the process of temporary or permanent object choice as well.

In general, then, we are speaking about perceptions colored by displacements onto objects in the present of feelings toward significant objects in the past. Thus, we are really using in its simplest form the concept of transference, in an attempt to understand multiple and interacting transferences in the couple.

IDENTIFICATION WITH THE AGGRESSOR

When the predominant transference is to a powerful, controlling, and frustrating early object, a particular way of attempting to master past hurts in present interactions which is commonly encountered in work with couples is identification with the aggressor (Avery, 1977; Fraiberg, Adelson, & Shapiro, 1975). Here an individual unconsciously attempts to turn around a difficult early relationship in which he or she had been the helpless victim (e.g., as a child of an emotionally depriving and withholding parent) so that he or she is no longer the victim but assumes instead the sadistic, controlling, powerful, upper hand in a current relationship with a spouse who is now put in the position of the vulnerable, needy, and helpless child. Because the two positions are perceived as "either/or" in unconscious fantasy, this is desperately and vitally necessary to do in order to protect the individual from a dreaded repetition of the earlier painful and helpless situation. In "sadomasochistic" couples, according to Avery (1977), each partner struggles to occupy the role of the aggressor and to force the other to accept the more vulnerable role. The purpose of the power struggles is to intimidate a potentially deserting partner into believing that the loss of the object will cause the partner more pain than his or her departure causes (Avery, 1977).

An example illustrates the operation of identification with the aggressor in a couple. A woman who had suffered much frustration as a small child was married to a narcissistic, vulnerable man who complained he felt chronically deprived of affection in their relationship. The wife would at times be warmly seductive toward her husband, but usually when she had a living room full of women for a meeting, and thus nothing could come of the overture but frustration. It emerged that she was inviting her husband to feel the anguish she had felt as a girl (but could not remember) when her hopes were repeatedly raised by her mother and then frustrated.

Avery (1977) gives a familiar illustration of a couple's desperate struggles for power and control in the following example:

> Enraged each time he failed to win his partner's agreement that she was the needier of the two, a patient habitually stalked out, announcing his intention to seek another lover. Soon after, he would call his "jilted" partner and meekly ask if she would come to fetch him. In angry and injured tones, she generally refused to pursue him; however, her response indicated that he was able to return to the relationship on her sufferance. The leverage had, for the moment, passed to her. (p. 104)

Once the jockeying for power is identified, the either/or view can be traced to its origins in the relevant genetic childhood frustrating or traumatic relationships for each member of the dyad.

SELFOBJECT TRANSFERENCE NEEDS AND MARITAL DYSHARMONY

Recent work on self psychology and the selfobject transferences may contribute to further understanding of certain aspects of marital dysharmony (Berkowitz, in press). Kohut (1971, 1972) has shown how, in cases where the individual's narcissism has been wounded or damaged early in childhood, attempts to repair or complete the self tend to proceed throughout life. This results either in a need to be constantly "mirrored," confirmed, and validated, or to be merged with an idealized, omnipotent other. An attempt at self-esteem regulation through an "idealizing" relationship may lead to the insistence on the partner's perfection and on uninterrupted attachment to him or her. Disruption of the attachment can lead to desperate, empty depression, narcissistic rage, and revengeful behaviors. An attempt to repair self-esteem through constant mirroring affirmation can manifest itself in implicit demands by one member of the couple for total and unconditional acceptance by the other. In a related vein, utilizing Margaret Mahler's work, Blanck and Blanck (1968) have described the wish to be completely understood by the partner without having to verbally articulate one's thoughts or wishes as indicating an underlying longing to replicate symbiotic union with a mothering figure.

BRIEF THERAPEUTIC CONSIDERATIONS

Couples therapy is interpretive (Titchener, 1966) and emphasizes a psychodynamic understanding of and insight into the current marital interactions in light of each spouse's own early experiences in his or her family of origin. As an illustration, the wife in a young couple would repeatedly and relentlessly press her husband with questions about his fidelity, asking whether he was attracted to other women, including even past relationships. He was unable to respond to her veiled request for reassurance which was based on long-standing characterological insecurity. She seemed to be asking, "Am I enough? Do you find me appealing?" Instead, he experienced her questions as the third degree, an interrogation and invasion of his private inner world and space, a feeling we were able to trace to his early relationship with an intrusive, divorced mother. As with his mother, he would respond with an automatic, profoundly guilty feeling, "confessing" certain facts and carefully trying to keep certain others to himself. The husband's guilty feeling was interpreted as related to his earlier interactions with his mother, and the wife's problem of jealousy, distrust, and insecurity about her appeal within her own family of origin was interpreted. The husband could then begin to recognize his wife's familiar sequence of questions as reflecting her insecure self-esteem and could respond to her with appropriate comforting and reassurance. She, in turn, could begin to forego the lengthy litany of questions and relentless pursuit of factual details.

In the treatment of marital dysharmony, one usually starts with a reluctant set of patients, no matter how consciously eager they are to solve their difficulties. Each tends to be invested in seeing the problem as residing in the marital partner in the here and now. No therapeutic alliance yet exists, and the patients are often guarded and distrustful of the therapist. Each partner fears the therapist's allying with one partner and abandoning the other (Avery, 1977). At the outset, members of the couple may be far more concerned with having the therapist take sides than being helpful to the couple as a unit (Berkowitz, 1981). The therapist, however, must maintain a therapeutic stance that is guided by the intention to be helpful to *both* partners—to help the couple mobilize its own resources and to facilitate the phase-appropriate growth and development of each spouse. A therapeutic alliance with both members of the couple is founded upon attempts to empathically understand each's life stresses, unresolved griefs, and feelings of abandonment. Despite each partner's frequent wish to locate problems in the spouse, the therapist tries to expand the couple's perspective to include their roles in generating, perpetuating, and resolving the conflicted marital interaction. In the context of the developing alliance, projections may be taken back, denied affects may be reclaimed (Berkowitz, 1977), and intra-psychic conflicts previously managed by externalization into the interpersonal marital setting may be re-internalized. At times it may be necessary for the therapist to gently confront both denied affects and distorted perceptions.

As Fraiberg *et al.* (1975) have underlined, where there has been repression and isolation of painful affects related to traumatic childhood disappointments and deprivations, the stage is set for the unwitting infliction of pain in current relationships. Where there is prominent reliance on identification with the aggressor, the therapist's technique should be designed to encourage the members of the couple to elaborate in detail and associate to the shut-out, frozen-out feelings lying behind their angry attacks on one another. Such an exploration should lead to the uncovering of unresolved grief in each spouse's early life, as this is triggered by sadness over current threats of separation and loss.

In time, the vituperative critical attacks and belligerent complaints of the partner's defectiveness will begin to recede as each individual's sense of inadequacy and insecurity is owned, acknowledged, and reclaimed. Already at this point there may be a greater capacity for empathy and a decreased tendency to react to every empathic lapse of the partner as if it were an intentional and personalized rebuff. This process is enhanced by the opportunity marital therapy provides for each spouse to see the other in more realistic perspective, including his or her more vulnerable side. Idiosyncratic motivations for behavior are traced to past experiences with significant early figures. Tentative reconstructions may be attempted based on evidence from observations of the marital relationship as well as the parallel transference manifestations toward the therapist. Main (1966) emphasized that, even with transference material, technically the marriage remains the endpoint of interpretation. It seems to me, however, that interpretations can usefully address a combination of transference and parallel here-and-now marital interaction, including interlocking defensive functioning and individual genetic reconstruction.

REFERENCES

Avery, N. Sadomasochism: A defense against object loss. *Psychoanalytic Review*, 1977, *64*, 101–109.

Benedek, T. Parenthood as a developmental phase. *Journal of the American Psychoanalytic Association*, 1959, *7*, 389–417.

Berkowitz, D. On the reclaiming of denied affects in family therapy. *Family Process*, 1977, *16*, 495–501.

Berkowitz, D. The borderline adolescent and the family. In M. Lansky (Ed.), *Major psychopathology and family therapy.* New York: Grune & Stratton, 1981.

Berkowitz, D. Selfobject needs and marital dysharmony. *Psychoanalytic Review*, in press.

Blanck, R., & Blanck, G. *Marriage and personal development.* New York: Columbia University Press, 1968.

Brenner, C. *Psychoanalytic technique and psychic conflict.* New York: International Universities Press, 1976.

Brodey, W. M. On the dynamics of narcissism: I. Externalization and early ego development. *Psychoanalytic Study of the Child*, 1965, *20*, 165–193.

Dicks, H. Object relations theory and marital studies. *British Journal of Medical Psychology*, 1963, *36*, 125–129.

Fraiberg, S., Adelson, E., & Shapiro, V. Ghosts in the nursery. *Journal of the American Academy of Child Psychiatry*, 1975, *14*, 387–421.

Framo, J. Symptoms from a family transactional viewpoint. *International Psychiatry Clinics*, 1970, *7*, 125–171.

Kernberg, O. *Borderline conditions and pathological narcissism.* New York: Jason Aronson, 1975.

Kohut, H. *The analysis of the self.* New York: International Universities Press, 1971.

Kohut, H. Thoughts on narcissism and narcissistic rage. *Psychoanalytic Study of the Child*, 1972, *27*, 360–400.

Main, T. F. Mutual projection in a marriage. *Comprehensive Psychiatry*, 1966, *7*, 432–449.

Paul, N. L. The role of mourning and empathy in conjoint marital therapy. In G. Zuk & I. Boszormenyi-Nagy (Eds.), *Family therapy and disturbed families.* Palo Alto, Calif.: Science and Behavior Books, 1967.

Sandler, J. Countertransference and role responsiveness. *International Review of Psycho-Analysis*, 1976, *3*, 43–47.

Sandler, J., Dare, C., & Holder, A. *The patient and the analyst: The basis of the psychoanalytic process.* New York: International Universities Press, 1973.

Semrad, E. *Teaching psychotherapy of psychotic patients.* New York: Grune & Stratton, 1969.

Skynner, A. C. R. *Systems of family and marital psychotherapy.* New York: Brunner/Mazel, 1976.

Titchener, J. The problem of interpretation in marital therapy. *Comprehensive Psychiatry*, 1966, *7*, 321–337.

Wynne, L. Indications and contraindications for exploratory family therapy. In I. Boszormenyi-Nagy & J. Framo (Eds.), *Intensive family therapy: Theoretical and practical aspects.* New York: Hoeber, 1963.

Zinner, J. The implications of projective identification for marital interaction. In H. Grunebaum & J. Christ (Eds.), *Marriage problems and prospects.* Boston: Little, Brown, 1977.

Zinner, J., & Shapiro, R. Projective identification as a mode of perception and behavior in families of adolescents. *International Journal of Psycho-Analysis*, 1972, *53*, 523–530.

Zinner, J., & Shapiro, R. The family group as a single psychic entity: Implications for acting out in adolescence. *International Review of Psycho-Analysis*, 1974, *1*, 179–186.

CHAPTER FIVE

Marriage as a Developmental Process

CAROL C. NADELSON
DEREK C. POLONSKY
MARY ALICE MATHEWS

Recent developments in formulating a psychology of adulthood, proposing that there are phases with specific tasks, has resulted in some redefinition of the developmental process and emphasized its evolution throughout the life cycle. These phases have important implications for couples, since the stages of an individual's life cycle occur within the context of relationships which, in turn, have their own phases. In this chapter, we will describe the developmental phases of marriage and relate them to individual developmental phases.

Marriage is a dynamic, changing interaction and not a "static" arrangement, with rigid role assignments and predictable outcomes. It can be conceptualised as a continually evolving relationship where changes in roles, tasks, ambitions, and expectations occur. Individual developmental changes must be superimposed on this relationship. Rather than assuming that change has negative consequences, this process can be viewed as similar to other developmental processes: stressful, but having the potential to lead to progress and growth. If complementary shifts do not occur in both partners, the homeostatic balance of the relationship may be disturbed.

THE CHOICE TO MARRY

Although the number of people who choose to remain single has increased during the past decade, about 95% of contemporary Americans do marry at some time in their lives (Glick, 1975). This represents a slight increase in

Carol C. Nadelson and Derek C. Polonsky. Department of Psychiatry, Tufts University School of Medicine, Boston, Massachusetts.

Mary Alice Mathews. Department of Psychiatry, Harvard Medical School, Boston, Massachusetts.

numbers over the early part of this century. Despite the fact that an increasing proportion of those who are under age 30 have never married, the proportion of those who reach 40 without marrying is lower than it has ever been.

There are many complex reasons for choosing marriage, conscious and unconscious, reality and fantasy based. Pressures for family continuity, succession, and inheritance represent the needs of society. For the individual, however, marriage is a way to find fulfillment of personal desires for happiness, companionship, emotional and economic security, and the desire for children. Family expectations and pressures include the desire for generational continuity. An additional societal pressure toward marriage comes from the workplace, where there are reports of discrimination against single people and indications that those who are married are seen as more stable and reliable (Jacoby, 1974).

Many of the psychological theories that have been offered to account for mate selection are variants of exchange theory. They propose a marriage market analogous to the economic market in which goods and services are exchanged (Edwards, 1969; Elder, 1969; Goode, 1966; Murstein, 1970; Waller, 1938). The assumption is made that the greater the desirability of the characteristics a person has to offer to the opposite sex, the "more" he or she will obtain in a spouse. There is an implicit assumption of certain "universal" values and attitudes, for example, that most women place a high emphasis on status-conferring ability in seeking husbands and that men emphasize physical attractiveness in seeking wives. These views, of course, neglect the importance of personal values and psychological variables as well as the irrational determinants of falling in love. The marketplace analogy supports the view that one is not "chosen" because of insufficient assets. It does not account for deliberate choice (Nadelson & Notman, 1981).

Identification with parents and the wish to recreate a similar family constellation is also an important determinant. Strong dependency needs, failure to develop a secure independent identity and the intolerable fear of isolation or loneliness may propel an individual into marriage. While marriage can facilitate the developmental step towards adulthood and enable the partners to separate from their families of origin and establish an intimate and shared relationship, the fact that individuals choose to marry is not in itself indicative of psychological health or maturity, nor is the converse true.

External pressures from parents and/or peers, which arise from watching friends marry and the desire to avoid being out of step or isolated, may also be an important pressure toward marriage. The decision to marry, then, is a function of complex emotional and developmental forces that evolve from the process of working through adolescent concerns, separation–individuation issues, and solidifying identifications. It may also represent the acting out of unresolved developmental conflicts. The failure to resolve these conflicts can result in a premature flight into marriage with a transfer of dependency wishes from parent to an idealized partner.

Currently a sizeable number of young people are postponing marriage, since the benefits of economic security and sexual gratification are available without commitments. With greater educational and career options open to women, increased economic needs, the desire for financial security, and decreased motivation to have large families, the premarital phase has lengthened and the number of couples who live together without marriage has increased.

As indicated in Chapter 1, expectations of marriage have changed enormously during this century. In addition to security and continuity of family, the search for love and companionship within a marriage makes it different from the contractual arrangement within families that existed in the past. This change has added to the stresses and pressures that couples confront during the course of their marriage, but it has also increased the potential for personal fulfillment in marriage.

CHOICE OF A PARTNER

Prior to marrying, most couples go through a process of mutual assessment in order to decide if the partner is "right" (Murstein, 1970). Romantic fantasies and unconscious processes, however, cannot always be tested or assessed even if a couple live together, since perceptions and expectations color and distort each individual's ability to be objective. The choice of marital partner is one of life's most difficult decisions, particularly because of the transference aspect. If the relationship with the potential partner is viewed as a replacement for important childhood relationships, the specific features or characteristics of the individual one has married may not be realistically considered and the discrepancy may later be the source of discord, unrealistic perceptions and projections.

Unconscious signals, however, also enable potential partners to recognize the possibility that they can jointly work through unresolved intrapsychic conflicts. Identification with the loving aspects of parents and parental introjects are also important intrapsychic determinants through which the partners can relieve rivalries and repressed sexual feelings, allowing for the fulfillment of frustrated longings and producing new opportunities for self-realization (Nadelson, 1978).

There is a degree of profound unconscious ambivalence in the choice of a partner. The level of psychological readiness to make a commitment to an intense relationship is an important factor in the success of marriage. While some individuals have attained a level of intrapsychic differentiation and individuation that prepares them to cope with the tasks of marriage, others are burdened by unresolved early conflicts, unrealistic expectations (conscious or unconscious), or severe psychological deficits that make the resolution of marital tasks more difficult. Those individuals who enter a marriage in less differentiated developmental stages can grow toward maturity within the marriage; however, those who either cannot cope or cannot resolve infantile and/or narcissistic issues are vulnerable to disturbance if their goals for the marriage differ from their spouse's goals (Nadelson, 1978).

Since the fantasy about the chosen partner must eventually be compared with the reality of who that person is, each individual, must confront inevitable disappointment. Kohut's (1971) concepts of mirror and idealizing transference provide a useful framework for understanding object choice and the evolution or marital conflict. From his perspective, the partner is necessary to the self because each has a degree of narcissistic vulnerability that leads to narcissistic expectation as well as to projective identification. Thus, whether self-cohesion and self-esteem are maintained by idealizing the self (mirror transference) or the partner (idealizing transference), each demands from the partner the fulfillment of an absent part. Hence, each is bound to be disappointed if his or her needs are not met. Marriage, then, can become a repository for old conflicts and unmet needs (Main, 1966), and mutual defenses and collusive "joint resistance" can prevent working through of these conflicts (Dicks, 1963).

Marriage can also foster growth and development in a positive direction, since the establishment of a close and sexual relationship offers the opportunity for partners to work through the prohibitions and inhibitions of childhood in the context of the establishment of a new level of object relations (Blanck & Blanck, 1968). When this occurs in the postadolescent phase, after identity issues have been resolved, infantile pressures are less intense, and the danger of object loss or identity diffusion is less likely to occur. When anxiety is diminished and greater flexibility is possible, conflict resolution is less narcissistically propelled.

MARITAL LIFE CYCLE

Individual life phases have been described as lasting approximately 7 years, with transitional phases of about 3 years between each stage (Gould, 1972; Levinson, Darrow, Klein, Levinson, & McKee, 1978). There has been considerable criticism of "stage theory" as a developmental construct, because it narrowly defines "crises tasks" that may not be universal. Furthermore, theories have generally been based on data derived from studies of men, and do not consider women's lives. Neugarten (1979), referring to women, nonetheless has emphasized the proliferation of roles and juxtaposition of transition points. This synthesis provides a context from which to look at coinciding and diverging points of individual and marital growth, and it has been clinically useful.

Berman and Lief (1975), using individual life stage models, have described several marital stages, each of which focuses on a different aspect of

Table 5-1. Marital Tasks

Stage	Age	Task and conflict
1	18–21	Shift from family of origin to new commitment.
2	22–28	Marital commitment, ambivalence about choice; stress over parenthood.
3	29–31	Crisis about commitment, doubts; divergent growth.
4	32–39	Productivity; spouses may differ in means of being productive.
5	40–42	Summing up and evaluation of success and failures.
6	43–59	Resolution of conflict and stabilization of concern about aging may lead to depression and/or acting out.
7	60 and over	Support and enhancement; conflicts relate to fear of abandonment, loneliness, and sexual failure.

the marital interaction (see Table 5-1). Within each stage, they have defined specific tasks.

The marital phases listed below can be seen as part of the process of the development and growth of the relationship itself, and marriages can be understood as moving through this series of phases, at varying paces. These differ at different ages and in different circumstances. The focus of this conceptualization is on the individual's developmental phases, is age-related, and does not address marital phases where there are significant age differences or where the individuals are at different points in their life cycles.

1. Idealization;
2. Disappointment, disillusionment, disenchantment;
3. Productivity, parenting;
4. Career resolution;
5. Redefinition, child launching;
6. Reintegration, postparenting.

Idealization

In this phase, beginning with courtship, there is an idealization of the partner, as a projected ego ideal. Each partner maintains the fantasy that the other will fulfill his or her needs and expectations. Negative traits and troublesome aspects of the interaction, such as vulnerabilities or dependency needs, are denied. For the couple who marries young, this phase may coincide with separation from the family of origin so that the resolution of those issues may, in part, overdetermine and intensify the idealization. For the couple who marries later this idealization may occur in the context of other life concerns, for example, health problems. These may intensify the need to idealize the self and/or the partner. Those with "narcissistic vulnerabilities" may need to maintain this state, because they cannot maintain a separate and cohesive self.

It is unusual for couples to seek therapy during this phase because it is the period of high energy, excitement, and idealization. It is "being in love." While, occasionally, a young couple may request counseling to talk over concerns, the dilemma during this phase is more often for the family, who are less blinded by the idealizations, and who might have some serious reservations about the marriage. Although their observations may be accurate, it is usually impossible for these to be heard. Parents may say nothing because they wish to avoid antagonism, hoping that the relationship will end, or they may become involved in an intense struggle, which usually reinforces the idealization and creates further distance from parents. Individual dependency conflicts, then, continue to be unresolved.

Similarly, if one partner is in therapy, the therapist may see unconscious determinants that portend a difficult marital course, but the ability to predict is limited and pressure may lead to rejection of therapeutic efforts. A cautious, reasoned, and objective stand is necessary, while maintaining a sense of humor and humility about one's potential omnipotence.

Disappointment, Disillusionment, Disenchantment

The impact of living together and facing the mundane issues of life evokes disappointment and often anger, anxiety, or depression. Couples often feel confused, bewildered, and deceived when the promise of the perfect relationship vanishes or diminishes. The period of coming to terms with the perceived limitations of the relationship and the partner is stressful. At times it may be intolerable and threaten the viability of the relationship. Indeed, as Bjorksten and Stewart note in Chapter 1, most divorces occur during the first two years of marriage.

Irresolvable conflicts in the resolution of this phase may reflect characterologic difficulties and may result in an attempt to mold the partner in the direction of the ideal and thus avoid the feared disappointment. At times, one partner may seek a new relationship so that the painful confrontation with his or her own limits and narcissistic injuries is not dealt with actively.

Since separation from parents may occur simultaneously with the need to work out a marital relationship, a couple may agree to bask in comfortable prolonged attachment to one or both sets of idealized parents, postponing resolution of separation and autonomy issues until parents die or other life issues intervene. Subsequently, conflict between the partners may erupt. At times, one spouse may insist on living closer to or farther away from his or her parents, making it necessary for the other to change the proximity and relationship to his or her parents.

For the older couple, this phase may be more easily mastered if disappointments have been mastered in the past. On the other hand, for those who have chosen a new partner to resolve past disappointments, and who continue to seek the ideal, the disappointment may be reminiscent of the past, and it may be potentially more difficult to tolerate.

Another important aspect of this marital phase is the ever-increasing familiarity with one's partner. As relationships develop, each partner feels freer to expose more regressed and infantile wishes to the other. If one partner has a low tolerance for these regressive manifestations, he or she may become frightened, anxious, disappointed, or even angry. This may precipitate symptoms such as depression or sexual dysfunctions, or acting out, perhaps in the form of sexual affairs, may occur. The stage may be set for difficulty in future communication if one partner learns that the other cannot tolerate him or her "in sickness and in health," but can only accept the healthy, mature, controlled person. Thus, the relationship may be jeopardized, as the more needy partner seeks support and companionship with others. The disappointment phase may end with distancing, even if the couple remain together.

During this phase, couples often seek therapy because of the reenactment of constellations resembling earlier object related conflicts, with attendant distortions in perceptions. This is particularly disturbing to the couple who may have felt that communication was good in the earlier phase of their relationship. The unconscious need to resolve earlier conflicts in object relations and the ways in which mutual projections and collusions serve defensive functions for the individual partners is an important determinant of the problems arising during this phase.

Most often, therapy is initiated at the request of one partner who views the other as the cause of the difficulties and attempts to enlist the support of the therapist in confirming this perception. Countertransference responses are more difficult for therapists if they are less experienced in working with couples, or if therapists allow the favoring of one or the other to cloud their objectivity. It is not difficult to see the "healthier" partner as correct. Attention must be paid to the ways in which partners can use each other to defend, via denial and projection of conflicts, to maintain a cherished position. In addition, a couple's relationship to parents is reenacted in the marriage. For this reason, individual meetings with each partner can provide a relevant individual developmental perspective.

Initially one partner may seek individual therapy and the therapist may not consider including the spouse. When the focus of an individual therapy is predominantly the marriage, however, it is important that the therapist consider seeing the spouse even if only for an evaluation. While this situation can create countertransference problems, because the therapist is allied with the original patient, and may consciously or unconsciously collude with him or her. This can be worked through. Even if there is no overt collusion, the partners may perceive that there is an unbalanced alliance. Conjoint therapy may be indicated in this event, or the couple may be referred to another therapist, while individual therapy with one partner continues.

Productivity, Parenting

When the disappointment phase is resolved, a new kind of commitment is possible. Each partner can find a way to be creative and productive and come to terms with the issues of separateness and autonomy. The couple must also develop an identity together, as a couple. If one partner begins to have interests outside the marriage that do not involve the partner and that the partner does not accept, these may be experienced as an abandonment or rejection.

For those in the child-bearing years a manifestation of productivity is parenthood. The resolution of the issues of the disappointment phase may enable a couple to make a decision about having a child. For some couples, the decision to have children may be made as a way of attempting to improve a marriage where disappointment continues. Some couples fear that they will lose the opportunity for parenthood and may decide to have a child regardless of the viability of the marriage. The decision may be a way of dealing with anxiety and fear of loss in the setting of increased marital disappointment, or an attempt to hang on to a wavering partner. If one partner "gives in," the price extracted for capitulation may have far-reaching consequences.

The state of resolution of earlier marital issues is critical for the success of this phase. The couple involved in career building, often finds that the decision about whether or not to have children is particularly difficult. They may not be able to anticipate the stresses or to make the kinds of compromises necessary to maintain dual careers. At times, the responsibilities seem so great, and the demand to be a perfect parent so overpowering, that the couple may decide not to be parents rather than risk being less than perfect. This serves a defensive purpose for people with low self-esteem and, for others, it may represent an attempt to differentiate from "bad" parents.

For those couples who have infertility problems, the focus of the marriage can shift towards the evaluation of the infertility and attempts to resolve it. Structured and regimented kinds of "directed sexual intercourse" accompanied by the self-concept of defectiveness are extremely stressful and may threaten the marriage. If pregnancy does occur, it may bring a couple closer or create greater separation. Often, the wife is assigned the role of the parent-to-be (with the need to take most of the responsibility for the child) and the husband has a less well defined role, with consequent isolation and distance in the marriage. Among the major role shifts of this phase is the necessity for the "child" position of the partners to be relinquished and replaced by a concept of parenting roles. The concrete reality of the demands of having a baby are difficult to incorporate prior to the actual event.

Further, the significant changes in roles that the new parents have to integrate into their self-concept are enormous, and difficult to anticipate. The shift from being somebody's child to being somebody's parent can be experienced with satisfaction and gratification or it can be a source of anxiety, fear, and competitiveness, if not done mutually, and either partner can be, or feel, abandoned by the other. The powerful, pervasive, and primitive needs of the newborn can stir up similar feelings in the parents, who may be threatened by the feelings of loss of control (Fraiberg, Adelson, & Shapiro, 1975). Marital conflict and competition about who is a better parent or who is doing more may emerge in this context.

The increased dependency and even regressive feelings of the new mother may increase her anxiety as well as that of the father. He may find it frighteningg to perceive her vulnerability and he may be unable to meet her needs. He may even need to flee in order to maintain his child–lover– narcissistic position, or to avoid a resurgence of old painful sibling rivalry issues.

The stresses and strains on a marriage brought by the "intrusion" of children have been discussed by a number of authors. Parenthood has been seen as negatively related to marital affection and intimacy, and a stage that threatens communication and mutuality (Abernathy, 1976). According to Grunebaum and Christ (1976), "the role of parent and spouse recurrently conflict" challenging the partners to communicate, empathize, resolve, and adjust.

There is even some evidence supporting the view that marital happiness decreases with more children, and that companionship is lowest during early child bearing and when adolescent children are about to leave home (Rollins & Feldman, 1970). Gould (1972) has stated that

> to maintain autonomy while sorting out the pressing demands of spouse, children, and employer is a task of greater magnitude than living with a spouse and much different than living alone, and required a more highly developed psychic apparatus if an optimal level of individuation is to be maintained. (p. 522)

The child-bearing phase also calls for a shift in relationship with the family of origin. Families that have not been able to support separation and individuation can become intrusive and controlling, making the shift in roles more difficult. Ensuing demands and stresses in marriage are related to the ages and needs of offspring, in each stage since the capacity for parenting tasks may differ. Conflicts between spouses about styles of parenting may increase the ambivalence of the partners to each other and to the marriage. Those styles that are unlike those positively remembered by parents or those that are too similar to those negatively associated with ones own childhood are especially apt to produce feelings of depression, futility, and helplessness. Clearly this phase is different for a younger couple than for an older couple or for those starting a second family.

Career Resolution

Careers and work are inevitable areas of concern during the productivity phase of a relationship. However, productivity in a marital relationship depends on realigning past attainments and directions within the context of a new relationship. For couples who marry later, these issues may be more settled individually, but they remain to be resolved within the relationship, especially if the couple are both in active careers.

There has been a major shift in family styles over the last two decades, with an increasing number of dual-career and dual-worker families. For these couples there is continual confrontation with the integration of family and job for both partners.

In a dual-career marriage in which both partners are engaged in high-commitment activities requiring more than 40 hours a week of work, as contrasted with marriage's where only one partner is employed outside the home or where both partners work at jobs that do not demand the same degree of ongoing responsibility, there is pressure to make even more adaptations. Modifications occur in many areas of life and require a complex process of decision making and allocation of responsibilities for family maintenance. The care of children may be the most difficult and conflictual area. Couples must often redefine gender-oriented activities and adapt emotionally to the stresses of new roles and expectations. Areas of conflict and dissonance stem from intrapsychic as well as sociocultural factors, since they touch upon self-esteem, competition, jealousy, unrealized expectations, and the resolution of dependency problems (Nadelson & Nadelson, 1980; Rapoport & Rapoport, 1971, 1976).

The administrative problems of the dual-career family can also be extremely troublesome. When two marital partners have roughly equivalent and demanding career roles, problems concerned with scheduling and coordination become prominent and constant. Careers that require a commitment to travel or the expectation that the couple must move geographically may cause stress for the partner who has fewer gratifications from the changes. Where the pain of numerous separations and object losses is great, it may be difficult for both partners to find career satisfaction simultaneously. Geographic changes may also diminish the optimal provision of children's needs for stability, continuity, and the development of peer relations.

Competition may be intensified in dual-career marriages and be a source of considerable stress. Within a conventional marriage, some aspects of competitiveness are resolved through gender enculturated role and personality differences, which relegate certain areas of family functioning to one individual, and other spheres to the other partner, for example, "My wife takes care of that" or "I don't know anything about cars." Competition is lowered simply because men ordinarily are not testing out new recipes and women aren't deciding whether to get a valve job on the car. Couples who choose a dual-career life-style must work out practical details of family care, and deal with their "deviant" social roles as well as their own conflicts resulting from the disparity between their intellectual positions and their earlier parental introjects. Success requires patience, flexibility, mutual respect as well as common ideals and goals. It requires reorganizing and tolerating competitive and angry feelings and being able to find ways of coping with the tension they produce (Nadelson & Nadelson, 1980).

Since two incomes are currently becoming more of an economic necessity, there are questions to be faced about the choice of job, the sense of self-esteem and satisfaction in the job and the demands of family. In a traditional relationship, the husband may resent the demands of dependent children, and spouse. He can handle this by denial, avoidance, or abdication, with withdrawal into work. In those marriages where the partners' major focus is on complementary role functioning with marked role divergence, the spouses may grow in different directions with decreased feelings of sharing and understanding. With both partners working, some of the complimentarity of role functioning is not possible and adaptation to diversified demands may be difficult.

There are indiations that couples experience a downward drift in the sense of marital satisfaction in their 30s, compared with their 20s. There is increasing difficulty in making marriages work, and increasing complaints of inability to communicate with spouses (Gould, 1972). If the marital commitment is significantly ambivalent, the marriage may not survive, and withdrawal into work, alienation, and affairs are common (Rapoport & Rapoport, 1971, 1976, 1978).

Redefinition, Child Launching

If a couple enters the middle years of their lives and of their marriage simultaneously, both partners must confront a number of stressful issues including changes in object ties, self image, and aspirations. These changes are precipitated by the changing needs of children and parents, physical changes, and the fulfillment of, or disillusionment with, one's dreams and goals. This, in turn, forces an awareness of the finiteness of time. There is a need to come to terms with previously denied limitations and failures, and this involves mourning, reassessment, and redefinition. There may, at this time, be a shift in emphasis in the relationship toward more concern with companionship, empathy, and sharing. For those who married later, so that the marriage is young, but the couple are middle-aged, the individual phases may not be synchronous and this may result in conflict. Similarly, if the age difference in the partners is great, the divergent life stages that each partner confronts may cause stress (Nadelson, Polonsky, & Mathews, 1979).

During this phase, one or both parents often have adolescent children, and the issues of control and autonomy that emerge as adolescents challenge their parents stir up these same issues for parents. There may also be a discrepancy in views about handling children. This may precipitate marital discord and further intensify the adolescent's conflict. This may be made more difficult by the reawakening in parents of their own early conflicts around separation. Thus, there is an opportunity for couples to provide mutual support and understanding or to become polarized and competitive, with each partner needing to be seen as the accommodating good parent.

The emerging sexuality of adolescents may also be quite difficult for parents to tolerate. It can stir up their own conflicted feelings and may precipitate competitive feelings or even yearnings for what was "given up" by marrying. Repressed sexual feelings may emerge, and sexual acting out may occur.

As children begin to leave home, separation issues are revived, and previous failures may be repeated. The launching period has been seen as one of the most stressful periods for the marriage, representing the culmination of parental commitment and the actualization of parental expectations. Once children leave, the couple again has to deal with more time with each other. When offspring marry, although often a relief, difficulties may be experienced. If the major comfort in the marriage stemmed from the parenting role, the couple may have difficulty giving it up. They may even experience depression, or they may withdraw from each other. The task of welcoming a "new child" may be a difficult challenge.

The postparental period may be one of high productivity and partnership. If, however, there is a discrepancy in age, ability, physical stamina, or interest, the partners may grow apart. Frequently one partner, usually the husband, approches retirement, while the other, usually the wife, has finally achieved independence and success. The role reversal that occurs may be stressful. Marital problems caused by dissonance in stages of career growth are increasingly frequent. For the husband, this period usually hearlds the plateau of his career, whereas, for many women today, the launching of children may be followed by a period of career development and growth. These differences may precipitate unanticipated marital stress, stirring up unacknowledged competitive and dependency issues.

If the marriage has been satisfying, the couple can usually weather the predictable midlife changes as well as the narcissistic blows of the aging process. If good communication and satisfying intimacy have been maintained, the reverberations of midlife changes can be contained within the marriage. Unpredictable changes like premature death of a spouse or debilitaing illness or injury or divorce at this time is another matter.

At midlife, women, with a sense of accomplishment from successful child rearing and with new freedom to develop, may experience a release of energy, self-confidence, and self-assertion that can lead to the pursuit of new goals and interests in the world (Benedek, 1950). As women work through separation–individuation issues again, feelings of insecurity and inferiority subside, and they can become less inhibited and more autonomous. Neugarten (1979) has described midlife personality changes, with men becoming less aggressive and competitive and more expressive and nurturing. If, on the other hand, the character structures of the partners are rigid and early issues are unresolved, or the evolution of the marital relationship has deteriorated, then the personality changes that occur in the second half of life can skew the partnership in an increasingly unsatisfactory way. If the midlife changes are not mastered, one or both marital partners can become more egocentric, stagnant, and depleted. Losses are felt to be personal defeats and insults. Men may complain of domineering mothers and controlling wives and may be troubled by unmet dependency wishes. This may be in reaction to the wife who has become more independent, more assertive, and less adoring. Women may fear, and be guilty about, their increased aggressiveness and may become depressed or withdraw from husbands whose dependency demands are experienced as invasive and undermining.

Reintegration, Postparenting

Retirement brings mixed reactions from couples. Some wives feel intruded upon by their increasingly dependent husbands. However, those who have developed a wide range of interests continue to grow and enjoy this stage even more than preceding stages. Good marriages have been reported to remain good and often improve in the years between 60 and 89 (Lowenthal & Haven, 1968). In this last stage, ambivalence diminishes and the marital relationship enjoys a shift toward greater sharing and empathy. Some couples, however, cannot arrive at this happier stage of resolution if they have not mastered the previous stages of their relationship and evolved adaptive patterns of coping and problem solving. Where joint resistances to change are built into their interaction, where avoidance patterns have predominated, where motivations for the particular marital choice have been conflicted, unrealistic, or outgrown, where resentments have grown over the years, the capacity and commitment to continue the relationship and adapt to the next stage of life together may be minimal or absent. Studies have shown that retirement can be especially painful to a couple who haven't developed the ability to communicate (Thompson & Chen, 1966).

CONCLUSION

We can conceptualize an evolutionary process in marriage. The individual partners change, and are confronted with different life stresses, and the marriage changes as it has to adapt to the emerging demands and realities.

At each phase there is potential for resolution or acting out, which can precipitate a need for treatment. Likewise we must be aware that marriages have their own independent course, a life cycle that may or may not be consonant with the individual life cycle of the partners.

REFERENCES

Abernathy, V. American marriage in cross-cultural perspective. In H. Grunebaum & J. Christ (Eds.), *Contemporary marriage: Structure, dynamics and therapy*. Boston: Little, Brown, 1976.

Benedek, T. Climacterium: A developmental phase. *Psychoanalytic Quarterly*, 1950, *19*, 1-27.

Berman, E. M., & Lief, H. I. Marital therapy from a psychiatric perspective: An overview. *Journal of Psychiatry*, 1975, *136*(6), 583-592.

Blanck, R., & Blanck, G. *Marriage and personal development*. New York: Columbia University Press, 1968.

Dicks, H. V. Object relations theory and marital studies. *British Journal of Medical Psychology*, 1963, *36*, 125-129.

Edwards, J. Familial behavior as social exchange. *Journal of Marriage and the Family*, 1969, *31*, 518-526.

Elder, G. Appearance and education in marriage and mobility. *American Sociological Review*, 1969, *43*, 510-533.

Fraiberg, S., Adelson, E., & Shapiro, V. Ghosts in the nursery. *Journal of the American Academy of Child Psychiatry*, 1975, *14*, 387-421.

Glick, P. A demographer looks at American families. *Journal of Marriage and the Family*, 1975, *37*(1), 15-26.

Goode, W. Family and mobility. In R. Bendix & S. Lipset (Eds.), *Class, status and power* (2nd. ed.). New York: Free Press, 1966.

Gould, R. L. The phase of adult life: A study in developmental psychology. *American Journal of Psychiatry*, 1972, *129*(5), 521-531.

Grunebaum, H., & Christ, J. (Eds.). *Contemporary marriage: Structure, dynamics and therapy*. Boston: Little, Brown, 1976.

Jacoby, S. 49-million singles can't be all right. *The New York Times Magazine*, February 17, 1974, pp. 12-13; 41; 43; 46; 48; 49.

Kohut, H. *The analysis of the self: A systematic approach to the psychoanalytic treatment of narcissistic personality disorders*. New York: International Universities Press, 1971.

Levinson, D. J., Darrow, C. N., Klein, E. B., Levinson, M. H., & McKee, B. *The seasons of a man's life*. New York: Alfred A. Knopf, 1978.

Lowenthal, M., & Haven, C. Interaction and adaptation: Intimacy as a critical variable. In B. L. Neugarten (Ed.), *Middle age and aging*. Chicago: University of Chicago Press, 1968.

Main, T. F. Mutual projection in a marriage. *Comparative Psychiatry*, 1966, *7*, 432-449.

Murstein, B. Stimulus-value-role: A theory of marital choice. *Journal of Marriage and the Family*, 1970, *32*, 465-482.

Nadelson, C. Marital therapy. In T. J. Paolino & B. S. McCrady (Eds.), *Marriage and marital therapy: Psychoanalytic, behavioral, and systems theory perspectives*. New York: Brunner/Mazel, 1978.

Nadelson, C., & Nadelson, T. Dual-career marriages: Benefits and costs. In F. Pepitone-Rockwell (Ed.), *Dual-career couples*. Beverly Hills, Calif.: Sage Publications, 1980.

Nadelson, C., & Notman, M. To marry or not to marry: A choice. *American Journal of Psychiatry*, 1981, *138*(10), 1352-1356.

Nadelson, C., Polonsky, D., & Mathews, M. A. Marriage and midlife: The impact of social change. *Journal of Clinical Psychiatry*, 1979, *40*(7), 292–298.

Neugarten, B. L. Time, age, and the life cycle. *American Journal of Psychiatry*, 1979, *136*(7), 887–894.

Rapoport, R., & Rapoport, R. N. *Dual-career families*. New York: Penguin, 1971.

Rapoport, R., & Rapoport, R. N. *Dual-career families re-examined*. New York: Harper, Colophon, 1976.

Rapoport, R., & Rapoport, R. N. (Eds.). *Working couples*. New York: Harper & Row, 1978.

Rollins, B. C., & Feldman, H. Marital satisfaction over the family life cycle. *Journal of Marriage and the Family*, 1970, *32*(1), 26–28.

Thompson, P. W., & Chen, R. Experiences with older psychiatric patients and spouses together in a residential treatment setting. *Bulletin of the Menninger Clinic*, 1966, *30*, 23–31.

Waller, W. *The family: A dynamic interpretation*. New York: Dryden Press, 1938.

CHAPTER SIX

Adultery and Marriage:
Three Psychological Perspectives

HARVEY S. WAXMAN
JANCIS V. F. LONG

Over 25 years ago Kinsey and his associates (Kinsey, Pomeroy, & Martin, 1948; Kinsey, Pomeroy, Martin, & Gebhard, 1953) estimated that half of married men and 25% of married women had affairs, while a 1969 survey suggested that the figures might be 60% and 40% for men and women respectively (Hunt, 1969). By 1981 Wolfe (1981) found that among the 106,000 women she surveyed, 69% of those over 34 had had an affair since their marriage. Thus, adultery at some point in married life appears to be the norm rather than the exception.

Life's deepest emotions of love, hate, jealousy, betrayal, and loss are potentially present in adultery, as are those conflicts between autonomy and dependence, adventure and security that lie at the heart of our intricate negotiations with important others from earliest infancy, and throughout life. Through the legal and religious proscriptions, particularly for women, that have historically surrounded this act, adultery has embodied a society's conception of sin, contract, and double standard of behavior for men and women. It is not by accident that adultery has been a pre-eminent focus of the novel for centuries. The breaking of sexual exclusivity in marriage serves to focus attention on the boundaries—psychological, social and sexual—that give marriage its particular character and define its variations between cultures and among different couples. Dicks (1967), a British marital theorist and therapist, considered adultery, when it becomes known to the spouse, to be the most serious threat to marriages.

Harvey S. Waxman. Department of Psychiatry, Beth Israel Hospital, Boston, Massachusetts, and Department of Psychiatry, Harvard Medical School, Boston, Massachusetts.

Jancis V. F. Long. Faculty, Washington School of Psychiatry, Washington, D.C.

At the same time, it is useful to note that for some, adultery is *not* a matter of great intensity. There are times when it is unknown to the spouse, and relationships are maintained without major disruptions. In Cuber and Haroff's (1965) and Komarovsky's (1964) in-depth interviews with married couples, many accounts were given of affairs that were tolerated as expected (if not wholly appreciated) behavior, and others that had been kept secret from the spouse, apparently without destroying the marriage. Though we do not know the quality of the marriages, 84% of the adulterous respondents to Wolfe's survey had not told their spouse of their affairs. There are relationships in which an affair is known tacitly, or even openly or collaboratively. In 1927 Judge Lindsey (cited in Neubeck, 1970) noted that from his observations "couples who mutually agree that adultery is all right . . . are far more common than even students of these matters have any idea of." The very word adultery today sounds slightly old-fashioned, heavy, and disapproving. The cooler, less consequential "affair" is usually perferred.

Nevertheless, in any marriage that has included passionate loving and sexuality, adultery, at least at first, is rarely a cool issue. Crimes of passion, which account for a large proportion of all violent crimes, and the empathetic interest engendered by real and fictional stories of rejected, secret, or divided love, attest to the familiarity of the intense psychological conflicts that can surround the adulterous relationship. Some of these conflicts are central to the understanding of intimate relationships and their vicissitudes throughout life. How and when do people balance contradictory longings for dependence and independence, for adventure and security? When are old loves discarded for new ones, or new ones renounced in the name of constancy? When is the matrix of intimate relationships enlarged to include both the old and the new? What, psychologically, is involved in the boundary-drawing around a married couple that makes sexual intimacy outside it such a charged matter? How do values of society become internalized and blended with an individual's developmental history to produce his or her psychological response to others? What explains the lowering of erotic intensity over time in long-term loving relationships? Where does jealousy, that blow to the head that has few rivals for intense psychic pain, come from? While this chapter cannot address these kinds of questions directly, we will suggest a framework for thinking about adultery that we believe has implications for understanding this and other forms of intimate behavior. In brief, we suggest that a person's psychological development, specific dynamics of the marriage they are in, and certain ubiquitous factors about the marriage relationship in general should each be given consideration in deciphering the psychology of an affair, or of the marriage from which it originates.

Psychoanalytic theory has given relatively little attention to the psychology of the extramarital affair. In Freud's case histories, affairs are frequently referred to but usually as the background to another behavior or neurosis. In later theory, with a few exceptions mentioned below, adultery is usually referred to in the context of promiscuity or immaturity of object relations (e.g., Kernberg, 1974, 1977; Neubeck, 1970). More surprising is the fact that affairs are scarcely discussed in the fast-growing literature on marital theory and therapy. A recent volume edited by Paolino and McCrady (1978), which provides excellent reviews of current writing on marriage from the psychoanalytic, behavioral, and systems theory standpoints, contains virtually no references to extramarital sex. Ransom (1980) has also recounted that research through 43 volumes concerning marital and family therapy revealed only seven direct discussions of adultery, and similarly little mention of love. He explains these omissions by the fact that the major theories of family therapy reduce individual emotions such as love or desire to "signs or symptoms of something else." Psychoanalysts focus on neurotic and immature development, while "family systems theory is engaged in a serious effort to see how far it can go in explaining interpersonal behavior without having to resort to any individual variables" (p. 254).

In this chapter, we suggest that both the developmental focus on maturity, and the "systems" approach to the dynamics of the marital dyad may be important to understanding certain affairs, but that in many cases, an approach that takes into account certain aspects of long-term marriage that tend to prevail even among emotionally mature and relatively harmonious couples is needed. For example, the single most obvious reason why someone has an affair is the pursuit of erotic experience. Sex is desired with someone new because the newness of the partner adds an intensity to the experience. Moreover the experience sought may not only be sensual. In an affair, a person may be pursuing emotional intensity, variety in object relations, the forbidden or secret for its own sake, some specific form of sexuality, attraction to a particular kind of person not represented by the spouse (who may have other attractions), or simply one particular person from whom love is felt. The question is whether such pursuits occur only in the presence of developmental impairment, or unsatisfactory marriages, or whether they are an independent cause of extramarital affairs.

ADULTERY IN THE PSYCHOANALYTIC LITERATURE

Early in the psychoanalytic movement, both Freud and Jung considered the matter of adultery and both decided that it might be a necessity for, respectively, "strong" and "complex" individuals. In 1908 Freud proposed that neuroses were the result of conflict between the demands of sexuality for free expression and the demands of a civilization that proscribed sex except between married people. Faced with such demands, "strong natures" would "openly oppose the demands of civilization," while "weaker ones . . . faced with the conflict between the pressure of cultural influences and the resistance of their constitutions take flight in neurotic illness." Such flight was appropriate for these "weaklings" who "obviously plagued by guilt for their fantasized transgressions would only be led to greater guilt by an act of unfaithfulness (Freud, 1908/1959).

Twenty-five years later in *Civilization and Its Discontents*, Freud again returned to the view that the weak alone submitted to society's demands for an "indissoluble bond between a man and one woman," but this time noted that the "stronger natures" might also do so subject to the "compensatory condition" of security (1933/1961). In between these two opinions, Freud had written in some detail about the relationship between "sexual impulses, short lived in themselves" and "lasting and purely affectionate ties," the process of moving from one to the other being the requirement for "the consolidation of a passionate love marriage." As usual, he did not offer unbounded optimism for the success of this process, one of the difficulties to be encountered being the tendency among men for there to be a "wedge between affectionate and sensual feelings which leads them to seek their erotic gratification among debased women" (1921/1957).

In *Marriage as a Psychological Relationship*, one of the rare contributions to the psychological issues of long-term marriage, Jung (1954) places his focus not, as Freud, on the conflict between biology and society, but on character differences between the spouses. He suggests that in midlife, some people will become conscious of their "complex natures" and long to express and unify their varied facets. This may lead to their finding themselves intolerably confined by the "simpler" nature of their spouses, where this is the case, and to their finding themselves, "outside the marriage" in "what we are wont to call unfaithfulness." Although Jung, too, sees only a few carrying this off successfully, he maintains that "one should take great care not to interrupt this necessary development by acts of moral violence," that is to say, conventional restrictions.

It is no surprise that Wilhelm Reich (1971) inveighed more openly against the sexual restrictions of conventional marriage. The "basis of marital misery," he claimed, is the conflict between economic dependence, moral demands, and habituation "which work towards permanence of relationship," and "full sexuality which can be satisfied by one and the same partner only for a limited period of time"

Karen Horney (1927/1973) addressed the "problem of the monogamous ideal" and concluded that both the "centrifugal and the centripetal forces in matrimony" originate in the Oedipal situation. She suggests that marriage is entered into with a "perilously heavy load of unconscious wishes" which predispose the reality to be a disappointment, and that the unconscious equation of the marital partner with the parent who was earlier desired and renounced revives the incest inhibitions that operated in the earlier case. Thus the growing familiarity of a married couple may promote both disappointment, and reduced sexual excitement, both of which become problems that appear to be alleviated by a new sexual partner.

No trend was set by these early psychoanalytic considerations. Few would go as far as Caprio, who in his book *Marital Infidelity* (1953) set himself the task of uncovering "some of the unconscious motivating factors involved in the problem of infidelity," and concluded that "infidelity like alcoholism or drug addiction is an expression of a deep basic disorder of character . . . which has led many women into prostitution" (p. 7). Nevertheless, adultery has tended to be considered as a moralistic rather than analytic issue. One key reason for this is that Freud was convinced of the insatiable nature of the libido, and focused very largely on the dynamics and psychological vicissitudes of controlling it by morality as internalized in the superego. In later schools of psychoanalytic thought, ego psychology and object relation theory, the lack of attention to adultery appears to stem from a focus on, respectively, management of the emotions and the capacity for object relations.

A central problem, and one we feel has been a disservice to the understanding of adult intimate relations of all kinds, has been the tendency for psychoanalytically oriented theories of human development to be conceived of as reaching an end point in "maturity." In reviewing the literature of marital theory, Geothals, Steele, and Broude (1976) pointed out that both Erikson and Fairbairn present a happy-ever-after view of the mature relationship that (the words are Fairbairn's, but the sentiment could be either) envisages "a relationship involving evenly matched giving and taking between two differentiated individuals who are mutually dependent and between whom there is no disparity of dependence (Fairbairn, 1954, p. 145). Erikson (1968) adds that "mutual genital love faces toward the future and the community" (p. 71), implying, presumably, not exhibitionism but rather the compatibility of mutual mature genital love with stability and social productivity. How, with such theories, can one then explain the adultery and divorce statistics? Only one way. Not perhaps inevitably, but certainly by implication, object relations and ego stage development theories suggest that difficulties in the adult intimate relationship indicate that at least one of the parties was not as adult as might be desired.

The outcome of this theoretical direction can be seen in Kernberg's three recent papers on the prerequisites and structural features of long-term passionate love (Kernberg, 1974a, 1974b, 1977). Again, a very optimistic view of the mature passionate couple is presented in which "sexual passion . . . constitutes a permanent feature of love relations."

Kernberg points out a number of instabilities that exist within the mature, passionate love relationship. Among them are the capacity of such experiences to engender unfulfillable longing for fusion, and disappointment when it cannot be adequately achieved. What he does not do justice to is the continued tension that appears to exist between lovers' desires for security, intensity, and mutuality within the boundary of the exclusive dyad, and the conflicting desires for the intensity that derives, in part, from novelty, insecurity, and the breaking of boundaries.

146

Before discussing in detail the proposed perspective on adultery, we would like to make a parenthetical observation. Whereas psychology and psychoanalysis have treated adultery as though it were not there, or not for the grown-ups, storytellers from earliest times have found it endlessly fascinating. Tanner (1979) has suggested that "it is the unstable triangularity of adultery, rather than the static symmetry of marriage that is the generative form of Western literature as we know it" (p. 12). From the time of Homer to the present, fiction has provided a wealth of psychological insights concerning adulterous intimacy and improved our understanding of the nature of marriage. We learn how psychological boundaries are made and broken, the attractions of the secret and forbidden, the interpersonal power struggled for in marriage. Through a novel such as Eliot's *Middlemarch* we feel society's long arm (and its limitations) in affecting our most private attitudes. And through the anguish of many heros and heroines we experience the pain of marriage to a person not loved, or of the infidelity of one that is.

The novel, with its ability to, as Powell (1976) has suggested, "imply certain truths impossible to state with exact definition" (p. 85), has been able to convey the subtle dimensions of such human experience far better than scientific writing. The ideas are often better too.

DEVELOPMENTAL PERSPECTIVE

Though the developmental perspective may have received an exaggerated focus in the psychoanalytic literature, it is nevertheless a useful viewpoint from which to seek an understanding of adultery. For that purpose, a developmental continuum on which the sense of self and the capacity for mature object relations can be located may be considered.

Of course at one end of the scale there will be no examples. People whose sense of self is always shattered or disintegrated tend to have no meaningful psychological interaction with others. However, those capable of limited "part object" relationships, though haunted by fears of self-fragmentation, do have a rudimentary capacity to relate. It would often seem, however, that it is only the physical aspects of the other person, the capacity to provide physical excitement and sensual comfort that is important. Both marriages and extramarital relations of people at this developmental level tend to be highly unstable, shallow, oriented toward sexual performance, and bizarre.

> Mr. B was married during high school when his girlfriend became pregnant. He was intensely ambitious, driven by unperceived fears that he was not successful, and grandiose. He traveled extensively and worked long hours so that his wife rarely saw him during the marriage. The investment of time and energy paid off handsomely at first, and Mr. B acquired a Mercedes, a boat, a house in an exclusive suburb, and a string of girl

friends. These girl friends were "glamorous" and led a lavish existence with Mr. B in which he would shower them with expensive gifts. Mr. B and the girl friends would quickly tire of each other, however. When Mr. B faced a series of business reversals, the turnover in girl friends became more and more rapid.

Intimacy is also problematic for the so-called narcissistic characters. Although the sense of self and the capacity for relating is more developed, the fragility of their self-esteem causes them to seek in others, qualities that will bolster and supplement their own self-image. Two factors frequently lead to instability in their marriages. First, the spouse is treated as an appendage to the self of the narcissistic character, with his or her own needs barely perceived, much less fulfilled. Secondly, the narcissist is prone to disappointment when the mate does not fully provide the necessary self-enhancement. An affair may begin in response to such disappointment. However, extramarital relations for these people are likely to continue the pattern established in the marriage. The lover represents an attribute, such as a rich person, and the affair contains little intimacy.

It should be noted here that so-called narcissistic concerns can be present at all points in the developmental continuum. People able to sustain intimate relationships of various kinds may also have affairs primarily to achieve some external aim. The middle-aged person who seeks in an affair assurance of continuing sexual attractiveness, or the social climber who uses sex to get near people of high status, "uses" the lover is a similar way. Furthermore, these "instrumental" aspects may also be enhancing factors of relationships even when intimacy is also present. An interesting question for developmental theory is the possibility of mixed levels of maturity among a person's different object relations.

Mr. and Mrs. S were both 24 years old when they married; however, while Mrs. S was a law school student, Mr. S was a freshman at the local state college, because he had joined the army at the end of high school. Their relationship was very turbulent, and the central issue was their difference in status. Mrs. S would sit in class and wonder whether she would appeal to the "attractive men who moved in her world." When she had the chance, she began an affair with one of the most intelligent and aggressive students in the class. Mrs. S had not been very interested in sex within her marriage, and similarly the sex in the extramarital relationship was not very important to her. Mr. S had many qualities that Mrs. S appreciated and that kept the marriage going. However, neither Mr. S nor Mrs. S considered Mr. S to be very successful, and Mrs. S felt that she needed to know whether she could attract a successful man.

A third category of people for whom problems in the capacity for object relations may be a primary determinant of adultery is the group of those for whom some aspects of the personality remains unintegrated with the sense of self. A repressed conflict or unacceptable wish exists in dissociated or unconscious form. Such people have the capacity for empathetic relatedness, but in matters pertaining to the repressed dimension they may be inhibited or anxious. An affair may allow for an expression of the dissociated aspect of the personality. The impetus for affairs of this type is similar to that described above by Karen Horney (1927/1973) and Dicks (1967).

> When Mr. D married his wife while both were in their early 20s, he valued her for providing an island of stability in what had been a troubling and tumultuous sexual life for him as a child and adolescent. Mr. D was deeply ashamed of his transient and exploitative homosexual encounters. Mrs. D insisted that he suppress that activity, which he did with relief and some unacknowledged regret. Mrs. D's main preoccupation was "family routine." She had no interest in creative or pleasurable sex, and only had perfunctory tolerance for "traditional sex." Mr. D accepted this arrangement in the name of achieving respectability. After a decade of marriage and suppression, and after several years of psychotherapy in which he came to understand better the basis of his sexual behavior, Mr. D began to look more actively outside of the marriage for sexual gratification. During this time, Mrs. D, who had not sought psychotherapy, did not change her attitudes. It was acceptable to her for Mr. D to seek sex outside of the marriage, so long as she didn't know about it, and he didn't disrupt the fabric of family life.

Even in the absence of marked difficulties in a person's sense of self or important repressed conflicts, many people emerge from childhood with an apparent predisposition to destablizing traits in adult relationships. Clearly the guilt, jealousy, and triangular sexual relationships that are the hallmark of the classically conceived Oedipal period take up a permanent configuration with some people. The seeking of sexual situations in which the real or imagined jealousy of a rival is a major factor, for example, seems likely to stem from unresolved Oedipal issues. Similarly, people who are having affairs often seem to be reliving their adolescence. Though we take issue with this view as a major explanatory factor, it seems likely that where marriage engenders a compulsive desire to fight for independence from the spouse, by indulging in extramarital sex, certain unresolved themes of individuation from adolescence are being acted out.

MARITAL PERSPECTIVE

Some affairs are understood better as a response to a person's marriage than as a manifestation of developmental difficulties. These are affairs which might not have occurred, or would not have had the same form, if the person had been married to a different spouse. A number of extramarital situations exemplify this, for example, the attempt of a spouse to extricate himself or herself from an unsatisfactory marriage; the attempt to compensate for missing qualities in a spouse within an otherwise viable marriage; the attempt to revitalize a drifting marriage; the attempt to gain revenge against a spouse for injuries suffered at his or her hand. In each such case the married partner uses the lover in part to adjust to, react to, or accommodate the spouse.

> Mrs. F was a drama teacher from a Jewish family. Her father was a psychologist and her mother, a teacher. Her decision to marry her husband at age 20 surprised and dismayed her family and friends. He was from a non-Jewish working-class family. Mrs. F found Mr. F to be ebullient, "real" and exciting in comparison to her parents whom she considered dull and intellectual. She was also excited by the prospect of "helping make something of Mr. F." He, in turn, saw his wife as a step for him in the direction of respectability. After a few years, however, her husband's inability to control his temper became increasingly troublesome to Mrs. F. Mr. F was fired from work for continually telling off his bosses. At home he would explode into rage and frequently attack Mrs. F physically as well as verbally. She maintained that she still loved her husband and wanted to work to improve the marriage. However, while attending a summer drama workshop, she began an affair with another participant. Mrs. F appreciated the calmness of the relationship, in comparison with the turmoil of her marriage, and the pleasure of jointly pursuing common interests with someone whose background and views were similar to her own.

Of course, this affair bears signs of "characterological immaturity." Mrs. F believed she had used Mr. F for her own needs, rather than truly accepting him, and her guilt for this may have kept her from acknowledging to herself, even when she was in physical danger, that the marriage was a mistake. A "better" response might have allowed conscious awareness of her mistake, and a verbal attempt to terminate the marriage rather than the acting out of her unconscious perceptions in the affair. Yet, overemphasis on the difficulties of solving problems through acting out rather than insight obscures Mrs. F's attempt to leave a destructive partner and find one to whom she could relate on a different and fuller basis. While acting out by having an affair may not be a perfect or very mature way of extricating oneself from a troubled marriage, a critique of the means should not entirely obscure the positive aspects of the ends. If Mrs. F were to repeat her choice of a destructive partner, we could more clearly invoke the developmental issues, but some second marriages do not repeat the errors experienced in the first.

People with widely differing character structures are often able to mesh effectively (at least initially) in a marriage. However, the equilibrium that has been achieved is hard to maintain as time passes. Most typically, someone who is valued for providing an island of stability at the end of adolescence can appear to be the personification of dullness in middle age; someone who is valued as "easy going" early in the marriage can come to be seen as passive and lethargic. Further, despite the "shared life" that marriage to some extent provides, the experiences of individuals in a couple, as well as their receptivity to them, can be widely different and pull the individuals in separate directions.

> Mr. and Mrs. G lived in an apartment with their 3-year-old son and Mrs. G's mother. Mr. G was a passive man who did what he was told and initiated little, either inside or outside his marriage. Mrs. G was ostensibly domineering and assertive, though she had been unable to separate from her mother. At first Mr. G's passivity was seen by his wife as cooperativeness and kindness, but after several years of marriage she came to resent his lack of initiative, especially in bed. Mrs. G began an affair with her employer and left very obvious clues about this affair which her husband ignored. Even when Mr. G, coming home from bowling late at night, saw Mrs. G's car parked outside her boss's house, he said nothing, though at that time he was compelled to acknowledge to himself what was happening. Mrs. G began to invite her employer to dinner, and on one occasion her son asked, "Mummy why are you holding hands under the table with Mr. X?" Several weeks after this episode Mr. G moved out of the apartment, having only halfheartedly confronted his wife, and without making any attempt to stop the affair.

Again, developmental issues are involved for both participants in this marriage. But it appears that Mrs. G's affair was primarily an attempt to reach Mr. G and jolt him out of his passivity. Clearly she was becoming increasingly dissatisfied with the marriage, especially sexually, while Mr. G was obstinately unaware that there were problems. Had Mr. G responded to his wife's provocation by recognizing the affair or even suggesting marital therapy, it is likely that he could have not only perpetuated the marriage, but also improved it.

> Dr. E and Mrs. E were both grandiose characters. Each represented a feather in the other's cap. Dr. E valued his wife for her beauty, and Mrs. E was proud of her husband because he was a physician. This balance was maintained for about 5 years until Dr. E revealed that he had had sex with one of the nurses at his hospital during one of the nights he spent there on duty. Mrs. E was enraged by this and unconsciously deeply threatened. She immediately began an affair with a professor at the college where she worked, who was known as a "womanizer." She flaunted this affair in the college community as well as in front of her husband. For example, she would be at the professor's house at midnight when the husband returned from being on duty at the hospital, and she would leave the phone number so that he could call her there. Mrs. E talked glibly of equality: "what's fair for him is fair for me." Beyond that, she was clearly enraged at her husband and taking revenge. At the next level, she was deeply threatened with feelings of worthlessness in her belief and fear that the husband had found a woman that he felt was more attractive. She had to prove to herself that she could replace the husband just as quickly as she felt he had replaced her.

Revenge may never be simple, and is rarely sweet, but seems to be a very common cause of adultery. The fear of it, moreover, is one of the most frequent inhibitors of the desire to seek sex outside marriage. As one person in marital therapy recently stated, "If I was unfaithful to you, I wouldn't expect for one moment that you would be faithful to me. I think that is the main reason that I am faithful to you."

SITUATIONAL PERSPECTIVE: THE VICISSITUDES OF LONG-TERM MARRIAGE

While Kernberg's view of the ever-deepening love relationship provides us with a model of the ideal marriage, what people typically report, even in those marriages that they themselves consider good, tends to be rather different. What people talk about are compromises they have made within themselves and with their spouses to make their marriage work. This brings us to the third perspective we suggest is useful for understanding adultery, one which is least mentioned in the professional literature. Important factors in many affairs are the nearly universal conditions that arise in the context of long-term marriage. Among these are the tendency for there to be a decline over time in a relationship's erotic and romantic intensity; the fact that love and sexual desire may be experienced for someone despite an existing committed love for a spouse; the tendency for couples to develop, within their marriage, stereotyped psychological roles that may inhibit the development of other aspects of their personalities. These are issues, we suggest, that may occur in the context of emotional maturity and good marriages. Some people come to terms with them by having affairs, others by sublimation, sacrifice, or repression expressed in a great variety of ways.

In the sexual behavior surveys (Cuber & Haroff, 1965; Dicks, 1967; Hunt, 1969; Kinsey *et al.*, 1948, 1953; Komarovsky, 1964; Wolfe, 1981), the observation is frequently made, directly or obliquely, that sex with the same person over long periods of time tends to become less exciting. Though the loss of initial excitement can be compensated for by the increasing depth of the emotional relationship, evidence suggests that the desire for sexual excitement and novelty remains strong even among people who are capable of committed love in an empathetic relationship. It is perhaps more accurate to say that the craving for sexual novelty rarely disappears, but that sometimes a good marriage will lead people to forego or sublimate this craving. At other times, social mores or the perceived costs of an affair will prevent the desire from being acted on. A deeply rewarding marriage will make the pull towards new sexual excitement less strong, but when the inevitable frustrations and tensions occur, even in a good marriage, the desire for an affair can reassert itself.

Sex may not be the only aspect of a new relationship that is pursued in an affair. The related excitement of intense romantic love may be equally or more important. De Rougemont (1957) suggests that "romance is by its very nature incompatible with marriage even if the one has led to the other, for it is the very essence of romance to thrive on obstacles, delays, separations, and dreams, whereas it is the basic function of marriage daily to reduce and obliterate these obstacles" (p. 52). Kernberg notes that the very capacity for mature genital love and passionate psychological involvement may be a destablizing element in marriage if people long to recapture the intensity they have known. A woman doctor of 45 with two grown children who claimed to have been happily married for 23 years wrote in an unpublished autobiographical essay, "I simply cannot bear the thought that I may soon reach the age when I shall never again fall in love, or walk up someone's apartment stairs oblivious to everything but a hundred fantasies of what it will be like when we make love."

As Jung implied in his account of the "complex" person, most people are capable of responding to a wider range of personality features than are usually encompassed by any one individual. Most married people have meaningful and intense nonmarital relationships that supplement the marriage and provide fulfillment of various kinds. It may even be a matter for concern if the spouse is a person's only significant relationship. Nonmarital relationships are usually not problematic unless the unmet dimension concerns sex or intimacy itself.

The second situational factor of long-term marriage concerns the seeking of alternative intimate experience for positive reasons while not relinquishing the primary relationship to a spouse.

Mr. R, a 45-year-old business consultant, had been married for 8 years and had a 3-year-old daughter. Though he loved his wife and claimed there was no doubt in his mind that he had found the spouse with whom he would spend the rest of his life, he would sometimes complain mildly and humorously about her excessively rational, calm attitude to life. When he met a woman at work who was more vivacious, spontaneous, and far less given to rational calculation, Mr. R was instantly attracted. Because of his closeness to his wife, he discussed his feelings with her, and she said, rationally, that she would make no objections to his having a relationship with the other woman, provided he spent sufficient time with her and their child, and also that he be discreet so that she would not have to discuss the matter with others. Mr. R visited his friend once or twice a week for two years, claiming that he enjoyed the contrast between her and his wife without wishing that either would be more like the other. The affair ended when its security and domesticity seemed to be taking on the character of a second marriage. She wished to be free to seek a real marriage, and he felt relieved to have fewer claims on his time and emotional energy. According to Mr. R., his marriage suffered only during the early stages of the affair when his preoccupation with the other woman had temporarily reduced his sexual interest in his wife.

Prosky (1974) and Williamson (1977) have drawn attention to the role specialization and stereotyping that may develop in a marriage. One partner comes to represent a certain value or style and is forced by the interaction of the couple to play the assigned role more exclusively than he or she would like. In the case above Mr. R enjoyed his role in the affair as the more balanced sober partner, in contrast to his marriage where, with his full cooperation, he tended to play the slightly out of hand *enfant terrible*. The very capacity for complexity and role diversity characteristic of a mature level of development may come into conflict with an almost unavoidable tendency for personality stereotyping in long-term relationships.

A special case of role stereotyping occurs where a quasi parent–child relationship is established between the spouses. We are not talking here of the recapitulation in marriage of deeply disturbed early relationships as discussed in relation to the developmental perspective, but rather a more subtle process in which mature and loving people, in the course of balancing issues of autonomy and intimacy, may come to see a spouse as a person who threatens their autonomy in some way. This dynamic may be exacerbated where social norms reinforce the authority of one spouse over another. Volumes have now been written on the ways women have been kept in childlike dependent roles by legal and social norms that give husbands parent-like authority over the conditions of their lives. In other setttings, women have been assigned the role of infantilizing the supposedly irresponsible male.

The decline of intensity, the possibility of attraction and love in a mature context for more than one person, and the struggle for psychological autonomy within a committed and intimate relationship are only three broad problems of long-term love to which an affair may come to be seen as a solution. Clearly there are innumerable variations of each problem, and innumerable solutions, sexual and nonsexual. Where an affair does occur, there are a wide variety of ways in which it is integrated into self-image, life arrangements, and the marriage in question.

CONCLUSION

Any theory of intimacy would have to address two obvious questions. What accounts for the universal tendency of humans to bond with others and erect to some degree barriers of exclusivity around the relationship? And what accounts for the almost as universal tendency to experience restlessness within the exclusive relationship and risk security in the pursuit of new experience? Though both these tendencies are instantly recognizable, the first has received more systematic study than the second.

Biologists and sociologists have classified some of the functions of exclusivity in marriage with regard to maintaining the species, protecting and training the helpless young, and creating a social and economic unit within society. Attachment theory as developed by Bowlby (1969) and the ethological school suggests models to explain the growth of love within an exclusive bonding process between parents and infants. Freudian psychoanalytic theory took the insatiable libido as a given and focused primarily on the dynamics and psychological vicissitudes of controlling it via guilt, the superego, and repression. The inheritors of Freud, particularly the object relations school and thought, focused on impairments in the capacity for relating stemming from early difficulties in the parent–child interaction. All these are crucial contributions to understanding the dynamics and difficulties of intimacy. We do not yet have dynamic theories to explain the vicissitudes of intimacy that do not stem from developmental difficulties. Though novels are rich in examples of the woe, the joy, and the variation that can be experienced in marriage, we simply cannot answer in a systematic longitudinal way the question, "What happens to couples?"

In this chapter we have tried to show that at least three perspectives are necessary to identify major variations in the meaning and motivation of different kinds of affairs. Developmental impairments in achieving committed and relatively harmonious object relationships seem to be paramount in a number of extramarital affairs. In others, the person is primarily working out some feature of the marriage relationship with his or her partner. In still others, the affair may be a response to certain situational features of long-term marriage that exist even in the presence of "mature" spouses, and good marriage relationships. To have attempted to explain the affairs presented in the case examples by one perspective only would, we feel, have been to miss essentially different features of each. By presenting this tripartite approach to adultery, fully aware that there are other perspectives as well, we have hoped to suggest a useful structure for analyzing the complicated agendas involved not only in this particular form of intimacy, but of all situations in which human beings become psychologically enmeshed with each other.

REFERENCES

Bowlby, J. *Attachment and loss.* New York: Basic Books, 1969.
Caprio, F. S. *Marital infidelity.* New York: Citadel, 1953.
Cuber, J. F., & Haroff, P. B. *Sex and the significant Americans: A study of sexual behavior among the affluent.* Baltimore: Penguin, 1965.
de Rougemont, D. *Love in the western world.* New York: Anchor, 1957.
Dicks, H. *Marital tensions.* New York: Basic Books, 1967.

Erikson, E. *Identity, youth and crisis.* New York: W. W. Norton, 1968.

Fairbairn, W. R. D. *An object relations theory of personality.* New York: Basic Books, 1954.

Freud, S. Civilized sexual morality and modern nervous illness. *Standard Edition,* 1959, *9,* 179–204. (Originally published, 1908.)

Freud, S. Group psychology and the analysis of the ego. *Standard Edition,* 1957, *18,* 67–143. (Originally published, 1921.)

Freud, S. Civilization and its discontents. *Standard Edition,* 1961, *21,* 59–145. (Originally published, 1933.)

Goethals, G. W., Steele, R. S., & Broude, G. J. Theories and research on marriage: A review and some new directions. In H. Grunebaum & J. Christ (Eds.), *Contemporary marriage: Structure, dynamics and therapy.* Boston: Little, Brown, 1976.

Horney, K. The problem of the monogamous ideal. In *Feminine psychology.* New York: W. W. Norton, 1973. (Reprinted from *International Journal of Psycho-Analysis,* 1927, *9,* 318–331.)

Hunt, M. *The affair: Portrait of extramarital love in America.* Cleveland: World, 1969.

Jung, C. Marriage as a psychological relationship. In *Collected works* (Vol. 17). Boston: Pantheon, 1954.

Kernberg, O. Barriers to falling in love and remaining in love. *Journal of the American Psychoanalytic Association,* 1974, *22,* 86–511. (a)

Kernberg, O. Mature love: Prerequisites and characteristics. *Journal of the American Psychoanalytic Association,* 1974, *22,* 743–768. (b)

Kernberg, O. Boundary and structure of love relations. *Journal of the American Psychoanalytic Association,* 1977, *25,* 81–114.

Kinsey, A. C., Pomeroy, W. B., & Martin, C. E. *Sexual behavior in the human male.* Philadelphia: Saunders, 1948.

Kinsey, A. C. Pomeroy, W. B., Martin, C. E., & Gebhard, P. H. *Sexual behavior in the human female.* Philadelphia: Saunders, 1953.

Komarovsky, M. *Blue collar marriage.* New York: Vintage, 1964.

Neubeck, G. A study of extramarital relations. In *The extramarital sexual relationship.* Englewood Cliffs, N.J. Prentice-Hall, 1970.

Paolino, T. J., & McCrady, B. S. (Eds.). *Marriage and marital therapy.* New York: Brunner/Mazel, 1978.

Powell, A. *Hearing secret harmonies.* New York: Popular Library, 1976.

Prosky, P. Family therapy: An orientation. *Clinical Social Work Journal,* 1974, *2,* 45–46.

Ransom, D. Love, love therapy and marital theory. In K. Pope (Ed.), *On love and loving.* San Francisco: Jossey-Bass, 1980.

Reich, W. *The discovery of the orgone.* New York: Farrar, Straus & Giroux, 1971.

Tanner, T. *Adultery in the novel.* Baltimore: Johns Hopkins University Press, 1979.

Williamson, D. S. Extramarital involvements in couple interaction. In R. F. Stahman & W. J. Hiebert (Eds.), *Counseling in marital and sexual problems. A clinicians' handbook.* New York: Williams & Wilkins, 1977.

Wolfe, L. *The Cosmo report.* New York: Arbor House, 1981.

CHAPTER SEVEN

Combined Concurrent/Conjoint Psychotherapy for Couples: Rationale and Efficient New Strategies

LEE BIRK

People experiencing trouble in their most important and intimate relationship, in general, have had to face a rather stark choice between "marriage counseling," which can be seriously, even fatally flawed in its superficiality and its circumstantial but often near-exclusive concentration on dyadic transactions, and psychotherapy or psychoanalysis, which so totally slights dyadically focused work that it is ordinarily carried out by two different therapists, one for each for the two individuals who together (whether they are married or not) comprise a mated couple. I believe that this stark choice is not necessary and in this chapter will outline some efficient new strategies for psychotherapy with couples, which, in their origins are "hybrid," and which, in the tradition of "hybrid vigor," I believe, enhance both the power and the scope of couple therapy.

INADEQUACY OF BOTH CONJOINT THERAPY AND CONCURRENT THERAPY, USED ALONE

Problems with Conjoint Therapy Alone

The most sophisticated marriage counselors and couple therapists have always strived to gain as full a psychodynamic understanding as possible of each member of the couple, and in conjoint therapy they endeavor to cultivate in both members the fullest possible understanding of self and partner. They attempt to facilitate understanding of the psychodynamic

Lee Birk. Department of Psychiatry, Harvard Medical School, Boston, Massachusetts, and Learning Therapies, Inc., Newton, Massachusetts.

forces within each partner, which operate to shape their attitudes, behavior, and lives, both as individuals, and as a couple. On a practical level, however, multiple dyadic disputes, distortions, negotiations, and fights and reconciliations often make it necessary to devote much time, energy, and effort to interrupting distractive interactional patterns and to developing and incorporating new and better ways of interacting and communicating. This complicated task often precludes careful and effective attention to subtle identifications and hard-to-grasp transference issues. Yet, these form the basis for much of the feeling the two people have toward each other. Almost every experienced couple therapist acknowledges that individual issues are frequently central to the troubles of a couple.

Problems with Concurrent Therapy Alone

Psychoanalysis or individual psychoanalytic psychotherapy can productively help people to understand themselves. They gain insight into crucial idiosyncratic sensitivities and tendencies to drift into transference distortions which, if unchecked, can blight the potential for two people to live together in some harmony. But individual psychoanalysis or psychotherapy by its very structure is "individual," with no built-in opportunity to observe the *actual behavior* of two mated individuals as they act and react with each other. This structural inattention to the complex details of who does exactly what to whom can make it difficult to reach an accurate diagnosis of what is really happening with a couple. If concurrent therapy is used alone, the therapist forfeits all possibilities of direct intervention in the dyadic process, and of identifying, interrupting, and interpreting interactions "on the spot," in an effort to get the two people to act and react differently with each other, rather than allowing them to retrace the same well-worn ruts that are determined by their fixed neurotic perceptions, and their established habits.

Classical psychoanalysis, for both members of a couple, especially simultaneous psychoanalysis for both, with literally no treatment of the couple together as an interacting system, has in fact been known to break up marriages. Conjoint "sessions," not even conjoint *therapy*, are often attempted at the desperate stage. This is something like treating pneumonia not when timely observations reveal cough, purulent sputum, spiking fever, etc., but when the first signs of cyanosis appear.

CONCURRENT THERAPY AS A STEP FORWARD

In the late 1940s Mittelmann (1948) precipitated a storm of controversy among his analyst colleagues by openly advocating that one analyst should concurrently analyze both members of a marital pair. His specific proposal was at best problematic, complex, and highly vulnerable to critique. Among his analyst colleagues at the time, there was total opposition to seeing the spouse, or any other single member of the analysand's family, *even one time, or for diagnostic purposes.* Unfortunately, at the time, it was commonplace for psychotherapists not doing analysis, but doing therapy with individuals, to copy psychoanalysis slavishly.

When concurrent therapy eventually became the mode for marital problems (Solomon & Greene, 1963; Martin & Bird, 1963), this was seen as a step forward, even though this method did not allow for the opportunity to observe the couple interacting as a dyad. Berman and Lief (1975) have well summarized the advantages and problems:

> One of the obvious advantages of this type of therapy lies in the screening of perceptual distortions. It is easier for just one therapist to sift out the distortions, and this technique avoids the possibility of each therapist identifying with his own patient and the consequent additional distortions this may create. If the therapist wishes to develop and make use of a transference neurosis, this is a far more effective technique than conjoint marital therapy, in which transference elements tend to be more muted. Concurrent marital therapy is also used effectively in cases where one partner markedly dominates the other, thus preventing the partner from having equal time or an equal share of the therapist's attention.
>
> Problems include the re-creation of the triangular sibling rivalry situation, issues of privacy and privileged communication, and lack of opportunity to observe the dyadic function. (p. 589)

CONJOINT THERAPY AS A STEP FORWARD

In the last 15 years, conjoint therapy has become the dominant mode of couple therapy, to the point where 80–90% of all marital therapy is now carried out in this way, or at least partly in this way. The advantages and problems again have been well summarized by Berman and Lief (1975):

> If the partners are seen together it is difficult for one partner to assign the blame and to continue to scapegoat the other, making that partner the "sick one." With both partners present, the focus is inevitably on the relationship.
>
> One problem in conjoint marital therapy is that there is no opportunity for private exploration, and since in many marriages there are some kinds of private information that the partners will never reveal, the therapy remains at the behavioral level. (p. 589)

Conjoint therapy for couples, when compared to simple marriage counseling, even when not combined with concurrent therapy, was an attempt, aimed at addressing both the problems of each individual (including transference distortions), and the dyadic problems (including unconscious contracts). Often, however, conceptual sophistication on the part of the conjoint therapist alone cannot overcome the considerable circumstantial obstacles of trying to get a husband and a wife to learn to understand themselves and their own particular transference distortions, while addressing simultaneously a warring couple's behavioral difficulties in real life.

COMBINED CONCURRENT/CONJOINT THERAPY AS A STEP FORWARD

Many therapists working with couples use a combination of approaches that exploits the advantages of the concurrent and conjoint techniques. The concurrent therapy facilitates in-depth work on individual issues, especially transference distortions, identifications, and other material that otherwise would likely not be brought up at all. Conjoint therapy offers the potential for diagnosis by direct behavioral observation and interaction. Thus therapists can often intervene interpretively in a troubled dyadic sequence with cognitively restructuring remarks to each spouse, in a manner that would be quite impossible if they were limited to conjoint therapy alone.

Some voices, notably that of Hollender (1971) have objected to the therapist's switching back and forth between individual and marital therapy. Many therapists, however, feel that the confusion, and the need to discuss matters thoroughly with both spouses in order to reduce it to a minimum, are worth the difficulty.

GROUP PSYCHOTHERAPY AND COUPLE THERAPY

An important parallel development within psychotherapy, along with the rising use of combined couple therapy, has been a growing recognition that group therapy may be more than "just" a useful adjunct, but may actually be superior to individual therapy in certain clinical situations (Birk, 1974a, 1974b, 1980, 1982; Birk, Miller, & Cohler, 1970; Guttmacher & Birk, 1971; Shapiro & Birk, 1967). The couple therapist can utilize the power of a group psychotherapy approach in working with couples (Blinder & Kirschenbaum, 1967; Boas, 1962; Framo, 1973; Gottlieb & Pattison, 1966; Leichter, 1962).

The strategic importance and epistemological advantage of group therapy is invaluable.

> Live data, drawn from live observation of the live interacting couple, the live interacting family, and/or an "artificial" but live interacting social group (as in group therapy), . . . were not only not a part of the method of psychoanalysis. . . .
>
> There is . . . [however] a large epistemological advantage accruing to the psychotherapist who creates the opportunity to observe his or her patient functioning within a social system. A therapy group is such a system.

The advantage referred to is no mere theoretical nicety; more often it is of crucial importance in how the therapy situation unfolds in that it can enable a therapist to transcend blanket empathy, support and endorsement for the socially dysfunctional patient, and to make accurate behavioral "diagnoses" as to precisely what the unhappy person actually does which "turns off" other people. (Birk, 1982, pp. 168–169)

GROUP METHOD FOR COMBINED CONCURRENT/CONJOINT COUPLE THERAPY

The basic method includes seeing each partner in group therapy, thus gaining the advantages of concurrent couple therapy and of group therapy. In addition the couple may be seen together, in a group of other couples, which provides features of conjoint therapy and of group therapy. The result would be called "combined concurrent/conjoint group couple therapy." In practice one might call it "group-group-group" because, in practice, that is what happens. For example, in treating five or six couples all the women might be seen in one therapy group while all the men meet "unofficially" by themselves without a therapist; then all the men might be seen in one therapy group while all the women meet "unofficially" by themselves without a therapist. Following this all the men and women might be seen together as a psychotherapy group of couples. Thus in one time block totaling about three hours, there are three "official" therapist-led group meetings, in sequence, one after the other, plus two "unofficial" peer-led group meetings.

Though the result may sound ponderous, our clinical impression is that this is a method offering great therapeutic leverage. This work began in 1972, and in 1979 the first 200 people (100 couples) were reported on. To date we have treated about 300 people (150 couples).

SUMMARY OF ACCUMULATED EXPERIENCE

To date we can offer no controlled research comparing this method with other possible approaches, but after this volume of clinical experience we feel well prepared to offer some clinical impressions.

1. The method is very hard to "sell" to prospective group-group-group members, but it is ordinarily possible to do so with enough preparation and tenacity. Very often we find a series of concurrent and conjoint individual meetings are both desirable for us as future group-group-group therapists and necessary to persuade the couple to give the method a try.

2. Once couples try it, they like it. Only 2 of 100 couples tried it and did *not* like it, and in each of these 2 couples 1 spouse did like it. Thus 99% (198 of 200 people) of those individuals who tried it liked it, found it valuable, and considered it more valuable than either conjoint but "individual" (i.e., non-group) couple therapy, or combined couple therapy involving concurrent individual sessions.

3. Most couples (both members ordinarily) made significant gains:

- Terminated with positive gains   70%
  ("*very* positive gains" = 25%)
- Left with little or no gain   5%
- Left prematurely with little gain   25%

4. Some couples (20%) split up during or soon after group-group-group. About three-quarters did so "positively," with apparent gains from treatment evident in the way they handled the divorce; the others divorced with no evident gains.

5. The method is long term (more than a year, generally) but often seems briefer than either pure couple therapy or pure group therapy for comparable gains to be made.

ADVANTAGES OF GROUP-GROUP-GROUP

1. Group-group-group has all the advantages of group therapy including peer interpretation, evocation of relevant material through multiple transferences, etc.

2. It has the advantages of concurrent couple therapy, amplified by the group advantages.

3. It has the advantages of conjoint couple therapy very much amplified by group advantages special for this group method, such as same-sex peer interpretation (which we have found *very* powerful), the potentiation of deep same-sex friendships, and useful intragroup same-sex identifications, both of which are particularly strongly evident in the "unofficial" peer-led meetings.

4. In complex and difficult couple problems, if therapy is to have a substantial and enduring impact, it needs to be moderately long term at least. Yet, as Grunebaum (1971) points out:

> The couple tend to induct the therapist into their own system. . . . If he works only with the couple for joint (three-way) meetings . . . he loses almost all of his therapeutic leverage within a matter of about 6 months. . . . After that they just don't pay any attention to him; what he says simply becomes incorporated into their fights. . . .

5. It utilizes therapeutically useful group pressure for reconciliation of initially divergent accounts. When the very same life events occur, yet the men hear one account and the women quite another, from each of the two spouses, this leads to a very strong pressure for the two people to forge one coherent, realistic shared account to which all presently in the couples group can subscribe. I have noted that couples often tell such divergent stories when they begin group-group-group that they are hardly recognizable as the same event, but as they make progress and near termination, *the two spouses tell essentially the same story*, without the vigorous prolonged multiple confrontations that proved necessary before.

6. "Secrets" within a couple are shared by the spouses within the men's group, or the women's group, as the case may be thus making a whole group and not just one ethically fallible, not totally wise therapist co-responsible for whether or not a particular affair, for example, really must be discussed, not just in the relative sanctity of the men's or women's group, but with the spouse and everyone else in the purifying cauldron of the whole couple's group. In pure conjoint therapy, individual or group, such secrets may simply never emerge: In pure concurrent therapy, therapists can easily be placed in an untenable position from which they cannot escape, and which ultimately may destroy the therapy as well as their alliance with one or with both of the spouses.

DISADVANTAGES OF GROUP-GROUP-GROUP

1. For people who are underinvolved with other people as individuals and overinvolved with their spouses, I believe the unmodified group-group-group approach can be seriously disadvantageous. Couples of this kind may be rather asocial, and cling to one another as if the spouse were the only other one in the world who really matters, or they may appear superficially to be very social, but on closer scrutiny, they often shun important *independent* human relationships. The disadvantage lies in the fact that such people experience the men's group (or the women's group), as mere preparation for "the main group" in which they will be reunited with their symbiotic partner. *Thus, "group-group-group" does not force an individual out of a symbiotic mode with his or her spouse anywhere near so much as does membership in a therapy group of people not involved with the spouse at all.*

2. In a parallel way, group-group-group puts heavy emphasis on *dyadic* disputes and distortions, and does not emphasize so much as is true for separate therapy groups, a *person's own problems as an individual*. If one or both of the spouses habitually uses dyadic issues (ordinarily unconsciously) to keep their own individual feelings and problems, they are using dyadic material as a defense, and group-group-group can play into this defense, or at least not undermine it effectively as other methods can.

3. While "the handling of secrets" was cited as an advantage over nongroup methods of couple therapy, in comparison to other methods it can be disadvantageous, in terms of how secrets are handled. The reason for this is that there appears to be a natural tendency for husbands and wives to talk with each other about what goes on in their own groups. This often begins innocently as each attempts to understand their own and others problems more fully, but the result is that it is hard to maintain impermeable confidentiality boundaries between the men's and the women's groups. In some group-group-groups cross-group confidentiality has been quite reliable, while in others it has not been.

> In the worst resultant episode to date, it turned out that one husband was the very last of 12 people—including his therapist, his wife, and both of the members of 5 other couples—to find out that his wife had been having a torrid affair and was planning to divorce him to marry this man. On the positive side, it should be pointed out that his wife was only finally induced to stop procrastinating and tell him the sad facts by the combined peer pressure of all the other men and all the other women in the whole group-group-group. Naturally he felt humiliated not just at the facts, but that he was the very last to know.
>
> Subsequently, many months later, he phoned me spontaneously to say that they were now being divorced, that he was recovering from the shock and that he was beginning to feel better: "I was at the time appalled to be the last to know. Yet it was really helpful to me knowing that everyone . . . [in both groups] felt I was being treated unfairly and just . . . didn't deserve that kind of treatment. . . . I was pretty depressed as it was . . . but without the vote of confidence from everyone in the group, I really think I might have done something [suicidal] to myself. . . . It was terribly hard, but I'm recovering."

This clinical anecdote, though it did turn out well in this case, illustrates that the handling of "secrets" can be as murky and treacherous in this form of couple therapy as in other more traditional forms. "Secrets" are *generally* handled much better in a group-group-group than in traditional couple therapy but not so well as they can be handled with still newer group-based methods of couple therapy.

ALTERNATIVES TO GROUP-GROUP-GROUP: ONE FURTHER STEP FORWARD?

Concurrent Therapy in Separate Groups plus Conjoint Couple Therapy

Although the group-group-group technique is one of the most effective, efficient, and engrossing of the therapies, for some people it has defects—listed above—which must be addressed. For this reason, for those couples who tend to operate in a fused manner, and/or have a preponderance of individual over dyadic issues, we recommend concurrent therapy in separate groups.

For this concurrent work with each spouse, *two totally separate mixed psychotherapy groups are used*. These groups are mixed in terms of sex, type of problem, and marital status. Some, but not all, of the individuals in these groups are in therapy because of marital problems. Typically the groups for each spouse are moderately intensive (two meetings weekly) although on occasion one spouse is treated in less intensive (one hour weekly) or more intensive (three hours weekly) therapy groups. The conjoint work also varies in intensity according to apparent clinical need, from "prn only" (when issues arise) to once to twice monthly or weekly.

Obviously then there are some striking advantages in terms of flexibility over group-group-group, permitting the couple therapist to focus the intensity of the therapy more or less precisely where it seems to be needed most, by the individuals involved.

There are other specific advantages, and these may be crucial for the treatment of those couples who are "fused," who have more severe problems as individuals than in their dyadic relationships, or for one or both of whom "secrets" make the case particularly difficult.

Beyond these generalities, more experience with this new method is necessary before we can say much about comparative outcome data with any great confidence.

One of the simplest and most feasible ways to combine concurrent and conjoint work, group therapy, and more thorough and far-reaching investigative work with the two individuals who comprise the couple, is to work with each member of the couple in concurrent individuals psychotherapy while also seeing the couple together in a weekly couple's group. At a practical level this option is open to any therapist who sees couples and is willing to lead one couple's group, while carrying on concurrent therapy with each spouse in separate groups requires that the therapist be a person who does many groups as a regular part of his or her practice.

INDICATIONS FOR NON-GROUP METHODS

From the perspective of one who from his own experience has come to believe in the practical superiority, in general, of psychotherapy within social systems—group over individual, conjoint couple over pure concurrent individual, group concurrent over individual concurrent, group conjoint couple over individual conjoint couple, etc—what are the indications for *non-group* couple methods?

1. Couple work that can be accomplished successfully on a short-term basis (in six months or less).

2. Sexual dysfunction in one or both members of the couple.

If either member of the couple presents with a frank sexual dysfunction, such as a partial or absolute inhibition of sexual arousal or of orgasm, or with either of the hyperexcitatory dysfunctions, premature ejaculation or vaginismus, whatever couple therapy may also be needed, it is essential also to work with the couple in sex therapy. Not to do so, given the brevity and success rate of modern sex therapy techniques, constitutes, in my opinion at least, inexcusably bad clinical management.

At the core of sex therapy is, of course, the basic behavioral strategem of using a competitive response, sensual and sexual pleasure, to displace and supplant maladaptive responses such as anxiety, shame, guilt, embarrassment, fear, "spectatoring" or "monitoring." As in many other behavioral treatment paradigms, desensitization is accomplished very gradually by means of a series of experiential "tasks" which need to be fun, not work. These are prescribed or assigned by the therapist to the couple at a controlled place which allows assimilation, desensitization, and genuine pleasure. (Birk, 1982, pp. 182–183)

While we have successfully treated couples with sexual dysfunction problems in short-term behavioral sex therapy groups, giving each couple, each week, an experiential assignment, we have found it unacceptably difficult and energy-consuming to *prepare* that is, couples—to persuade them to do it—for short-term sex therapy in a group format. Further, we have not found it really fair or practical to disrupt a long-term couples group by insisting on taking the time, *each week*, to ask enough questions to be able to make an intelligent behavioral prescription for the following week.

3. Couples who feel realistically that, because they are public figures, they cannot comfortably make group therapy a feasible alternative. It would, however, be easy to be overinclusive about this category; among the couples we have treated successfully in group-group-group are executives, physicians, psychiatrists, professors, rabbis, and ministers.

Being part of a mated couple tends to bring out the most immature and primitive, as well as the best and highest, most mature and genuine human sharing. Psychotherapy in general is a very complicated subject; psychotherapy for couples is even more so. Our best stance as therapists is one of continued respect for the importance, complexity, and subtlety of it, *combined with an abidingly empirical attitude*.

REFERENCES

Berman, E. M., & Lief, H. I. Marital therapy from a psychiatric perspective: An overview. *American Journal of Psychiatry*, June 1975, *132*(6), 583–592.

Birk, L. Intensive group therapy: An effective behavioral–psychoanalytic method. *American Therapy*, Fall 1974, *1*(1), 29–52. (a)

Birk, L. Intensive group therapy: An effective behavioral–psychoanalytic method. *American Journal of Psychiatry*, January 1974, *131*(1), 11–16. (b)

Birk, L. The myth of classic homosexuality: The view of a behavioral psychotherapist. In J. Marmor (Ed.), *Homosexual behavior: A modern appraisal*. New York: Basic Books, 1980.

Birk, L. Psychotherapy within social systems. In A. Jacobson & D. Parmelee (Eds.), *Psychoanalysis: Critical explorations in contemporary theory and practice.* New York: Brunner/Mazel, 1982.

Birk, L., Miller, E., & Cohler, B. Group psychotherapy for homosexual men by male–female cotherapists. *Acta Paedopsychiatrica Scandanavica*, 1970, Special Supplement 218.

Blinder, M. G., & Kirschenbaum, M. The technique of married couple group therapy. *Archives of General Psychiatry*, 1967, *17*, 44–52.

Boas, L. V. E. Intensive group psychotherapy with married couples. *International Journal of Group Psychotherapy*, 1962, *12*, 142–153.

Framo, J. L. Marriage therapy in a couples group, *Seminars in Psychiatry*, 1973, *5*, 207–217.

Gottlieb, A., & Pattison, E. M. Married couples group psychotherapy. *Archives of General Psychiatry*, 1966, *14*, 143–152.

Grunebaum, H. Personal communication, February 1971.

Guttmacher, J., & Birk, L. Group therapy: What specific therapeutic advantages? *Comprehensive Psychiatry*, 1971, *12*, 6.

Hollender, M. H. Selection of therapy for marital problems. In J. H. Masserman (Ed.), *Current psychiatric therapies* (Vol. 11). New York: Grune & Stratton, 1971.

Leichter, E. Group psychotherapy of married couples' groups—some characteristic treatment dynamics. *International Journal of Group Psychotherapy*, 1962, *12*, 154–163.

Martin, P. A., & Bird, H. W. An approach to the psychotherapy of marriage partners: The stereoscopic technique. *Psychiatry*, 1963, *16*, 123–127.

Mittelmann, B. The concurrent analysis of marital couples. *Psychoanalytic Quarterly*, 1948, *17*, 182–197.

Shapiro, D., & Birk, L. Group therapy in experimental perspective. *International Journal of Group Psychotherapy*, 1967, *17*, 211–224.

Solomon, A. P., & Greene, B. L. Marital disharmony: Concurrent therapy of husband and wife by the same psychiatrist. *Diseases of the Nervous System*, 1963, *24*, 21–28.

CHAPTER EIGHT

Interrelationship between Psychoanalysis and Brief Sex Therapy

ROBERT DICKES

Brief sex therapy was first introduced by Semans in 1954. He developed the stop–start behavioral technique for premature ejaculation, reporting a successful outcome in six cases. Semans did not follow up on this report and it received little attention, as did brief sex therapy in general. On the whole, the treatment of sexual dysfunction remained in the province of psychoanalysis and general psychiatry until Masters and Johnson published their classic work on the physiology of sexual excitement (1966) followed shortly (1970) by their work on sex therapy.

Masters and Johnson utilized a behavioral technique employing sensate focus exercises as one of the bases of their approach to sexual problems. They advocated a 2-week course of treatment based on graded sensate focus exercises beginning with nongenital touching and ending with intercourse. They first reported a cure rate of over 90% for premature ejaculation and a very high rate for other types of sexual dysfunction. Masters and Johnson's publications and their technical approach then formed the basis of the burgeoning sex therapy movement.

Many people have seized upon the apparently simple format of the sensate focus approach and declared themselves sex therapists. Some of these people have had little or no training. Some have had a few courses. Most of these courses took little account of dynamic psychiatry and even less account of psychoanalytic theory and clinical knowledge. Only a few people have had basic training in psychodynamic therapeutic techniques and have had clinical experience in psychotherapy and in family or marital therapy. Furthermore, to the best of my knowledge, no residency training program

Robert Dickes. Department of Psychiatry, State University of New York–Downstate Medical Center, Brooklyn, New York, and Department of Psychiatry, New York University School of Medicine, New York, New York.

prepares people to become qualified as sex therapists. Almost nothing is taught about the Masters and Johnson techniques, at least as a clinical experience in the actual treatment of patients. In general, the treatment of sexual dysfunctions by any method is overlooked by many psychiatrists.

It is also true that psychoanalysts have shown little interest in the behavioral techniques of brief sex therapy. They scoff at the reported results. I have heard analysts talk in terms of transference cures and flights into health as if the releif of the symptoms were indicative of a bad outcome. Some have said that the relief of the sexual difficulties by means of brief therapy approaches may only lead to the worsening of other neurotic symptoms. They believe that the reduction of pressure in one area necessarily leads to increased pressure in another area, especially if the unconscious, unacceptable drive impulses are ignored. Further, they believe analytic formulations should be avoided in brief sex therapy.

It is no wonder that the complementary relationship between psychoanalytic treatment approaches and brief sex therapy has not been stressed in the psychiatric and psychoanalytic literature. Many psychiatrists, as sex therapists, avoid dealing with unconscious forces and some deny the existence of such factors. In my opinion, such denial limits one's ability to function adequately as a sex therapist in today's milieu of a markedly changed patient population. There are numerous cases in which the combined approaches are beneficial, and occasionally ongoing analytic therapy is benefited by brief sex therapy conducted by another therapist. Brief sex therapy frequently requires dynamic insights and interventions. The following illustrations apply.

The first example relates to an analytic patient. This patient, suffering from secondary impotence, was referred to me by his previous analyst who unexpectedly had to discontinue his practice after the patient had been in treatment for approximately 2 years. Some characterological change had occurred in the patient, but his sexual difficulty, impotence, had remained as severe as ever. He complained bitterly about this and felt that his previous therapist had neglected his major complaint.

Much negative transference from the patient's father to the first analyst then focused on me. It took some time before a good working and therapeutic alliance could be developed (Dickes, 1975). Eventually the patient settled down and was able to associate appropriately, listen to interpretations, and expand his recollections of childhood. Much about his marriage also was clarified. He had married under duress. His wife-to-be claimed she was pregnant and threatened him with a lawsuit if he didn't marry her. Fearful of facing a judge, he capitulated and married, only to discover that the woman was not pregnant. He then began to experience intermittent sexual failure, which developed into complete failure. He said this was reasonable since he hated his wife and could not stand the smell of her genitals, which he claimed "stank worse than any other woman's." Extramarital attempts at intercourse were also disastrous, however, since he was unable to have an erection. Due to his sense of guilt he believed that this was a proper punishment. Thus, in an odd way he seemed comfortable with his impotence. Meanwhile much information concerning his father emerged.

In brief, his father was punitive, denigrating, and extremely hostile to any of his son's attempts at mastery. His father never lost the opportunity to belittle him, could beat him at any sport, and always did. The patient, for example, was an excellent handball player. In spite of this, his father would regularly beat him 21 to 0 and then ridicule him in front of his friends, pointing out that his son "was nothing but a strikeout and would never be a man." These critical parental attitudes were all transferred to me and required considerable working through.

During this process much was also learned about his mother, who was psychotic. Space prevents me from describing anything more than one set of memories related to his sexual difficulties. He recalled that even in his earliest childhood his mother had what he, at first, called "fits." Any frustration and failure led her to "faint away." As repression lifted, it became clear that she would have a tantrum, but with considerable sexual display. She would throw herself onto the floor and thrash about kicking her legs and feet up into the air. Her movements always led to her skirt hiking up above her thighs and exposing her genitals since she wore no underpants. The patient finally recalled her thrashing increasing to a crescendo, at which point she would urinate, wetting herself. She, of course, "stank." All of this was done in front of the fascinated but horrified boy who was stimulated beyond his capacities. This led to an altered state of consciousness which I have termed a hypnoid state (Dickes, 1965). When his mother recovered from the "fits," she would berate the father in a crazy way. The patient also said that his wife berated him in much the same way. The equation of mother equals wife became very clear to him as did the distinctions between them. At an unconscious level, the women in his extramarital affairs also represented the forbidden woman, namely his mother.

As these matters were clarified, one would have expected some improvement in the patient's sexual symptoms. All therapists are aware, however, that recall and working through do not always lead to changes in real life. Such was the case with this patient. He left for summer vacation in an apparent state of stalemate.

He returned in September. I was immediately aware of a suppressed excitement and exultation in the man and awaited developments. He then announced triumphantly that he had finally become successful sexually and was having an affair. He then told me that he had talked with the woman whom I knew he was seeing, and persuaded her to go off with him for brief sex therapy, which they did during August. The treatment had been successful.

He then waited for me to attack him for what he felt was his defiance of me. He fully expected me to beat him down as his father did. He also expected to be dismissed from treatment for daring to seek out another type of therapy. I disappointed him and simply told him that I was glad to hear of his success and asked him to continue associating. Over a period of weeks, as more negative transference was resolved, the patient became aware that it was the analytic work that had allowed him to defy me as father and become successful. So great had been his transference hate originally that he could never have allowed a therapeutic success to develop, since that would have been a capitulation to me as representative of his father. The remainder of his successful analysis is irrelevant to this discussion.

It could be argued, at this point, that a successful result would have occurred anyhow, even if it would have taken longer. I don't believe that this would necessarily have been the case. Nor do I believe that, for the sake of a technical purity, a patient should be content to wait a year or even a few months for a success that could be obtained at once. Further, successful action induces useful changes that improve the alliances and the realistic relationship of patient to analyst. I believe that I noted a decided change in the patient's ability to function as an analytic patient. The satisfactory resolution of the transference neurosis was speeded up, leading to an earlier and much happier result for the patient. No closed system concept applies, and success released energy for more useful functions.

The second illustration concerns a young couple in brief sex therapy. They entered treatment mutually agreeing that the wife was the patient. Both complained that vaginal entry was, at times, difficult and sometimes painful. Orgasms could only be obtained by manual stimulation and rarely with vaginal containment of the penis. Both were painfully aware that something was wrong, but they were in total ignorance of the causes of their difficulties. They were very much in love and totally committed to one another. A careful history following the usual format of a joint interview followed by individual interviews with each failed to reveal any serious psychopathology.

I must add that serious sexual difficulties can and do exist in the absence of major psychological problems. Many therapists still do not accept this fact. Over the years I have noted, however, all sorts of combinations. Elsewhere, I've written: "I've observed many severely psychotic people whose sexual adequacy may be described as truly astounding, and I have observed many people with far less than adequate sexual functioning, who are not all psychotic. I have also treated some psychotics who came with severe sexual dysfunctions. These patients did very well, sexually and often better than some neurotics" (Dickes, 1974, p. 22).

The lack of evidence of serious psychopathology in this couple led me to recommend brief sex therapy as the method of treatment rather than psychoanalysis or psychoanalytically oriented psychotherapy. Sensate focus exercises were suggested. These began with nongenital caressing under good conditions. The couple, seen weekly, returned with enthusiastic reports and progress was rapid and uneventful until the phase of vaginal entry was reached. Immediately, the presenting complaints surfaced and further progress ceased. Their sexual experiences were carefully examined for possible causes. The young woman noted that she was reluctant about entry even in favorable times when she was moist and would eventually be able to come to orgasm. She enjoyed kissing, touching, and foreplay. Further study of the woman's actual behavior revealed that, at other times, she was reluctant about any foreplay that would lead to intercourse. On these occasions she would be dry, and entry, if accomplished, was painful. Orgasm would not result, even though her husband showed no performance difficulty.

Over a period of weeks it became clear that the difficult experiences more or less coincided with visits to the young woman's parents. At this point analytically oriented people might exclaim, "Ah, ha! The Oedipus complex rears its head!" Indeed, they would be right.

Further study of the couple's relationship revealed that the young woman's father had been violently opposed to the marriage, and for months had not only refused to talk to his daughter's suitor but had tried to interfere with their meetings. The girl's mother was very much in favor of the marriage, and for very good reasons. The husband-to-be was of good family, handsome, and already successful. He was, as the saying goes, "a really good catch." The girl's mother eventually persuaded her husband to agree to both engagement and marriage. Throughout the engagement, however, he was rarely civil to his prospective son-in-law. Only after marriage and the birth of a son, a matter of great importance to the new grandfather, did he become friendly to the young man.

The patient had been very upset by her father's behavior. She had been very close to him; they had similar interests and had even taken trips together without the mother. There were other clear indications of the Oedipal fixation but these lacked enough intensity to interfere with her ability to love a man or to have interfered with her life. The difficulties were restricted to sexual activity. A diagnosis of hysteria, for example, was not indicated.

The young husband had reacted with considerable resentment to his father-in-law's behavior and had retaliated in kind. He answered only when spoken to and visited only under considerable duress. He and his wife would argue about these matters but never seriously enough to interfere with their love—that is, up to this time.

I did not opt for depth disclosures of the Oedipal fixation, but for the apparently superficial confrontations that would make the couple aware of their behavioral reactions and allow them opportunities to work through their angry feelings. I cannot give the details of this working through, nor can I discuss the implications of and relationships between childhood fixations and their later effects. I can only point out that a knowledge of dynamics can permit a therapist to choose between several approaches.

In this couple, awareness of their response patterns to the parents and the serious implications for their own future were sufficient to lead them to behavioral change. The young man loved his wife enough to give up his hostile behavior to his father-in-law, thus reducing his wife's anger. This permitted her, in turn, to see that her husband's "closing off" of her father had led to her "closing off" to her husband. It was enough at this point to explain to her that there are all kinds of "closing off," both psychological and physical. This psychologically minded and bright young woman got the point immediately.

The result of this limited approach led to an uneventful and successful treatment. Attention to the psychic economy led to a shift in cathexis that allowed the couple to improve without any direct dealing with the unconscious depth factors. This is often a key point in brief therapy. It requires knowledge of the significance of the Oedipal complex, however, to permit the choice of ego-syntonic interpretations which were so effective in this instance.

Not all cases, however, respond so readily even when the preliminary interviews show no immediate evidence of basic problems that could interfere with a rapid resolution of the symptoms. Many times these problems only become apparent during the course of the graded exercises. As the reader may know, it is reported that premature ejaculation is the easiest to cure of all the dysfunctions. This is not always the case.

A couple in their late 20s came for help. The only complaint was the husband's premature ejaculation, which occurred intermittently. The couple had been married for 6 years and came for treatment at the wife's insistence. The husband told me, in the one-to-one interview, that prematurity had troubled him since adolescence but usually only in the first few encounters with a new girl. He said that if he came rapidly it was generally at the beginning of the evening and that by the second time around, he was "okay." At least, he said, "none of my dates ever complained." I might add that all his liaisons were short lived—due, he believed, to his unwillingness to make any serious commitment to a woman. "After all," he said, "I was going to professional school and it made no sense to get too involved."

Treatment procedures were agreed upon and stage-one sensate focus exercises were described and instituted. Essentially, these consist of body caressing without touching erotic areas such as the genitals and breasts. The couple returned and reported that they had enjoyed the caressing but had become too excited to stop and had gone on to intercourse. The man was once again premature! He excused this on the grounds of being too excited and, after all, it had been natural to go ahead.

Associations gradually revealed a general characterological prematurity. When the couple would go out, for example, he would be ready a half hour early and then badger his wife to hurry. He could not understand her annoyance at his nagging. It was at this point that the patient's oral character structure began to emerge. He was also a "horn tooter." That is, even before a red light turned green, he would begin to blow his horn in his impatience to get moving. All of us have been subjected to this kind of annoyance. It is necessary, however, to recognize the early oral fixation in this type of behavior and to take account of this in one's treatment plans. Character-ological ego-syntonic behavior, when detrimental to an individual, must be dealt with in any treatment plan. Knowledge of psychoanalytic, dynamic formulations may therefore become important in any short-term therapy.

The importance of developing patience and learning to withstand mounting tension was explained to the couple. The wife was advised to help her husband to control his impulses to immediate action. This was stressed especially for the sexual situation but it was also pointed out to the man that his impulsive behavior also interfered with his career development and other nonsexual activity. No mention was made of oral fixation, nor were any other analytic formulations presented as such. Knowledge of these formula-tions, however, permits the therapist to gain an appropriate understanding of the basic structure upon which the symptom rests. This allows the therapist to use these insights in a way acceptable and therefore useful to the patient. Progress in treatment continued. The man began to modify his general behavior and all seemed to be going well.

The stage of vaginal containment was surmounted and movement initi-ated. The man was, by this time, able to manage higher degrees of sexual excitement and reported that vaginal containment and motion could last at least a half hour. I asked if his wife was able to be orgasmic in this time period. His immediate reply was that he didn't know. His wife responded that she couldn't be orgasmic, since he spent most of the time motionless and would not let her move. When questioned about this, he at first denied it, but finally admitted that his wife might be right. No change in his behavior ensued over the next few weeks.

When I discussed this with the couple, the wife suddenly reminded herself of what she termed a "weird" remark on the part of her husband. She quoted him as saying when she was menstruating, "How can you go to the bathroom with a Tampax inside you? Do you take it out?" She said he didn't seem to know what was wrong with the remark. He admitted saying this but claimed that it was only a simple slip and of no consequence. He refused to discuss it further when I asked him what came to his mind about the remark. He said simply that everything was blank—a remark that analytically applies to his castration complex. The blank signified a denial of the female genital, which, in the minds of some men, is viewed as a wound, the end result of a forbidden masturbation based upon incestuous attachments. This will seem farfetched to non-analytically oriented people, but such mental entities do exist in the minds of at least some people.

The patient's sudden change from cooperative behavior to one in which he complained of confusion and unwillingness to go further indicated a powerful unconscious force at work and an increase in resistance. I therefore suggested a period of individual treatment for the young man. This was accepted. In the very first of these sessions, I focused upon his increasing negative transference. Underneath his love for his father, who had died when the boy was 12, was considerable hate, not only for what was viewed as his father's desertion, his death, but for other actions recollected as well. These included endless demands for perfection and the role of avenger for the daily misdeeds his mother saved up and recounted when his father came home. Father would then punish him, beating him with a belt, not caring which end of the belt hit the child.

All of this emerged with tremendous intensity and eventual relief. He also developed an understanding of his continual unwillingness to do anything for his mother. His wife had questioned and criticized him for this attitude of indifference to his mother, and this had angered him. He was equally unwilling then to please his wife. He had transferred his attitudes toward his mother onto his wife and other women.

Upon the completion of the above work, couple therapy was reinstituted. Treatment eventually ended successfully. I believe that knowledge of transference, an analytic concept, significantly aided in the treatment of this patient. Not all cases of premature ejaculation are simple and easily cured. Many require interpretations based upon dynamic principles.

When brief sex therapy was popularized by Masters and Johnson, a selected group of patients was admitted to their program. These patients were carefully screened and only those most likely to succeed were selected for treatment. Thus, an active, well-informed, and well-motivated group formed the core of the first reported successes. I believe this to have been a suitable approach for a new form of treatment that had to prove its value in the face of much opposition. Since the introduction of brief sex therapy, however, the situation has shown a marked change.

A much broader range of the population has been made aware of the possibility of treatment. This large segment of the public has been informed by the media of the therapeutic possibilities. Before these people come for help, however, many require repeated referrals by agencies or urging by private professionals. Thus, a new type of patient is seeking help. A less active, less successful, and often less psychologically attuned group is asking the therapist to solve its problems. Many of this group of patients put the burden of "cure" on the therapist. These people are also sicker. So large is the influx of this type of patient that Kaplan (1974) commented that the original types of patients are no longer available. They are, and do appear, but they are a small minority and do not constitute the bulk of the patient population as they did in the beginning. These facts have implications for therapeutic approaches.

It must be emphasized that the majority of patients now presenting for brief sex therapy are much more passive and dependent and less psychologically equipped for a rapid resolution to their sexual problems. Attention must now also be focused on evidence of psychological difficulties in many areas of activity. Some of these problems must be dealt with first and then related to the sexual problems.

For example, a couple sought treatment because the man was unable to ejaculate. Ordinarily, specific sexual exercises would be suggested to help him overcome his ejaculatory difficulties. His history revealed him to be a "constipated" man. During his entire courtship he never gave his wife a gift or took her out to dinner. He went to the movies only grudgingly.

After their marriage even this movie going ceased. He would not give his wife a weekly allowance for household expenses, but doled money out to her irregularly and never in large enough amounts to meet the bills. Proper household furnishings were, of course, out of the question. The man was even sparing with words and thoughts. In brief, he was a thoroughly anal character whose miserliness related to early anal withholding at the time of bowel training.

It was my belief that the man was more suited for individual long-term therapy but he would not accept this idea nor would he pay for it. A decision was made to accept the couple for treatment but to shift the immediate focus from the man's sexual difficulty to his general behavioral patterns.

This type of brief sex therapy can be classified as a special case of time-limited therapy (Mann, 1973; Sifneos, 1972). An attempt was made to apply a behavioral technique based upon the analytic concept that this man's behavior related to his bowel training. Analysts do use behavioral approaches, although they use them differently. Sooner or later, patients with street phobias are required to face the fact that they must go into the street. All insight work must eventually lead to behavioral change if success is to be achieved. This is obtained by resolving basic unconscious conflicts, thus permitting the patient to shift the unconscious problems to consciousness. A reduction in anxiety then allows the patient to agree to actively fight the phobia by going out and then dealing with the emerging difficulties.

The patient under consideration was first offered the suggestion that he take his wife out to dinner one night of the week and to a movie another night of the same week. The decision of how to arrange this was to be his. This proviso was explained to the couple and was based upon the need to avoid any hint of coercion. The idea of giving or doing something to please his wife, without her asking, therefore in his view demanding, was revolutionary to this man. He eventually mastered his withholding impulses and only after the first tasks were accomplished were new ones suggested.

It took some months before sexual assignments were made. These were introduced only after the man himself succeeded in overcoming his urge to withhold. He was always permitted to make the choices, even of the sexual exercises. This was done in order to avoid repeating his mother's controlling behavior especially in relation to the timing of stool output in early childhood.

These so-called remote causes, therefore the more deeply unconscious ones, have become more important in the treatment of the types of patient populations seen today. It is rare for patients to proceed smoothly from the first steps of sensate focus to full-scale satisfactory intercourse without demonstrating some difficulty and resistance at some time during the course of the assigned activities. The points at which these occur and the manner in which they present themselves offer insights into the patients' unconscious dynamic problems, which are reflected in their behavior and interpersonal reactions. An understanding of these problems aids the therapist in determining how and when to intervene. An apparently superficial approach may focus on recent events, but can actually touch upon remote and unconscious conflicts as described in the case just presented. Changes in the patient's dynamic structure can occur and then modify the aberrant behavior. Thus, there is no contradiction between analytic theory or practice and proper brief sex therapy. The special skills that dynamic training offers can be used as aids in the resolution of patients' difficulties.

Many believe that Masters and Johnson's discoveries concerning the female orgasm have outmoded analytic concepts about human sexuality. This is untrue. Freud stressed the idea that a clitoral orgasm was immature and that a vaginal orgasm was the sign of normal sexual maturation. Masters and Johnson, on the other hand, pointed out that all female orgasms were characterized by a consistent physiological pattern involving both clitoral and vaginal responses. They concluded that clitoral and vaginal response patterns could not be separated. This discovery has been used as evidence that Freud's remarks about the female orgasm, in terms of clitoral and vaginal types, are incorrect and that, therefore, analytic ideas should be discarded.

It must be remembered, however, that Freud was reporting on a wide variety of subjective psychological response patterns and not on physiological patterns. It must also be remembered that Masters and Johnson also noted a wide range of subjective psychological responses even though the physiological response regularly involved both the clitoris and vagina. Women have reported that their subjective pleasure response during orgasm was experienced sometimes in the clitoral area and at other times vaginally and in the deep pelvis as well. Even wider areas of response have been reported. Thus the range of subjective response is quite large. This full range of subjective pleasure should be available to all normally mature women depending upon the circumstances of the lovemaking.

Freud's remarks concerning clitoral orgasm refer to those women who even under the best of conditions have been unable to experience the widespread uninhibited response, but only note localized, superficial responses, interpreted as clitoral. When discussing this localized response, Freud therefore referred to those women who had shown marked inhibition.

No actual contradiction exists between the approaches of Freud and Masters and Johnson. Freud never discussed actual physiology, while Masters and Johnson dealt with a basic physiological response when discussing the clitoral–vaginal reaction. Although both organs regularly react, part or all of the subjective pleasure response may be inhibited due to unconscious conflict. This was Freud's contribution.

Analysts and sex therapists, however, do use different technical approaches. In general, analysts avoid direct questions and await the results of free associations. Sex therapists, on the other hand, frequently ask detailed questions about performance and insist that patients be explicit and detailed in their reports about their sexual behavior and responses. In the past, analysts were taught to avoid pointing out that their patients' associations about sex were so general that no information concerning the actual sexual behavior emerged. The theory of technique seemed to indicate that one need only wait, and any attempt by the analyst to point to the failure to associate to sexual material was suspect.

When I was a candidate in a psychoanalytic institute, one of my patients had a sexual problem, among many others. I followed the usual procedures involved in free association and free-floating attention. One day when the patient was associating to her sexual difficulty, which involved fear of penetration, I pointed out that her associations failed to clarify what she was experiencing or what was happening. I later presented this session to my supervisor, who informed me that my infantile sexual curiosity was interfering with the patient's associations and that to inquire about sexual responses was a form of seduction. As you can see, he took a dim view of my pointing out the lack of information. Yet I had been unable in 2 years to get a clear picture of this woman's fear of penetration and what was wrong.

I discovered, by showing the lack of detail to the patient, that she failed to lubricate and thus penetration was painful. Among other things, foreplay was minimal. No wonder there was trouble! Brief therapy here would call for explanations and advice related to sensate focus exercises. Analytic approaches called for associations, which led to concealed difficulties between the spouses and infantile unconscious conflicts. This associative approach aims at wider goals, such as character change as well as behavior change. Brief sex therapy aims at behavioral change and therefore symptom removal. However, both methods have symptomatic relief as a goal. Not all patients are suitable for analysis nor are all patients suitable for brief sex therapy. No conflict should exist between the two disciplines. Ideally, each therapist should have several technical approaches available for the treatment of patients.

Today, I believe fewer analysts would disagree with the idea of obtaining information concerning patients' actual sexual activity and response by means of appropriate technical interventions. This information, using the knowledge gained about the physiology of human sexual excitement, can highlight physical and emotional difficulties. This allows for discreet confrontations and interpretations that can speed analytic progress. Thus, again, no conflict exists between the two methodologies and knowledge gained from either source is of benefit to the patient, which, after all, is what it is all about.

It has been the thesis of this chapter that the discoveries of Freud and of Masters and Johnson are not in opposition, but are, indeed, complementary to one another. In spite of this, many sex therapists have avoided utilizing Freud's contributions when treating their patients. Yet, Freud's revolutionary concepts concerning the importance of unconscious drives and childhood difficulties to the development of eventual sexual dysfunction have remained classic. Several clinical case reports have been presented that explicate the theme that the treatment results of brief sex therapy are improved by the use of dynamic insights.

A case report of sex therapy concomitant with psychoanalysis is also briefly reported. The brief sex therapy aided in furthering the analysis by improving the patient's ability to associate and work profitably in the analysis. Each technique enhanced the other, rather than having interfered with the patient's progress. The behavioral techniques based upon sensate focus exercises and the use of dynamic understanding of the unconscious forces at work within the patients are not in opposition but reinforce one another.

Technical approaches based upon the above principles should be part of the basic training of psychiatrists and sex therapists. Such training should include clinical experience.

REFERENCES

Dickes, R. The defensive function of an altered state of consciousness. *Journal of the American Psychoanalytic Association*, 1965, *13*, 356–403.

Dickes, R. The concepts of borderline states: An alternate proposal. *International Journal of Psychoanalytic Therapy*, 1974, *3*, 1–28.

Dickes, R. Technical considerations concerning the therapeutic and working alliance. *International Journal of Psychoanalytic Psychotherapy*, 1975, *4*, 1–25.

Dickes, R. The new sexuality: Impact on psychiatric education. In T. B. Karasu & C. W. Socarides (Eds.), *On sexuality*. New York: International Universities Press, 1975.

Kaplan, H. S. *The new sex therapy*. New York: Brunner/Mazel, 1975.

Mann, J. *Time-limited psychotherapy*. Cambridge, Mass.: Harvard University Press, 1973.

Masters, W. H., & Johnson, V. E. *Human sexual response*. Boston: Little, Brown, 1966.

Masters, W. H., & Johnson, V. E. *Human sexual inadequacy*. Boston: Little, Brown, 1970.

Semans, J. H. Premature ejaculation: A new approach. *Southern Medical Journal*, 1956, *49*, 353–357.

Sifneos, P. E. *Short-term psychotherapy and emotional crisis*. Cambridge, Mass.: Harvard University Press, 1972.

CHAPTER NINE

Marital Discord and the Wish for Sex Therapy[1]

DEREK C. POLONSKY
CAROL C. NADELSON

Over the past several years there has been an explosion of information about sexual physiology and performance and a proliferation of clinics offering sex therapy. Supermarket checkout counters are gold mines of information about almost every aspect of sexuality. Magazines offering self-assessment and self-treatment programs sell abundantly.

The easy availability of sexual information has encouraged many people to focus more attention on their sexual relationships. Couples are discovering that they "ought" to be bothered if their sexual relationship does not fit some predetermined norm, despite what they really feel. With this focus on sexual problems, expectations about what sex therapies offer has increased, unrealistically promising a quick way to happiness. In this context the clinician has seen a change in the way couples present, focusing on a sexual problem rather than a troubled relationship. The success of the Masters and Johnson technique and of other sex therapy programs and the public awareness of directed short-term therapy approaches has led people to request this treatment. They often expect that they will be instructed in a foolproof method with guaranteed success.

Prior to the work of Masters and Johnson and the development of so-called "direct sex therapy," the "traditional" approach to sexual difficulties was long-term psychotherapy or psychoanalysis, to understand the unconscious conflicts that contributed to the symptoms. The results achieved were not spectacular or even very good. Too often, after the end of a long period of treatment, patients had a sophisticated understanding of their conflicts

1. Reprinted by permission from *Psychiatric Annals*, 1982, *12*(7), 685–695. Copyright © 1982, Charles B. Slack, Inc., Medical Publishers.

Derek C. Polonsky and Carol C. Nadelson. Department of Psychiatry, Tufts University School of Medicine, Boston, Massachusetts.

and perhaps some improvement in their relationships, but little change in their sexual functioning. The pendulum then swung to the opposite pole and purely behavioral techniques were promoted. These also did not produce spectacular results for a large number of couples. The integration of the behavioral techniques of direct sex therapy with "traditional" psychotherapy met with considerable resistance. Behavioral approaches have been devalued as "transference cures" by psychotherapists, and psychodynamic views have been seen as irrelevant by behaviorists.

Increasing attention has been paid to the need to attend to the interrelationship between these approaches in therapy. In addition, many clinicians have emphasized that sex therapy cannot be successfully carried out if the marital relationship is in difficulty or if there are significant intrapsychic impediments. Thus the clinician must have a more complex understanding of etiology and treatment (Dickes, Chapter 8, this volume; Glick & Kessler, 1980; Nadelson, 1978, 1979a, 1979b; Sager, 1976).

CASE REPORTS

Dr. A had been married for 14 years when he sought consultation for intermittent impotence and feelings of dread and anxiety when he thought of having sexual relations with his wife. If they did manage to have sexual intercourse, he would experience relief at having "done it," and he would feel that he did not have to think about it again for a few weeks. He never experienced any pleasurable anticipation. Dr. A had been treated in intensive psychotherapy for this problem several years earlier. Although other symptoms had improved, his sexual problem was unchanged. Mrs. A was uncomfortable discussing sex and felt that the problem was her husband's and he ought to "fix it." She believed that they had a good marriage, and if the sex did not improve she could "put up with it." The couple was evaluated both individually and together, and although conjoint therapy was recommended, the decision was that Dr. A should be seen alone. The therapist agreed to proceed in this way, intending to work through the resistance with Dr. A and bring Mrs. A into therapy, in some way, later. This decision was made in order to build a positive alliance, especially with Mrs. A, whose anxiety and mistrust were apparent.

In therapy the first issue to be addressed was Dr. A's perception that the problem was "all his fault." He found it very difficult to look at his wife's role in their sexual problems. He seemed to ignore that Mrs. A was uncomfortable with outward displays of sexual affection, and that she had suggested that he solve "his" problem, even if it involved having sex with another woman.

As the therapy progressed Dr. A began to examine his early relationship with his parents, particularly his competition with his father and his conflicts with competence and aggression. Over several months, he worked actively in treatment, periodically coming back to specific sexual encounters with his wife. As he began to experience less conflict about being competent and aggressive, and as his sense of self-esteem began to improve, he began to experience sexual feelings. The earlier sense of dread about sexual intercourse began to fade. Intermittently, however, his symptom would return, particularly after a sexual encounter. He would worry about not being able to repeat the performance and then lose his erection. His wife was encouraging and supportive. From Dr. A's point of view, the result was extremely gratifying. He felt better about himself, was more assertive and was sexually more successful. Although it was the "sex" that brought him to therapy this time, it was using a combined approach with an evaluation of the couple, attention to individual intrapsychic dynamics and some directed sexual instruction, that led to a significant improvement.

When Dr. A talked about his dread of sexual encounters, specific suggestions were made. This diminished some of his anxiety, and enabled him to have a positive sexual experience. It is doubtful that any change would have taken place had he simply entered into sexual therapy, or if he had gone to a clinic that offered surrogate therapy, since he would most likely have been unable to perform as directed because the crucial intrapsychic issues would not have been touched.

Who Is to Blame?

As with many marital interactions, there is often an attempt to blame one partner and to define him or her as the "patient" or "wrongdoer."

Mrs. B was in her mid-30s and married for 10 years when she requested referral to a "sexually oriented" therapist. She stated that she was unable to experience sexual pleasure and that she had an aversion to physical intimacy. She and her husband had seen a couples therapist for 2 years and then a pair of sex therapists for 9 months. The sex therapists finally "gave up" and told her that she ought to see an individual therapist. She followed this recommendation and was in psychotherapy for 2 years.

Initially, her therapy focused on problems of self-esteem. She then began to work on her sexual inhibitions. As she talked about her marriage, it became apparent that she felt distant from her husband. She saw him as unable to understand her feelings and unavailable for her or for the children.

The couples evaluation revealed that Mr. B held the view that he had been the victim of an unresponsive wife. He felt that the burden of sexual frustration was too much to bear and he finally announced his intention to seek a separation. After he left, Mrs. B was struck by the lack of noticeable change in her life. She began to wonder what she had received from her husband if his leaving was so unremarkable. As her self-esteem improved she was able to talk more about her dissatisfaction with her husband and to move toward increasingly autonomous behavior. When Mr. B became aware of her growing independence, he wanted to move back home. However, she stood firm and said no. She began to see other men, and soon became involved with a man whom she described as caring and considerate in a way that contrasted sharply with her husband. As the relationship continued, her sexual feelings increased and she experienced a sense of excitement and anticipation. After 6 weeks of dating, the relationship was sexually consummated and she found her responsiveness rewarding and gratifying.

This example illustrates the problem of attributing pathology to one partner without attending to the interactional dynamic. Further, couples therapy had missed an important element in the husband's unavailability and unresponsiveness, and it focused only on the wife's intrapsychic difficulties. The sex therapy was not sensitive to individual psychodynamics, and also focused on the wife as the partner with the problem. The husband's difficulties were not perceived. They were masked by the focus on the wife. Mr. B had, in fact, suffered from premature ejaculation, but his wife's sexual aversion served to protect him from confronting his symptom and his anxieties about sexuality and intimacy.

Is It a Sexual or a Marital Problem?

The camouflaging of marital difficulties with a sexual problem is illustrated by the case of Mr. and Mrs. C. They were both in their late 40s and had been married for 18 years. They were seeking sexual therapy at Mrs. C's insistence because Mr. C had been impotent for the previous 6 to 8 months. Mr. C, however, dated the onset of the problem to 5 years previously when he began to notice a waning in the intensity of his erections. Couples therapy sessions were often filled with intense and, at times, acrimonious bickering. After several weeks of meeting, Mr. C requested an individual meeting. During this session he admitted to a sexual affair in the past year, stating that he found himself able to perform perfectly well with the other woman. He realized that he was not attracted to his wife, and that he was angry and resentful toward her because she had changed after they married.

Initially, he believed that she would be a "traditional" wife, and that he would be the "man of the house." Over the course of the years she had become more independent, leaving him feeling betrayed and rejected. He was seen for several individual sessions and it became clear that he was recreating an earlier parental conflict. He viewed his wife as undermining, unsupportive, and critical, and he spent a great deal of time examining her behavior for confirmation of these perceptions. During subsequent joint meetings, an attempt was made to shift the focus from the sexual difficulties in the relationship to an examination of the distorted perceptions each had of the other. After several months, Mrs. C admitted that she felt better because her husband's limitations were clearer to her. They subsequently terminated treatment. They were never able to resolve the problems in their collusive system, where Mr. C saw Mrs. C as aggressive and critical and she saw him as withholding and distant.

This couple illustrates the need to understand that the focus on a sexual problem can be a way of avoiding other issues. Mr. C initially presented because of "impotence," and Mrs. C indicated her willingness to engage in couples therapy to alleviate the sexual problem. They did not indicate that the marital relationship was troubled. When it became clear to Mrs. C that the solution to the problem was not to be found in sexual therapy, but rather in facing some of the difficult feelings they had about each other, she chose to end therapy and continue living in a situation that provided stability and security, but not much emotional satisfaction.

The following couple illustrates another aspect of this problem, where there seems to be an absence of genuine intimacy and mutual caring and the partners are angry and dissatisfied, utilizing mutual projections that support distortions. In this case it comes as no surprise then that there are sexual difficulties. In the absence of warm feelings, it is hard to imagine that there would be a dramatic transformation in the bedroom. Frequently, couples appear to look toward "sex therapy" as the cure for these troubles and at times there is even a sense of self-righteous concern when they say, "look what I am prepared to do to demonstrate my seriousness and commitment."

Mr. and Mrs. D specifically requested sex therapy to deal with Mrs. D's declining interest in sexual relations with her husband. In the first interview Mrs. D acknowledged her lack of willingness to have sexual relations and her feeling that she was being unfair to her husband. However, as the session progressed, she began to talk about her anger with him and stated that she could not bear to be physically intimate with him. After meeting with Mr. D, it became clear that he dealt repeatedly and unrelentingly in double-bind situations. For example, he would state "Of course you have power—you may do anything you want." He would then proceed to disqualify the statement and tell Mrs. D that what she wanted to do was impossible because he did not want it. In their parent–child relationship, the marital dynamic became clearer. Mr. D saw himself as the agreeable, permissive, understanding, reasonable parent and he colluded with his children in seeing his wife as angry, aggressive, complaining, and unsatisfied. On several occasions he characterized his wife as overly concerned and intrusive with his son, but he did not acknowledge that he in fact did share her views.

The two were able to recognize and acknowledge that sexual therapy had no place until the marital difficulties and intense struggles between them were addressed.

Is There Serious Individual Psychopathology?

We have seen many couples presenting with requests for sexual therapy with serious psychopathology found in one partner, necessitating treatment for that problem.

Mr. and Mrs. E called the clinic to request sexual therapy. Mr. E had had premature ejaculations for the duration of their 5-year marriage. Initially, it appeared as if this would be a straightforward sexual therapy case. However, when Mr. E was seen alone, a severe depression became manifest. This related to his father's recent physical decline and imminent death, which reawakened guilt feelings about a younger brother who had committed suicide while he was an adolescent. Mr. E had never told his wife about his brother's suicide. Mr. and Mrs. E were seen together in therapy to allow Mrs. E to learn more about the feelings he had been unable to share with her. Her response was supportive and caring, greatly facilitating his recovery.

After Mr. E's depression improved, the couple indicated that they had been experimenting with the "squeeze technique" on their own. They felt much closer to each other and were feeling more sexual. They successfully solved the problem with some additional help from their therapist.

Sex Therapy or Marital Therapy?

The value, for the therapist, of being familiar with the techniques of sex therapy is underscored by the frequency with which sexual difficulties surface in couples after they have been in treatment for other problems. A recent study of 100 "happily married couples" reported that even in this group 40% of the men had either erectile or ejaculatory dysfunctions, while 63% of the women had either orgasmic or arousal difficulties (Frank, Anderson, & Kupfer, 1976; Frank, Anderson, & Rubinstein, 1978). While this may have been temporary or situational, it does suggest that there are substantial numbers of people with sexual difficulties and that all therapists should take a complete sexual history as part of a routine evaluation, and have some familiarity with the indications for and techniques of sexual therapy.

Mr. and Mrs. F came for therapy because they had not been getting along for several years. Mr. F had experienced recurrent rejection early in his life and had developed a need to protect himself from the vulnerability he experienced in close relationships. He consequently attempted to maintain a distant and "safe" relationship with his wife. Mrs. F came from a family where her weak masochistic mother was terrified of her distant, punitive, and explosive father, causing her also to be frightened of intimacy.

During couples therapy both partners gradually became aware of the origins of their need to maintain distant relationships. As both experienced more affection and formed a trusting relationship with the therapist, their marital relationship began to change. They became more responsive and were able to express their needs to each other.

After 8 months they began to talk about their sexual problems. Mr. F was impotent, a fact that had been hidden until this time. The focus of the therapy was then changed and their sexual difficulties were addressed. If the couples therapist had not been able to do sexual therapy, it is likely that the couple would not have resolved their sexual problems, since they were not prepared to trust and work with another therapist. In his relationship with the therapist, it had taken Mr. F a long time to be trusting and feel safe enough to expose his vulnerability and "defectiveness."

THE EVALUATION FORMAT

The initial comment of a couple might be as nonspecific as "I have a sexual problem," or "I don't enjoy sex," or it may be very specific and technical, such as "I have premature ejaculation." Frequently the couple then asks for "sex therapy."

Ensuing discussion of the evaluative process, which includes a complete evaluation of each partner and the couple together, often raises many questions. "Why do we have to do that when it's a sexual problem?" or "I just want sex therapy, that's all." The clinical material we have presented above provides some perspective on our belief that it is important to learn about each person as an individual, and also to see the couple in the context of a relationship. In our experience, partners tend to be candid, open, and often give some insight into their motivation for treatment when they have an individual session. We sometimes learn that one partner has come because he or she is guilty about an affair, a lack of commitment, or lack of interest in the relationship. The focus on the sexual problem can be diversionary, even consciously.

It is also necessary to define the presenting problem, to learn how long it has been a problem, what techniques have been used to treat it and why treatment is sought at this particular time. In addition, this relationship and other relationships can be understood, and we can learn about the family history. Previous sexual experiences, sexual attitudes of family, and sexual education are important areas of information. We also attend to each partner's capacity to experience pleasure and evaluate life satisfaction. Sex is frequently the focus of a host of other problems.

During the couple's meeting we attempt to assess their interaction, as well as how they relate to the evaluator. We also obtain a consensus, if possible, as to how a couple defines the problem for which they are seeking treatment. It is not frequent that the agendas of each partner are different. This must be discussed openly before a commitment to treatment can be made. A treatment plan is then formulated with the couple and evaluator discussing it and reaching an agreement.

It is important to note that even if sex therapy is recommended, and a directed approach is agreed upon, individual psychodynamics must continue to be part of the thinking of the therapist. Seldom, in our experience, is direct sex therapy alone effective (less than 15% of our cases).

At times the therapist may not feel that the problem is primarily sexual, but the couple may insist on defining it that way. If the couple is defensive and unable to accept an alternative interpretation of the difficulty, so that other techniques are precluded, it is possible to follow the couple's wishes, as with Dr. and Mrs. A, and initiate a behavioral approach. It is likely that in this situation the couple needs to maintain some control over therapy. If interpretations are insistent or premature the couple usually withdraws from therapy, seeks another therapist who will provide what they request, or drops out entirely and seeks other solutions, even divorce. We find, most often, that if a direct sex therapy approach begins, the couple rapidly experiences their own resistance and inability to follow the directions of the therapist and usually will return, more cooperative.

The therapist with a multifocal approach is in a unique position to evaluate a couple and to present a treatment plan which includes both marital and sexual therapy at different phases or, at times, in combination. A couple may begin with couples therapy or individual therapy, and then move into sexual therapy, and vice versa. There has been much debate in the literature about the efficacy of mixing these approaches and/or using the same therapist. In our experience, within the context of couples therapy, direct sex therapy approaches can be employed and when appropriate, a couples therapy focus can be reintroduced.

At times, sexual therapy may be effective, enabling the couple to proceed in couples therapy, or one or both of them may seek individual psychotherapy. The impact of success, and the increased self-esteem that attends it may be instrumental in this shifted focus. If, however, sex therapy "fails," the patient may feel that you have proved your point, and may become more involved in individual or couples therapy.

One last and important issue relates to the couple's questions about the therapist. Because of public awareness and interest, couples often seek sex therapy with a well-informed and well-read background of the subject. Some have even tried much of what is recommended. This presents the therapist with a unique opportunity for a collaborative effort.

Questions such as—"What is your background?" "Have you had experience treating people with sexual problems?" "What are your results like; do people get better?" "What actually happens in sex therapy; do we do it in your office?"—are asked and, if the therapist is not defensive, a realistic discussion of fantasy and reality can be very productive.

Questions need to be answered after they have been explored thoroughly. The couple's anxiety, although it is not different from the anxiety of the person beginning individual psychotherapy, often requires an informational discussion to facilitate the evolution of a therapeutic alliance. Responses that are interpretive or those that evoke additional questions (e.g., "I wonder why you ask that?") tend to alienate the couple and reinforce their feeling that their concerns are not being addressed. Further, it is important for these questions to be used as an opportunity to learn of the expectations of the couple, and how they understand the process. A detailed discussion of approach and theory are helpful. Particularly since so many couples have made previous attempts at utilizing various techniques themselves, they wonder what difference it will make to have a therapist to work with. Their fantasies and fears must be addressed.

With regard to success rate, it is often reassuring to hear that all couples are different and unique, and that, while figures are helpful, success is difficult to quantify or assess when criteria are so unclear. Most couples do not want to be statistics, they want to know that the therapist is competent and committed. Obviously, this view has its limits, and a careful discussion should include a realistic appraisal of what can be expected.

CONCLUSION

Clinicians working with sexual and marital problems increasingly concur that a variety of treatment approaches must be integrated. Lief (1980) states, "A competent sex psychotherapist must be able to use a variety of therapeutic approaches and from among these to choose methods of intervention that fit the special and often unique circumstances found in a given clinical situation" (p. ix). When the focus is simply on one aspect, such as sex therapy, it is possible to miss the subtle, but crucial influences of interpersonal and unconscious dynamics, and the treatment is likely to fail. Although there are no good research data supporting this view, because it has not been systematically collected, clinical evidence increasingly favors this approach.

In our clinic we have seen a large number of couples who have failed in other therapeutic attempts, usually direct sex therapy. While it is difficult to document the specific frequency of this pattern, because referral patterns vary, we are impressed with the number who have serious marital and intrapsychic conflicts. Treatment with "sex therapy" has resulted in a sense that little has been accomplished. Most of these couples did not participate in follow-up, so those who had treated them would be unable to document the success or failure of the treatment. Other clinicians have reported similarly, including Masters and Johnson, and Kaplan (Kaplan, 1982; Masters & Johnson, 1970; Sager, 1975; Schwartz, 1982). They emphasize the necessity for caution in seeking a rapid cure, and have suggested that direct sex therapy techniques are applicable for only a small percentage of those presenting with sexual problems. It is important to remember that Masters and Johnson evolved their technique from a highly selected, motivated population, which may not be comparable to those patients seen in other clinical settings.

Increasingly couples present with a sexual complaint, which becomes the calling card for entry into treatment. While many of these couples have sexual symptoms, sex therapy is not necessarily indicated if other problems exist. Sager (1975, pp. 124–140) has developed five criteria for evaluating a couple's interpersonal status to determine suitability for sex therapy:

- Relative freedom from basic feelings of hostility, since this may preclude ability to cooperate. Marital therapy is indicated first for couples who are constantly angry with each other;
- General acceptance of each other as a sex partner;
- Motivation for help for him or herself as well as for the partner. It is important that each partner become aware of his or her own role in causing or perpetuating the dysfunction, and perceive the mutual benefits of improving the problem;
- Ability of each partner to postpone sexual gratification, since this may be necessary during the course of treatment; and
- Ability to accept a nondemand ambience during the course of therapy.

For many, the identification of sexual problems serves a defensive function. Initially, it may be important to respect this, since it facilitates the recognition that there is a problem. Most often, after sensate exercises have been suggested, the couple will return to the next session having done nothing. There is an unending supply of "valid" reasons (e.g., the World Series was on, the in-laws were visiting, or there was no time because of a tight work schedule, etc.). The couple usually becomes aware of their resistance when they find that the next week they also have "reasons." The therapist then can ask them to understand their behavior as an indication that there are other issues that must be addressed first. A change of focus in the treatment will occur, and the couple will no longer insist on "sex therapy."

It is important for clinicians to be familiar with the concepts and use of direct sexual therapy and to have a thorough grounding in psychodynamics and interpersonal processes. The information gathered from individual interviews can facilitate an understanding of what each individual brings to the marriage and attempts to "wring out of the partner" (Dicks, 1965, p. 269). It is also important during the initial evaluation to ascertain whether there is serious individual psychopathology that needs to be addressed before proceeding with couples treatment.

Flexibility in treatment approach is essential. As previously indicated, the therapist can shift his or her technique, at times focusing on individual issues or on the interpersonal interaction and at other times, becoming more directive with specific sexual instructions. Although there has been substantial debate about the advisability of this shift by the same therapist(s), we view it as an important, and at times, necessary component for successful therapeutic outcome. It is important to recognize that an alliance develops between the couple and the therapist that is not readily transferable to another therapist if the problem focus changes (i.e., if the couple begins to talk about sexual difficulties a referral to a "sex therapist" may be seen as a rejection or an indication that sex is not a valid therapeutic issue). Glick and Kessler (1980) state, "Because of the interrelatedness of these two problem areas, therapists who undertake to treat couples should become competent in both marital and sex therapy. Therapists should be in a position to move freely from one of these areas to the other" (p. 203). Frank *et al.* (1976) state that "any therapist who is assessing a couple with marital difficulties, but is unable or unwilling to confront the issues of sexual compatibilities, may be performing only half the required task. Equally obvious is the fact that any therapist in sexual counseling must have more than a minimal ability to deal with interpersonal conflicts within a marriage" (p. 562). For the therapist who has experience with individual, marital, and sex therapy, the opportunity to see the effects of moving back and forth utilizing different techniques is extremely gratifying. The changes that can be made in couples' lives is sometimes enormous, and may occur in a remarkably short time.

REFERENCES

Dicks, H. V. Concepts of marital diagnosis and therapy as developed at the Tavistock family psychiatric units, London, England. In *Marriage counseling in medical practice*. Chapel Hill, N.C.: University of North Carolina Press, 1965.

Frank, E., Anderson, C., & Kupfer, D. Profiles of couples seeking sex therapy and marital therapy. *American Journal of Psychiatry*, 1976, *133*(5), 559–562.

Frank, E., Anderson, C., & Rubinstein, D. Frequency of sexual dysfunction in "normal" couples. *New England Journal of Medicine*, 1978, *299*, 111–115.

Glick, I. D., & Kessler, D. R. *Marital and family therapy* (2nd ed.). New York: Grune & Stratton, 1980.

Kaplan, H. *ISD: A model for the treatment of ego-dystonic homosexuality.* Presented at the Integrative Psychiatry Symposium Series, January 23–24, 1982, New York.

Lief, H. Foreword. In S. R. Leiblum & L. A. Pervin (Eds.), *Principles and practice of sex therapy*. New York: Guilford, 1980.

Masters, W., & Johnson, V. *Human sexual inadequacy*. Boston: Little, Brown, 1970.

Nadelson, C. Marital therapy from a psychoanalytic perspective. In T. J. Paolino & B. S. McCrady (Eds.), *Marriage and marital therapy*. New York: Brunner/Mazel, 1978.

Nadelson, C. Evaluation of sexual dysfunction. In A. Lazare (Ed.), *Outpatient psychiatry*. Baltimore: Williams & Wilkins, 1979. (a)

Nadelson, C. Treatment of sexual dysfunction. In A. Lazare (Ed.), *Outpatient psychiatry*. Baltimore: Williams & Wilkins, 1979. (b)

Sager, C. J. The couples model and the treatment of sexual dysfunction in the single person. In E. T. Adelson (Ed.), *Sexuality and psychoanalysis*. New York: Brunner/Mazel, 1975.

Sager, C. J. The role of sex therapy in marital therapy. *American Journal of Psychiatry*, 1976, *133*(5), 555–558.

Schwartz, M. F. *The Masters and Johnson approach to the treatment of the ego-dystonic homosexual.* Presented at the Integrative Psychiatry Symposium Series, January 23–24, 1982, New York.

Marital Dissolution

CHAPTER TEN

The Divorced Woman: Processes of Change

ELIZABETH H. MAURY
RUTH A. BRANDWEIN

Stripped to its bare essentials, divorce is a major *change*. Most divorcing women change from living in a relationship where their husband is head of household, to becoming heads of their own households with their children. (Although some divorcing women don't have children, the majority do; Norton & Glick, 1976.) In this chapter we will focus on the divorcing woman with children, since her childless counterpart can slip back with relatively little difficulty into the status of the never-married woman.

Change in a person's life creates challenge, opportunity, and vulnerability. New strategies for daily living must be learned; old attitudes and patterns must be shed. Relationships change inside and outside the family and the meaning of one's existence must be examined. This process of relearning takes time. Although the pace may be most rapid during the first year or two following divorce, relearning continues as other life changes occur. Despite individual and demographic differences among women, it is possible to examine the impact of divorce on all women through the prism of time.

Divorce can be viewed conceptually as a change process with three stages (Maury, Brandwein, & Kohen, 1980). The first, "predivorce," stage involves the abandonment or rejection of the marital role, a process that usually begins before physical separation. This change is internal, psychological, and "within the family" until the couple "goes public" by physically separating. While this psychological process is occurring, the woman does

Elizabeth H. Maury. Exceptional Parents Unlimited/Association for Retarded Citizens, Fresno, California, and Central San Joaquin Medical Education Program of the University of California at San Francisco Medical School, Fresno, California.

Ruth A. Brandwein. School of Social Welfare, State University of New York at Stony Brook, Stony Brook, New York.

not change her social definition as wife. That happens only at the moment of separation.

In the second, "ex-wife," stage, the woman no longer lives with her husband, but still views herself or is viewed by others as an ex-wife. During this stage, the divorcing woman faces everything at once: becoming head of household; assuming financial responsibility for the remaining family; locating child care; finding or keeping a job; coping with the myriad of events of daily living formerly shared (at least in theory) with her husband; and in the midst of this, experiencing the complicated feelings that inevitably accompany a major life change, even when it is "for the best." This second stage, which normally lasts for the first year or two following separation, is often fixed in the minds of professionals and lay people as *the* divorce experience, rather than being seen as part of an ongoing process.

The third, "single-parent," stage is that of new, positive self-definition, based on integration of old and new roles. At this point, the divorced mother no longer sees "divorced" as the key element in her self-definition, but affirms herself as a single parent capably managing the affairs of her family. Not all women attain this stage. Some remarry while they are still coping with the issues of stage one or stage two. The women who reach stage three, we believe, enter into a relationship with a man (if they choose to do so), with much greater capability and determination to secure full equality and mature interdependence in the relationship.

This chapter examines these three stages of divorce, drawing on theoretical and interview data from our own group, the Women's Research Center of Boston (Brandwein, Brown, & Fox, 1974; Kohen, Brown, & Feldberg, 1979), as well as on theory and research of other authors. (Unlike many bodies of psychosocial literature, current research about divorce shows much cross-study congruence.) The chapter concludes with suggestions for human service professionals working with divorced mothers in each stage.

STAGE I: PREPARING FOR SEPARATION

Women have varying opportunities to plan for change or continuity as they move from marriage to divorce.

Control over the Divorce

Our data and others' suggest that women who initiate the divorce fare better than women whose husbands initiate the change (Kelly, 1978). The 19 women in our sample who initiated the divorce reported fewer problems in the immediate postseparation period than those who did not (Kohen, 1980). The decision making gave them a sense of control. They were able to face the psychological reality of separation before physical separation began.

Maintaining Changing Roles

Before separation, a divorcing woman may not only begin letting go of the marital role but may also identify competencies (such as a sense of humor, organizational ability, or job skills) and roles (such as mother or career person), which she can carry from marriage to divorce.

In our study, we identified three groups of women who had different role attainments and competencies prior to divorce (Fox & Brandwein, 1979). One group, whom we classified as "Young-Poor," had married young, bore one or two children, and were divorced by their mid-20s. They were poorly educated and had few job skills. A second group were the "Older-Poor." These women had been married almost 15 years on the average, had three to six children, were also poorly educated, and had marginal job skills. A third group, the "Well-Educated" group, were married from 5 to 10 years, had one to three children, and had at least some college education or marketable job skills.

During marriage, the "Young-Poor" mothers did not have time for success either as workers or as parents, so caught up were they in chaotic, impoverished marriages. They carried inadequate skills and poor self-images into divorce. The "Older-Poor" mothers, while having few job skills, usually had long, rewarding experiences as mothers. The "Well-Educated" mothers typically had both job experience or training at the professional level as well as success experiences as mothers. Hence, they were the best prepared during marriage for the roles they needed in divorce.

Analysis of how much control a divorcing woman feels in dropping the marital role, and of what roles she performed during marriage that she may be able to continue following separation, has important implications for predicting ease of transition to single parenthood.

STAGE II: LEARNING NEW ROLES AND CHANGING OLD ONES

Until physical separation occurs, most of the divorce process takes place within the privacy of the family. The separation publicly announces the conflict between the spouses. From now on, the divorced mother's actions will be on view to family members, friends, and fellow workers, as well as to formal organizations such as banks, social agencies, schools, and religious institutions.

Spheres of Action: Interrelated Dilemmas

The divorced mother must operate in three distinct spheres: the *internal*, the *boundary*, and the *external*. The *internal* sphere refers to her activities and relationships within her own family (herself and children). The *boundary* sphere refers to interactions with her extended family, friends, coworkers, and ex-husband. The *external* sphere refers to interactions with formal organizations as well as to contractual relationships with schools, employers, landlords, and service people.

As a divorced mother, she must decide how to provide what is needed in the internal sphere (to herself and her children) and how to obtain what she needs from the boundary and external spheres. She acts as gatekeeper, entrepreneur, and conduit among the spheres. Her problems represent cross-sphere difficulties. In the rest of this section, we will examine some of these difficulties and the solutions that must be found for them.

ECONOMIC CONSTRAINTS

In providing for her family, the divorced mother deals directly with the external sphere—agencies and institutions in the large society—and she faces three interrelated problems. First, she may lack adequate job skills or education to enter the job market. This problem hits almost all women, from the one who never completed a graduate degree as she followed her husband from job to job, to the woman who married right out of high school and had no paid employment during 20 years of marriage. How is she going to become marketable? She will need training or education, but while she is being trained, she will not be earning money. This dilemma forces many women to abandon hope for adequate jobs and take on low-level, dead-end employment or go on welfare. Such solutions do not lead to long-term financial stability.

Second, if she finds a paying job-training program or gets her tuition paid at a local college, how will she pay for child care, and of what quality will it be? Current estimates are that about 90% of paid, out-of-home group care is not of the quality that most mothers can provide (Fraiberg, 1977). Children left with neighbors or relatives may not fare better. Furthermore, child-care needs, while most acute with children under school age, do not disappear even through the teenage years. Mothers in our sample with teenaged children felt that their teenagers' need for supervision, although not of the minute-to-minute variety, was just as critical as for younger children.

After finding child care and receiving job training, the divorced mother faces employment discrimination—with women earning less than 60 cents for every dollar earned by men with the same training and experience—and she can expect to be the "last hired, first fired" (U.S. Department of Labor, 1979).

Society provides no solutions for any of these problems. By utilizing resources that may be available in her internal or boundary spheres, an individual woman may minimize her difficulties. For example, a woman who is well-educated, has been employed prior to divorce, and can maintain her employment following divorce may experience less financial chaos than one who starts with no job skills or education. Furthermore, if she worked during marriage, she may be familiar with the vagaries and upsets of securing child care.

If she's lucky, her ex-husband may continue to contribute to the family and the drop from before-divorce income will be less precipitous. It is important to note, however, that the probability of a divorced woman collecting any child support may be less than 60% in the first year after the court order and down to 20% after 10 years, as in one California study (Weitzman, 1974). Hence, except for families that were impoverished to begin with, practically all women and children face a steep decline in income following divorce, and the woman's earning capacity rather than her ex-husband's becomes the primary determiner of family income (Bane, 1976).

A divorced mother's extended family may provide financial assistance, perhaps by helping her to make house payments or by giving clothing or presents to the children. Nonetheless, all of these buffers against financial difficulty depend on personal resources. No systematic provisions for the divorced mother (except for the indignity and inadequacy of welfare) are available from the larger society.

DISCRIMINATION AGAINST A WOMAN HEAD OF HOUSEHOLD

The barriers a woman faces in maintaining economic security for her family are compounded by the difficulties of being a female head of household. Our respondents, as well as those from other studies, pointed out that there are no positive expectations of divorced women—successful divorced women are seen as a contradiction in terms. The choice to remain single and yet be a mother remains a nonlegitimated role, except for the widow, who is desexualized and viewed as an object of pity.

In our sample, all but four women reported examples of discrimination, ranging from difficulty in obtaining credit, to harassment by a judge during divorce proceedings. These instances were recorded separately from descriptions of sexual harassment, reported by all but two of our sample. Discrimination against women heads of household was even reported in one study where wives of men being held as POWs in Vietnam had taken charge (McCubbin, 1979).

PSYCHOLOGICAL IMPACT OF SOCIETAL DISCRIMINATION

These societal definitions also have psychological impact, both in terms of the mother's self-esteem, and in her relationships within the family. Studies have pointed to two major effects in her relationships with her children (Smith, 1970; Hetherington, 1979; Weiss, 1979). First, the children's ability to cope, especially if they are below adolescence, will be closely related to her own ability. A mother who is doing well will be more available to help her children deal with the change to a single-parent household. Second, stigmatization of the mother outside the home, as well as the absence of a second

197

adult to back her up, can affect her children's perceptions of her. They may see her as more equal to them in power, more on their level. This can be a plus or minus, depending on the mother's ability to accept this change in power.

During this second stage, when the divorced woman has shed her role as wife and not fully integrated her roles as a single parent, she runs the risk of living by other people's definitions. She may be defined by her parents and friends as emotionally or financially needy; by school authorities as potentially inadequate in raising her children; by the bank as a poor risk; and by an employer as either expendable labor or as unreliable because of her child-care responsibilities. She may be seen by the landlord as untrustworthy financially and/or morally. These stereotypes may or may not be applied in any particular case, but no divorced woman escapes them totally. They make her journey toward self-definition slow and precarious.

A divorced woman's family furthermore, is open to public scrutiny in ways that a two-parent family is not. Either the court or the welfare department—or both—may step in and make a judgment about the adequacy of her child rearing. There is always the implicit threat that she may be judged inadequate and that her children may be removed from her.

Spheres of Action: "Piecing Together" Solutions

As the divorced mother sorts through her particular strengths and vulnerabilities in the "ex-wife" stage, following separation, she begins the process of "piecing together" resources within herself, in her friends, neighbors, colleagues, relatives, and ex-husband, and in agencies and institutions that will help her move toward positive self-definition. Because societal supports are lacking, each divorced woman's "piecing together" is unique. And because life circumstances change, the pieces that fit at one time may no longer fit at another.

"Piecing together" begins during the "ex-wife" stage, as an immediate response to crisis. It begins as the divorced mother locates the resources to keep the family going, and develops long-term strategies for the survival of self and family. It continues once the acute issues come under control and the mother moves toward more positive self-definition. It remains a highly complex task. No person can do it without support.

INTERNAL RESOURCES

Earlier, we identified two inner resources a divorced mother may carry from marriage to divorce—her control over the decision to separate, and her past record as a competent mother and/or competent wage earner. Her children may also be important resources, if they provide either emotional or tangible support, through taking part-time jobs, caring for family members, or doing housework or repairs.

Within the boundary sphere, the ex-husband, the mother's family of origin (and in our study, in-laws, if the marriage was a long one), her friends, and her colleagues are all potential sources of support.

Studies show that the transition to divorce is easiest when the divorcing partners agree about money and custody (Westman, Cline, Swift, & Kramer, 1971). However, only a low percentage of divorcing couples, perhaps 20 to 30%, make stable arrangements on both of these issues (Weiss, 1975; Hetherington, 1979). Divorcing mothers, on the whole, cannot expect to count on ex-husbands for income, nor for a predictable commitment to the children. A reliable ex-husband should be regarded as a great (if perhaps temporary) comfort to the mother.

The woman's family of origin can also be either supportive or difficult. Some mothers in our sample felt forever grateful to their parents, who had provided both psychological and concrete support since separation. As one mother said, "Everyone should have a mom like mine." They did not feel belittled or demeaned by this assistance.

Others received help from parents, but felt pushed back into a child-like, dependent role. One mother whose parents had helped with child care and small loans said, "Their brain is in never-never land. They're such buttinsky parents. When my kind of woman gets a divorce, she's out of the adult female role and back into the daughter role as far as the family is concerned." Although they could count on support, these women felt their family relations to be a psychological burden.

Friends can provide assistance, embarrassment, or pain. Several women we interviewed had a wide range of friends on whom to call for child-care assistance, for small loans, or for companionship. One spoke warmly of women friends with whom she spent Friday evenings—"That's my time to howl." Some talked of close male friends, not necessarily sexual companions, who did things with the children or helped with small jobs around the house. However, many also reported negative experiences with male friends who, following the divorce, either shunned them or propositioned them.

We found in our study, as had others, that middle-class women relied more on friends for support, while poorer women turned more toward their families (Montalvo, 1976). In general, middle-class women had more options in obtaining services such as day care or home repairs. Since favors from families or friends might imply obligations in return, the middle-class women's ability to purchase services gave them more independence than the poorer women.

Colleagues at work, or work itself, may be either a hindrance or support to the divorced mother. Work may be her main chance to interact with other adults, especially if her children are young and she has no evening child care. Flexible time schedules or supportive colleagues were greatly appreciated by women we interviewed. Their jobs refreshed and sustained them in the midst of their many responsibilities. For other women, inflexible time schedules or difficult interpersonal situations made work intolerable. Women spoke of bosses who wouldn't give them time off to be with their children; of long commutes, of sexual harassment in finding or keeping a job.

EXTERNAL RESOURCES

When women in our sample talked of their contacts with social agencies or institutions such as hospitals, schools, the welfare department, clergy, or the courts, a fragmented picture of service and discrimination emerged. No woman had escaped negative encounters, but most had also found some positive resources. Resources obtained seemed a patchwork of what was available in a particular community and depended on the mother's skills in going after what she needed. The majority of women we interviewed had become highly knowledgeable about public services, credit policies, health care, and legal aid. Out of necessity, they became advocates and community organizers—starting day-care facilities, keeping job-training programs alive, staffing women's clinics and resource centers. They had learned to pull together and to find neighborhoods and communities responsive to their needs. Women in city neighborhoods where female-headed families were common and accepted felt much support, while women in outlying suburbs felt isolated by the prevailing norms of two-parent families (Bequaert, 1976). At least one woman in our sample had moved back to the city to live in an environment that would be more accepting of her and her family.

STAGE III: MOVING TOWARD SELF-DEFINITION

As divorced women begin to integrate the roles of household head, primary breadwinner, and "both mother and father" (as many women put it) to their children, they move beyond seeing themselves as ex-wives toward a positive definition as single parents. However, they continue to face the problems of multiple demands on their time and energy. Juggling roles and demands remains a severe logistic, if not psychological, problem, for most divorced mothers.

Rollins and Galligan (1978) have identified four ways of minimizing the overload problem. Their suggestions were: (1) identify whether the task or role is satisfying; (2) delegate tasks when possible; (3) find resources that can help with the task ("piecing together" again); (4) try to merge two roles or tasks into one. We saw these strategies at work to a greater or lesser degree in all the families we interviewed and often marveled at the women's resource-fulness.

Role Satisfaction

Women in our group cited two roles as bringing great satisfaction—mother and worker. Some women found satisfaction in both roles (although role demands tended to compete with one another), some primarily in one. Women who were not satisfied in either role tended to appear the most stressed by divorce (Kohen, 1980).

A divorced woman's satisfaction in her achievements as a mother or wage earner allows her to move beyond the ex-wife stigma. It's as if she can say, "I may no longer be a wife, but I'm a damned good mother/worker, and nobody can take that from me."

Role Delegation

Divorced mothers can normally expect help from their children on a day-to-day basis. Our data indicate that they delegate tasks to the children whenever possible.

At least three studies, including our own, have now identified a characteristic among children of single-parent families which Weiss describes as "growing up a little faster" (Fox & Brandwein, 1979; McCubbin & Dahl, 1976; Weiss, 1979). In our sample, we found that teenaged girls particularly were delegated major responsibilities for housework, babysitting, and cooking, and that school-aged children were often given serious responsibilities as well (such as an 8-year-old cooking meals for herself and mother). The "nontraditional" family of divorce seems to promote a very traditional work ethic!

Delegating household tasks to people outside the family appears to be problematic to divorced mothers. Because women are seen as skilled at housework and child care, friends, family, and neighbors assume that a single mother will continue to perform these tasks no matter what other obligations she has. If friends and family do not help out, the women must seek paid assistance. Only the middle-class women in our sample could afford a cleaning service or hire a babysitter for an evening. The poor women needed to rely on nonpaid services, and the price exacted, either in feelings of dependence or in sexual coercion, was often too high.

The difficulties for women in delegating tasks outside the family contrasted sharply with easy access to services that five male single parents we interviewed reported. These men made better salaries for their educational level than the women we interviewed, and hence were better able to pay for services they needed. More important, they were viewed by friends and relatives as needing help with family tasks and as heroes for even attempting to raise their children alone. All five said they were able to obtain, free of charge, babysitting and housework assistance from a wide range of people.

Piecing Together Solutions—Continued

As mentioned before, because there is no defined path toward successful divorced motherhood, because those who could serve as role models are usually too busy keeping their own families going, and because social supports are inadequate, each divorced mother must find resources on her own. To add to her task, she must find new resources as her needs and those of her family change.

Adequate income and adequate child care continue to be pressing needs even after a woman has achieved some stability and self-definition. Most mothers, even after several years of divorce, are still piecing together a combination of job and/or welfare, perhaps some child support, and an occasional loan or gift from family members. This financial pattern may be modal for divorced mothers.

Finding child care illustrates another patchwork arrangement, combining resources used in the boundary sphere with contractual arrangements in the external sphere. Arrangements for most families seldom last for more than a few months, so that even the best-organized and planful mothers report a continuing drain on their energies to assure adequate care for their children. Child care for a working divorced mother, with 8 hours on the job and an hour's commute each way, can often involve two or three different arrangements over the day, with additional plans for a child's illness or school vacation.

Role Merger

Merging of roles was undertaken by several mothers we interviewed who had combined their income-producing and child-care roles by becoming day-care providers in their own apartments. By earning income while caring for their own children, they eliminated child-care expenses. Most women, however, described how fragmented they felt because they could not integrate roles. They literally ran from early morning to late at night, preparing meals, taking children to child care or school, commuting to work, and then reversing the process, dropping with fatigue around midnight.

In our sample of divorced mothers, whom we interviewed from 1 to 5 years following separation, we concluded that 22 of the 30 had reached the third stage of the divorce process, in which they no longer saw themselves in the negative status of ex-wives, but as positively defined single parents. (Kohen, 1980). The eight women who had not been able to achieve self-definition were blocked by: (1) inability to find satisfaction in either the working or mothering role; (2) isolation from adequate social supports; (3) a family situation, such as a handicapped child, which created extra demands over and above the other responsibilities of single parenthood (Kohen, 1980).

They were still in the second stage of identifying roles and gaining competence, and had not yet achieved active control and integration of, roles.

Active control and integration often go along with behavior that is not traditionally defined as feminine. Our successful mothers defined themselves as "much too mouthy," or as women whom others "wouldn't dare" to cross. This assertive behavior goes against the grain of feminine socialization, and was acquired slowly and painfully through the many experiences divorced women have, taking charge of their own psyches and of their families. Yet, while most of the women in our sample described themselves as having come through hard times since separation, the majority felt it had been worth it to get out of the bad marriage. Most said that they felt stronger psychologically than during marriage and the early postseparation period, even though their life circumstances remained more difficult than when they had been married.

As a young mother with one child said "Things are different—not easier. When you're having a difficult marriage it can be pretty horrendous. Going through a growing period is difficult, too. This is difficult happy; that was difficult sad." An older mother with six children said, "It's easier now. It comes to attitude. You can do so much when your mind is free and you don't have any aggravation. Nothing is easier, but it feels easier. I have to live up to my own expectations—no one else's."

IMPLICATIONS FOR HUMAN SERVICE PROFESSIONALS

In the last 10 years, the exploding divorce rate has made divorce a subject no human service professional can ignore. Almost everyone who is seen is affected. If he or she is not divorced, he or she may be contemplating divorce, be in a relationship with a divorced person, or be the child of divorce. While divorce has certain universal aspects, these will be experienced in a unique way by each individual, and the perception of the event and its implications will change over time.

This chapter has conceptualized divorce as a process consisting of three stages: "predivorce," "ex-wife," and "single parent." Most clients seek professional help in the second, often most problematic, "ex-wife" stage. Hence professionals have tended to view the entire divorce experience as problematic rather than seeing it as providing opportunities for growth, change, and self-affirmation. In the paragraphs below, recommendations for working with women at each stage are discussed.

Stage I: "Predivorce"

If a client seeks professional guidance while struggling over whether to divorce, the professional can help the client identify some of the tasks ahead.

While most professionals have moved beyond the "save-this-marriage" approach, we should not gloss over the difficulties a woman faces as she moves out of marriage. She may decide separation is not right for her, she may begin to plan for education or job training that will enable her to be economically secure, or she may decide to postpone the physical separation until she is psychologically or economically ready. At this stage, helping the woman take an active role in planning and anticipating what lies ahead can reduce her feelings of powerlessness and lack of control over her situation.

Stage II: "Ex-Wife"

In helping a divorced mother during this transitional period, the professional can identify how presence or absence of community support and the lack of societal validation for female heads of household may affect the mother's capability to meet the demands of this period. The divorced mother can also be helped to understand how lack of respect for divorced women may affect her relationship with her children.

As human service professionals, our assistance to divorced mothers during the "ex-wife" stage may consist as much in helping to identify resources as in speaking to the anxieties of uncertain income, of taking a job, filling out an income-tax return, or accompanying one's son to a Little League banquet. Identifying resources involves a selective sorting through of inner strengths and competencies, of what other people can offer, and of community support. The professional can help the client systematically examine internal, boundary, and external resources, costs and benefits of each, and how they can be creatively combined.

Stage III: "Single Parent"

At this stage, the professional can offer practical advice and analysis of the "overload problem" and can discuss the solutions described above. More important, professionals can learn from divorced mothers the solutions they have devised, and present these as already developed models and patterns from which to choose.

In this discussion, we have deliberately focused on the social situation in which a divorced mother is embedded as she attempts to reorganize her life away from membership in a marriage and toward an identity as a single adult in charge of a household. This social situation is stressful, and stress has emotional ramifications. Human service professionals working with divorced women need to recognize the objective difficulties of the divorce situation as an important aspect of whatever emotional problems they may be experiencing. As one woman in our sample said, "My problems are real, not fantasies."

As human service professionals, we can emphasize the process of divorce by identifying at what stage in the process a woman is, helping her understand the special problems of that stage, and helping identify the resources she may have available in moving towards self-definition. We may need to help her discard some of her feminine socialization, at least that part that defines women as passive recipients rather than movers and shakers. And we can help her see that being defined by others adversely affects her self-esteem.

We may encourage divorced women to take assertion training, to look into filing a discrimination suit, to form self-help networks at home and on the job—nontraditional suggestions perhaps, but necessary if divorced women are to see themselves as controlling their destinies.

When the divorced woman no longer looks upon herself as divorced, but as a single woman with children, able to draw from her own values and sense of self-worth, she will be reaching the end of her journey through the divorce experience and can get on with the rest of her life.

REFERENCES

Bane, M. J. *Here to stay: American families in the twentieth century.* New York: Basic Books, 1976.

Bequaert, L. *Single women alone and together.* Boston: Beacon, 1976.

Brandwein, R. A., Brown, C. A., & Fox, E. M. Women and children last: The social situation of divorced mothers and their families. *Journal of Marriage and the Family,* 1974, *36,* 498–514.

Fox, E. M., & Brandwein, R. *Views of oneself as mother following divorce: Factors affecting attitudes towards offspring and self-image as a mother.* Paper presented at the meeting of the American Psychiatric Association, Chicago, May 1979.

Fraiberg, S. *Every child's birthright: In defense of mothering.* New York: Basic Books, 1977.

Hetherington, E. M. Divorce: A child's perspective. *American Psychologist,* 1979, *34,* 851–858.

Kelly, J. *Children and parents in the midst of divorce: Major factors contributing to differentiated response.* Paper presented at National Institute of Mental Health Workshops on Divorce and Children, Washington, D.C., February 1978.

Kohen, J. *From wife to family head: Transitions in self identity.* Unpublished manuscript, Family and Sex Roles Program, Survey Research Center, Institute of Social Research, University of Michigan, Ann Arbor, 1980.

Kohen, J. A., Brown, C. A., & Feldberg, R. Divorced mothers: The costs and benefits of female family control. In G. Levinger & O. C. Moles (Eds.), *Divorce and separation: Context, cause and consequences.* New York: Basic Books, 1979.

Maury, E., Brandwein, R., & Kohen, J. *The divorced woman: Processes of change.* Paper presented at the meeting of the American Psychiatric Association, San Francisco, May 1980.

McCubbin, H. Integrating coping behavior in family stress theory. *Journal of Marriage and the Family,* 1979, *41,* 237–244.

McCubbin, H., & Dahl, B. Prolonged family separation in the military: A longitudinal study. In H. McCubbin, B. Dahl, & E. Hunter (Eds.), *Families in the military system.* Beverly Hills, Calif.: Sage, 1976.

Montalvo, F. Family separation in the army: A study of the problems encountered and the caretaking resources used by career army families undergoing military separation. In H. McCubbin, B. Dahl, & E. Hunter (Eds.), *Families in the military system.* Beverly Hills, Calif.: Sage, 1976.

Norton, A. G., & Glick, P. Marital instability: Past, present, and future. *Journal of Social Issues,* 1976, *32,* 5–20.

Rollins, B., & Galligan, R. The developing child and marital satisfaction of parents. In R. Lerner & G. Spanier (Eds.), *Child influences on marital and family interaction: A lifespan perspective.* New York: Academic Press, 1978.

Smith, T. Foundations of parental influence upon adolescents: An application of social power theory. *American Sociological Review,* 1970, *35,* 860–873.

United States Department of Labor, Women's Bureau. *Earnings gap between women and men.* Washington, D.C.: U.S. Government Printing Office, 1979.

Weiss, R. *Marital separation.* New York: Basic Books, 1975.

Weiss, R. *Going it alone: The family life and social situation of the single parent.* New York: Basic Books, 1979.

Weitzman, L. Legal regulations of marriage: Tradition and change. *California Law Review,* 1974, *62,* 1169–1288.

Westman, J., Cline, D., Swift, W., & Kramer, D. The role of child psychiatry in divorce. In S. Chase & A. Thomas (Eds.), *Annual progress in child psychiatry and child development, 1971.* New York: Brunner/Mazel, 1971.

CHAPTER ELEVEN

The Quest for the Wanted Absent Parent in Children of the Divorced or Deceased[1]

LORA HEIMS TESSMAN

Linda's parents were divorced, and she decided that she wanted to shut her father out of her life. Yet she found herself writing a poem:

> I will walk forever till I find you
>
> It is too long the sun takes to rise
> and fill the earth with warm and fragrant light
>
> Meet me on the earth
> From the depths of my spirit I call to you
> Come with the rising sun.

An increasing number of children experience divorce-caused parental parting followed by a new family structure that may or may not include a stepparent, and may or may not involve continued contact with the absent parent. Others lose a parent through death. This chapter is concerned with the variety of transformations within the child, in the image of the lost or partially missing parent, and considers the effect of such transformations on his or her personality and behavior. Is the missing parent really gone from the life of the child? Where do the inner representations of the disrupted relationship go? What forms does a quest for a still-wanted absent parent take in childhood and later life relationships? What is the relationship between a quest and the mechanisms of identification, which has usually been considered as a central defense against loss? How does the image of the missing parent fuel the psychic life of the child in ways that can either

1. An earlier version of this chapter was presented at the Annual Meeting of the American Orthopsychiatric Association, Spring 1977.

Lora Heims Tessman. Psychiatric Service, Medical Department, Massachusetts Institute of Technology, Cambridge, Massachusetts, and private practice of psychotherapy and consultation, Newton, Massachusetts.

enhance or distort identification that become aspects of his or her later identity?

To explore these questions, I draw on experience with children and adults seen in psychotherapy or briefer kinds of consultations, who have suffered loss in different contexts. These include:

1. Children aged 10 or younger who have experienced parental separation or divorce, followed by the remarriage or recoupling of at least one parent, and who have had continued contact with at least three out of four parent figures.
2. Children in puberty or adolescence who have experienced family disruption either through divorce, or because of a traumatic death that occurred in the context of considering divorce (e.g., suicide in the context of arguments about divorce). In some of these cases, material is available about the relationships established by the individuals into their late 20s.
3. Children and adults who experienced the death of a parent during childhood.
4. Individuals who were either adopted as infants or whose parent died or left the parental relationship before their birth. In such cases, the quest for the parent is not based on the loss of an actual relationship, and therefore not intrinsically related to mourning.

Individuals in these situations suffered different kinds and degrees of loss, which affected the attempted resolutions. For example, parental death was a final loss, precluding any further reality testing about the nature of the lost person in direct experience. Parental divorce, resulting in an absent parent who is still more or less accessible for further reality testing, however, was most often complicated by the child's feeling of disloyalty to the home parent over still longing for the absent one. Loss was rarely a discrete event, for the trauma included the pre and post loss period of strife, distress, and adjustment in all who impinged on the life of the child. However, working through either kind of loss was deeply affected by the nature of the previous relationship to the still-wanted parent, and by the presence or absence of a sustaining human support network. This was most centrally the remaining parent, but often also a new, additional parent figure, that is, a stepparent or love partner of the home parent. It usually took considerable support and permission before the child could experience the grief and longing stimulated by the loss of, or altered relationship to, the absent parent, in a way that was constructive. These broader issues and a comparison of the psychotherapy process with individuals in each of these groups I have discussed elsewhere (Tessman, 1978). In this chapter, the focus is on a single aspect of coping with the loss of a parent, which may go unrecognized: The children and adults I encountered have convinced me that a quest for the missing wanted person goes on at many levels and in many guises, and that it can coexist with the mechanism of identifications as a means of coping with loss.

Reunion wishes and fantasies are a mainstay of all separated lovers, and have also been documented in relation to the bereaved (Deutsch, 1937; Parkes, 1972; Rochlin, 1965) as well as the divorced (Weiss, 1975) and their children (Wallerstein & Kelly, 1976). In the children and adults with whom I worked, such reunion fantasies provided a fertile field for richly conceived expectations of recreating those aspects of the past wanted relationship that were most exquisitely laden with affective pleasure or pain. Depending upon the nature of the past lost relationship, and the developmental level of libidinal wishes of the child at the time the loss was experienced, attempts at such recreation could occur through the medium of ideation, motor behavior, affective or somatic experience, or be evident in the later choice of loved persons. Although sometimes obvious, at other times the meaning of the phenomenon as linked to a quest was far from obvious or apparent. The diverse expressions of the quest included the following: searching; anticipations of reappearance, or of messages or letters; a sense of the presence of the person; daydreaming involving disguised fragments of the quest, pseudologia or "lying" in the service of inner integrity; use of transitional objects and transitional phenomena; magical gestures meant to recreate the lost relationship; acting out to defend against painful memory; hyperactivity, motor restlessness, wandering, some types of stealing; suicidal wishes and attempts; repeating and holding onto painful affects focused on the disruption of relationships or on the choice of loved persons in later life. When the form of the quest is recognized and becomes focused instead on memories, mourning, and associated alterations in the image of the wanted person in accordance with reality, the person has begun to accept what was lost and can turn more fully toward what might still be.

Examples will be limited here to only a few of the forms of quest enumerated above, and we will consider the relationship between the quest and identifications; and the quest, reality sense, and reality testing. To illustrate some of the possible manifestations of the forms of quest, here are some short vignettes.

Peter: A Mixture of Identification and Search

Peter was 3½ when his mother left home to pursue a career in law. His father had been quite willing to take custody of Peter and his 2½-year-old sister. He devoted himself to child care after working hours, and was attuned to the importance of keeping the children in the same day-care center they had attended before their mother left. Father had told Peter that mommy missed the children, but lived too far away, and so would not be able to visit, and they would not see her. After a period of regression to more infantile behavior and clinging to father, as well as to his favorite day-care worker, Peter seemed to accept the situation "well." At day care, he was described as taking a new sudden interest in cooking and in feeding the dolls. In playing house, he persistently now chose the role of "mommy" rather than "daddy," a contrast to his behavior before his mother left home. In this way, Peter was coping with the loss by identifying, or playing at becoming, "mommy." At home, he declared that he wanted to be the one to cook for daddy, and insisted on making "sagetti," which was the favorite food item his mother had often made for him. However, several months after she left, when out for a walk with daddy, Peter was apt to suddenly shout, "Get away, daddy," push his father away, and run down the street toward an approaching woman, calling "Mommy, mommy." It was only after the repeated discovery that the distant woman was not "mommy" that Peter would rush back into his father's arms, sobbing. This was the point at which his open grieving for the mother began. Thus, the repeated disappointment in his still-present expectation that mother would reappear forced him to face the reality of her absence and the associated pain.

This direct kind of searching or expectation of reappearance was common in very young children of the divorced and occurred in the majority of individuals shortly after the death of a parent. Older children of divorce were more often aware that their conscious wishes for parental reunion were a fantasy, while motor behavior such as restlessness, hyperactivity, or cutting classes were expressions of the unconscious expectation of recovering the gratifying parent by following to wherever he or she might be.

Emily: A Reunion Fantasy with a Never-Known Parent

A touching reunion fantasy was evident in the psychic life of Emily, a graduate student in her 20s who had been adopted as an infant. She was periodically troubled by wrist cutting. The wrist cutting was always precipitated by a disappointment in a potentially mothering person. This disappointment was perceived by the young woman as a desertion, signifying that the person to whom she was attached did not want her to live. Secretly, in a paper bag, which she took great effort to conceal in her clothing, she carried a much-used and partly mutilated soft, stuffed fur kitten, which she assumed had been given to her by her mother when she left her at the adoption agency. Possible separation from the toy kitten gave rise to panic reactions. This young woman continued to hope consciously each birthday that her mother, whom she had never seen, would somehow find and visit her for a birthday celebration, recognizing her daughter by recognition of the toy kitten. The week after her birthday, she was always deeply depressed.

Since Emily had no real experience with her biological mother (although she did with both adoptive parents), her loss was not one for which, through memory, she could grieve. Yet much feeling was focused on her "birthday," her day of birth, the only day in her past she could know for sure that she and her mother must have been together. One aspect of her quest for her mother was condensed in the meaning of the kitten, which, used as a transitional object, comforted her when she held it, and from whom separation caused anxiety. In fantasy it represented not only the concrete expression of her mother's love or gift to her as a baby, but was also endowed with the enduring print of her babyhood self in such a way that it was conceived of as the means by which her mother would recognize and therefore want to be reunited with her.

Endowing the transitional object with the power to make the mother actually appear is linked to early stages in cognitive development, as described by Piaget (1954) and others. During these stages the lost object is re-expected in the place and via the particular gesture associated with its appearance. Emily was still waiting for the reunion, holding her stuffed toy to bring it about.

Karen: The Repetition of Painful Relationships in Accordance with a Distorted Image

When Karen's parents divorced during her adolescence, she seemed to accept her mother's view of father as "vicious and rotten" and shrank from further contacts with him. She remained close to mother in adolescence, playing the role of half confidante, half head of the household. For example, she monitored her mother's dates, demanding that mother tell her whom she was seeing and setting limits on the hour when she had to be home, like a parent. In her early 20s, Karen found she was attracted only to men who were intimates of her mother and who treated her cruelly. The relationships were secret from mother. In therapy, the parallels between the men and her mother's and her shared image of the father became quickly apparent, as well as the fact that Karen had not again tried to find out for herself what her father was really like. She began exploring the meaning of disrupted relationships, first by making a visit to her first boyfriend in late adolescence, whose desertion had made her feel suicidal. She saw the ways she had alienated him, realized that she had not been simply rejected, and began to grieve for the wasted potential in the relationship.

Karen began to think more about her father, finding herself in a torrent of grief. For example, one day in the shower she found herself beating her fists against the sides, shouting about her father, "I hate you, I hate you," and eventually, "I love you," and she then began to cry uncontrollably. She found this relieving, unlike earlier episodes of loss of control of emotions, which had felt to her like "going crazy."

Karen then got in touch with her father again and found to her great surprise that, "He is not an ogre, but just human like the rest of us." Slowly, shyly, and cautiously, Karen rebuilt a warm relationship with her father, re-evaluating those aspects of strife between her parents that had indeed resulted in some irritability or "cruel" neglect and domination of her by her father in childhood. A more realistic view of her father was followed for

Karen by a love relationship with a man who could care about her. Although Karen had postponed throughout adolescence the transformation of her image of the father she longed for, because it would have alienated the mother she still felt desperately tied to, her secret quest for father drove her toward re-experiencing cruelty in her love choices. However, as her father was still alive and receptive to her, when Karen was less dependent on mother and her views, she could risk the reality testing that resulted in a transformation of her image of the father and the affective components experienced in her quest.

Karen's vehement rejection of her father in adolescence, followed by the disguised return to him, via other traumatic relationships in her 20s, was a pattern characteristic of a number of girls who could not risk leaving a mutually dependent alliance with their mothers during the period following divorce.

In each of the cases briefly sketched above, the child had to deal with a different difficult acceptance of loss of a parent figure and the implications this had for the image of the self. For Karen, the loss involved a drastically altered relationship with the father; for Peter a real desertion by his mother; and for Emily the loss of the fantasy she cherished—that her moher had loved and wanted her.

Psychic separation from a wanted person involves the slow and painful decathexis of the inner psychic representations of that person. It is these psychic representations, emanating at times from unconscious and non-verbal organizations of perceptions once experienced, which seem to remain ready to be externalized and reapproached in the external world. Images once imbued with love perhaps sculpt the form of hope eternal. What Peter, Emily, and Karen had in common was that they had not given up hope that they could somehow make their wish come true.

THE FUNCTION OF THE QUEST

There seem to be three reasons why the quest for the absent person so often has to be secret: (1) It conflicts with what the individual "knows" is rational; (2) it may jeopardize the security of other needed relationships, most of all to the home parent, by being "disloyal" to them; (3) it may arouse more pain and longing than the individual can cope with at the time. Simultaneously, however, a continuation of the "quest" defends against the deeper grief of coming to terms with a permanent "absence" of the lost person, or permanent major alteration in the relationship. The presence of the quest may result in a limit to what is invested in other relationships and in inner expectations. Yet, the quest and its representation may be imbued with either the most precious and individual vitality of the individual, (e.g., stimulating creativity) or the most stultifying renunciations and self-destructiveness. Quests that are either secret or unconscious tend to surface in therapy in preparation for grief.

When repeated loss of a parent, associated with severe deprivation, occurs prior to the time when the concept of object constancy is normally established, nurturance and the bodily states associated with it may be sought, rather than the maintenance of a particular image of the lost parent. However, in such cases, there may be an expectation that if one waits long enough, "lady luck" or fate will appear, to make things better. The ego modes associated with this kind of perception, in the absence of active attempts to bring about good fortune, are reminiscent of the earliest stages of a baby's expectations. Emily's wishes involved such expectations, as do those of many who suffer from deep and constricting depressions associated with a sense of helplessness about ameliorating one's deprivation.

For example, by the time her mother died when she was 11, Mary Ann had already suffered multiple losses. Living with an erratic grandmother, she had had contact with her mother only as a sporadic "treat." The child had jumped into the grave with her mother and was forcibly pried away from her mother's corpse. After mother's death further multiple changes of foster-home placements intensified her sense of deprivation and loss. For the rest of her life, she ceaselessly searched for mother figures and nurturance, but almost any mother would do. She left her first husband in order to move in with his mother. When she was an adult, her adolescent daughter functioned as her most attentive mother figure, but even she could not diminish Mary Ann's need for constant nurturing supplies, or "treats," in the form of alcohol, excessive food, or presents stolen for her by others. She encouraged her daughter toward incest, viewing her as the mother of the family.

After incest had taken place, she fantasized about a blissful mother–baby togetherness, should her daughter be pregnant by the father, rather than focusing any distress or empathy on the plight of the daughter. Mary Ann was driven toward wishful images of "treats" or bodily bliss, rather than images of persons loved or lost.

The pattern of expecting "rescue" from the environment can have other sources not discussed here.

Returning to the issue of the function of the quest, it might be said that the quest is a precursor of grief, which, however, is valuable in itself as a way of preserving a distillation of the affectively charged image of the self and other, which the individual treasures.

IDENTIFICATION AND THE QUEST

Identification with a lost love object or some of the love object's attributes has standardly been considered as a major defense against loss (Freud, 1915/1957). Internalizing the object in this way preserves it in the psychic world of the bereft, allowing him or her to withdraw the emotional invest-ment in that person as he or she existed in the external world. Variations in the kind of identifications with the lost person that are made depend not only on the developmental level of wishes operant in the bereft at the time of loss, but also on the quality of the past relationship, the balance of hostility and guilt versus loving feelings experienced toward that person, etc. In addition, it was clear that for the children who had lost a parent through divorce or death, the remaining parent's attitude toward the former spouse was reflected in whether the child felt permission to identify with positive rather than negative attributes, and whether the identification was experi-enced in an ego-syntonic way, or surfaced, for example, as an ego-alien symptom. Identification with devalued, punitive, depriving, injured, or dead aspects of the lost person are associated with self-devaluation and depression.

However, I was repeatedly struck by indications that identifications with the lost, wanted parent seemed to coexist with a still externally directed quest for him or her, based on an assumption, either conscious or un-conscious, that the lost one was still out there somewhere in some form, and that if one did certain things, either in the realm of ideation, motor behavior, or the repetitive experiencing of certain affects, the lost one would reappear for mutual forgiveness and further enjoyment. Thus, what was internalized seemed simultaneously to be ready to be again externalized and sought.

This apparently contradictory state of affairs can be resolved if one considers, along with Shafer (1968), that in psychic reality the object is immortal. He holds that "it makes more sense to speak of the various fates of the immortal object than to speak of object loss pure and simple." He reminds us that there is no "no" in primary process ideation in the uncon-scious. Death, for example, as nonbeing is a variation of "no" and therefore cannot be conceived. It is only in rational or secondary process thinking that concepts such as "no," death, or loss are fully recognized. Even so, negation of the loss may of course occur as a way of avoiding pain.

Identification and the quest may exist side by side, or emerge during different periods of time. In psychotherapy, it was useful to differentiate between the acting out of an identification, and acting out which constituted a component of the quest, for the implications for the individual were different. For example, Linda (whose poem was quoted) had a "nervous breakdown" at age 17. This included acting on a suicidal fantasy as well as the conviction that her mother might stab her with a knife. Among other meanings, this episode involved living out an identification with the paranoid psychotic episode for which her father had been briefly hospitalized years earlier, following the divorce. She now felt that she was identical to him in a variety of ways and knew that the rest of the family considered her as the most similar to father. This was identification. It seemed important at that point in her development to treat her differently than her father, if *possible*, in order to avoid confirming this sense of being identical. *Not* to hospitalize her, which was manageable in her case because a supportive human network could be mobilized quickly, was one way of attempting to do this. She remained in therapy another year and then left home for college. Years later, when she returned for a consultation in her 20s, she described being irresistably attracted to a man she did not otherwise like, but who was excited with her about dressing up as firemen to attend a Halloween party. Only after it was brought to her attention did she recall that playing "fireman" was what she and father had done tirelessly during her early years, incurring her mother's disapproval. This was a quest for re-experiencing that joyful, exciting part of the interaction. Another time, when a man she cared for left her, she found herself on the floor whimpering, "Daddy, daddy." This, too, was part of the quest and involved repeating painful affects experienced in relation to father's sudden leaving of home.

REALITY SENSE, REALITY TESTING, AND THE QUEST

Reality sense must be differentiated from "reality testing." The child's reality sense includes what he or she knows to be true from personal experiences and how these felt. Reality sense may be contradicted by one's later "reality testing" or by the perceptions of others around one. If it is contradicted in these ways, the child either loses trust in his or her own perceptions, or attempts to validate the perceptions in reality by recreating an experience which will prove that they are true. In most of the bereaved I encountered, reality testing was unimpaired. Yet, their reality sense did not fit their current situation. Part of this reality sense had been built around the interaction between the self and the lost, wanted parent. When loss through death occurred, some grieving, decathexis, grappling with guilt, overcoming fears of a similar fate through identification, etc., may all occur. Still there is something else left: The reality sense includes the experience of past affective sharing with a beloved. It was this that provided a strongly motivating force, pushing for validation in later perception, and fueling a quest. If a loved parent was dead, the child seemed to need continued validation of earlier experiences through the possibility of sustaining perceptions from the other parent (or others). This involves not only the usual help in dealing with the factual realities of the death, as well as the child's own mixed feelings, but the recognition that there is something that still exists of the relationship for the child and that this is the affectively shared experience. In order to complete mourning and invest fully in other relationships, it was important for the child to know that this was reality, rather than just existing in his or her imagination. The case of Amy illustrates some of this.

Amy: The Quest and the Sense of Reality

Amy, a creative, charming unmarried woman in her 30s, in an ingenuous fashion, combined aspects of identification with the father who died when she was 5, and poignant attempts to seek out his image in fantasy, through an imaginary companion and in the form of transitional objects and phenomena (such as singing, associated with father). She felt a fierce loyalty to her father and his memory and renounced committing herself to relationships that would have betrayed the unconscious promise between herself and her father to be true to each other forever. Therapy material detailing her rich associations during grief work is presented elsewhere (Tessman, 1978) and reference will be made here only briefly to the variety of expressions of her quest, direct and disguised.

As the only child of two devoted parents, the sudden death of her father in a distant city while on a business trip brought about many changes in Amy's life. Her mother wanted to spare the little girl from pain, and did not take her to the funeral service nor did she cry in front of the child.

Amy could not conjure up a mental image of her father as dead. When her mother remarried 5 years later, Amy insisted on keeping her father's last name herself and did so into adulthood. A theme of "belonging together" with the dead father persisted through adulthood and during a suicide attempt, when she had felt ready to "leave this world" as he had done. She was angry with her mother for not buying a space adjacent to her father's in the cemetery for Amy to be buried. In her 20s, she established a relationship with a man who was unavailable as a steady lover or husband and lived in a distant country. She had many fantasies that, although separated by time, space, and circumstances, the two of them belonged together and looked so similar that it was "like we have the same genes."

For this young woman, the recovery of memories of the father and the solidification of her image of him as real, based on the reality of their past feelings for each other, was an elusive, painful process, less accessible than the readily available fantasies of reunion in life or death. At the beginning of therapy with me, she expressed that she could "feel nothing" about her father's death, though she knew it had affected her. It was not until the second year of therapy that the affective links between her experience and continued quest for her missing father became useful to her. These included the following:

1. She had always looked through the holes in her mailbox hoping for red and blue edges of air mail letters. As she put it, "It's always letters from *far away* . . . white envelopes just don't turn me on, even if they are nice long letters from friends from home. The funny thing is that the anticipation is greater than the real thing. The pleasure is in anticipating . . . once I receive the letter, I don't care that much." Much later this was linked to her fantasy as well as experience (at age 4) of a loving letter from father.

2. As a latency-aged child, she used as a transitional object a sheet which she would put around her mouth at night, rocking her head. She dwelt at length on the question of whether when her father was buried, he was entirely gone and especially whether there was any skin left. Fantasies of her father's presence as a "friendly ghost," in the form of "Casper the Ghost" (a cartoon character), who is made out of a sheet, made the connection between her transitional object, the sheet, and the loss of cuddling and skin contact with the father when he put her to bed at night. Her father's shirt was Casper's sheet, which she put to her lips.

3. Another transitional phenomenon was that of singing herself to sleep, a song that was later replaced by her mother's sewing machine and in adulthood, by another humming sound. In therapy at this time, the most affectively laden preconscious wishes toward the father came up in the form of sudden song fragments, as rich in association as dreams. Through the song fragments, she began to recapture more memories as well as previously unconscious wishes. It was not until then that I learned that her father had usually sung her to sleep (she even remembered the songs) and that she had then perpetuated this interaction on her own. In addition, the singing was later (when she was 9 and 10) used consciously in an attempt to alienate or induce guilt in the prospective stepfather. Through her songs, for example, the song "Where have all the flowers gone? Gone to the graveyard . . . ," she recaptures memories of wanting to plant flowers on her father's grave, wondering how they would be fertilized, and feeling that her mother prevented her from carrying out the wish.

4. She assumed father would know and acknowledge her gift. "I thought of him as being someplace, definitely around. . . . I felt his presence and knew he was watching. . . . I had a lot of little conversations with him. Once this girl said sarcastically, 'Oh, I forgot to say my prayers to God,' and then she spat up to the sky . . . and I felt awful because I thought that she might have missed God and spat at my father . . . even though all the time I was definitely an atheist." I asked Amy what she thought her father would have minded most. She said, "I'm sure that he was hurt when mother got married again . . . that she could forget him so quickly; . . . how weird death is. . . . I mean, they disappear and just leave others' lives all fucked up." Her voice trembled. I said, "You *feel* his leaving now?" She answered, "It's so weird how powerful absence is. When we talked about him before, I remembered talking to him . . . and I didn't feel like crying, because we were talking about his *presence.* . . . Now it's his *absence,* and that hurts." She weeps. A little later she adds softly, "What kept me from being sad at 6 and 7 was that he was present for me—I was pretending all the time he was still there. When airplanes scared me, I would sing, . . . it was 'Our father gave to thee, anchor of liberty, to thee I sing,' . . . but later it had something else about . . . land where my father died. . . ." Later, she discovered an additional assumption, namely that as long as she sang, her father also could not feel alone, and therefore could not be dead. I will comment later on the recognition of the absence as a frequent turning point in the quest.

5. An additional way Amy stayed in touch with her father was through conversations with an imaginary brother whose father was still alive, and who, it turned out, wore glasses like her father did.

A turning point for Amy came when her grieving led her to search for more memoirs of them than she had gleaned from a few old pictures. One day she told me: "About my father, . . . what I discovered this weekend is *that he loved me*. It all started here when we talked about what he was really like . . . and I went home and rummaged around drawers some more and found an envelope of paintings and drawings. . . . I found this long letter he wrote me when I was 4. He drew a picture of himself with his glasses on and then an arrow and a kiss, *he was blowing me a kiss across the distance*. He made a great big heart on it with an arrow and the words, 'It's all yours.' There were four pages of love! My God, he knew I was alive and cared about me! It's not fair . . . his words 'I love you forever' made me cry again. . . . Forever was only for a year and then he was dead."

Next time, she added "The weird thing about that letter—I keep thinking that I never really knew before that he had a relationship, . . . I mean a *real* relationship to me, not just in my mind."

Amy had finally arrived at the feeling that she was loved in reality by her father. This could not be lost and therefore left her with less of a burden to recreate and remain true to the relationship on her own.

Children who, unlike Amy, had lived with a long or debilitating illness in a parent before death, tended to manifest a special feature in their fantasies of a reunion: In their image, they tended to repair the body of a parent who had changed through illness before death. Their losses begin at the time of the change in the relationship caused by the combination of the parent's incapacity, increased self-preoccupation, and other family member's stressed reaction. Guilt about their anger during this period of time further complicates grieving. The image of their quest most often is that of the parent prior to the time such troubles began.

For example, 10-year-old Vicky, whose mother had long been confined to a wheelchair before her death, developed the fear that her mother would rise from the grave and fly through the child's window to punish her. Although guilt played a role in this fear, her wish was embodied in the image of mother, flying unshackled from her wheelchair, to be mobile and playful with her as she used to be.

Seven-year-old Jerry, referred because of stomach aches 6 months after his mother died, complained of having to sit still with mother, whose "stomach and the rest of her" were wasting away. She had cancer of the colon. Jerry offered to draw a picture of a mermaid, which he said he always draws now, but throws away if she "doesn't come out right." His mermaid had long hair like his mother used to have and her lower half was a strong, beautiful fish tail. The mermaid's stomach had also changed, Jerry told me, "but whenever she said goodbye she didn't die." She just swam away and would, of course, return.

An interesting component of the image of the wanted, missing parent is that some individuals eventually manage to bring it under their control, using it in the service of the ego. For example, a man whose much-loved mother had died when he was 9 had always suffered from a sense of sexual inadequacy and inhibition. However, when he was near 50, and wanted to prolong his "staying power" in intercourse with his wife in order to satisfy her, he would, at will, conjure up the image of his mother dying to immediately diminish his sexual excitement, thereby prolonging intercourse.

THE PAINFUL AWARENESS OF THE ABSENCE OF THE PRESENCE

A shift in reality sense sometimes accompanied the grieving process in such a way that the bereaved person eventually came to face the absence of the previously cherished presence. The moment of facing the absence was intensely painful (as in Amy's case). It tended, however, to be followed by a reshuffling of expected gratifications sought from current relationships. This consisted of an attempt to come to terms with the reality that the expected love from the lost parent would not be forthcoming and hence might have to be sought in different ways from current relationships. When the quest is given up, symbolic rather than literal fidelity can remain. Such fidelity may re-appear in the content or vitality of the ego-ideal, becoming central to the individual's commitment to associated aspirations.

Once reality testing proceeds, it becomes more possible for the child or adult to proceed with grief. Only after this does the person usually allow him or herself to selectively identify with those characteristics of the lost person which he or she still valued, while continuing some degree of the quest by attempting to bring positive affects, themes, or endeavors shared with the wanted parent in the past into his or her new relationships. It is then that the continued "reality sense" of having truly loved and then lost a wanted person includes the perception that one's own contribution to that mutuality, one's own loving feelings, are still within; that they have survived the anger and can set one free to love again.

COMMENTS

For the children of the divorced, continued reality testing was usually possible to a greater or lesser extent. Input, derived from continued contacts, about what the parent was really like could help transform the magical images of childhood to both less-fearsome and less-magnetic proportions. This process was not available to some, either because of the withdrawal of the absent parent or the hostility of the remaining one. It seemed most difficult in some of the cases in which divorce coincided not only with the pubescence of the child, but also with the devaluation of the parent in the human support network surrounding the child. For numbers of children, the process of grieving and the continued quest was prolonged and complicated by repeated sequences of raised hopes, glimpses of fulfillment of these hopes, followed by frustration and despair. Promises made and broken were the prototype of this, and tended to lead to their being lived out in other relationships at the end of the adolescence. Children whose parents made a better second marriage or alliance, or who, after a period of time, again lived a satisfying life without a remarriage seemed in the best position to grapple with the quest.

For the children of the deceased, the drama took place between themselves and the image of the lost parent. He or she was not available in reality for testing the transformation of one's image or trying new modes of interaction. Nevertheless, one had to make peace with the image in order to have energies fully available to invest in new relationships. Previously unfinished mourning was usually a prerequisite. A sign of such peace often accompanying the shift of energy from a former quest was the expressed feeling "He (or she) would have liked the person I've become." In this sense, coming to terms with the meaning of the past relationship, with grieving, and with the quest were tasks that could be finished, while treasured affective links remained, sometimes surfacing especially at moments of inner renewal. For example, Wendy, whose loved father died when she was 10, was surprised when, as a married adult and after much grief work, tears sprang to her eyes as she realized her longing for her father's presence and expected response of celebration at the moment of announcing her pregnancy. "You see," she said, as she mused gladly (while still tearful) about possible echoes of her father's personality she might recognize in her baby, "he was a person who added a friendly touch to each event." Though her current event would not be blessed with his friendly touch, it was enriched by his memory.

In the psychotherapy of children who are reacting to family dissolution, working to sustain a human support network, preserving positive aspects of identification, and facing intense grieving comprise the bulk of the task, and are often painful. In contrast perhaps, the quest for the absent, wanted person retains the refreshing human combination of imagination with fervor, which insists that whatever was once good shall not cease to be. Though the hopeless quest must be renounced, the attendant energy prevails to help create future possibilities. Finders? Seekers. But are there some complications for keepers?

Some Implications

An affectively rewarding relationship with a parent, even when it is later disrupted or lost, appears to be strengthening to the personality, and continues to have an impact in complicated ways on later development.

In a sample of children of the divorced or deceased I have described elsewhere (Tessman, 1978), the primary correlation with overall propitious personality development turned out to be with the well-being and continued appropriate emotional involvement of the home parent with the child; while the second most important factor revolved around ways of coping with the altered relationship with the absent parent. Some years after parental parting, there often was a striking contrast in the functioning of those children who retained their basic enthusiasm for life, compared to others, in whom a course of depressive impoverishment of the personality reflected an inner state of resignation.

A sustained period of pleasurable and rewarding affective engagement with at least one parent appears to be central to the resilience of the child, guarding against depressive impoverishment, even though other complications for development might ensue. The "quest" is one of those complications. Here is another: Children who become very "special" to a parent, in contrast to that parent's disappointment in their mate, had more than the usual difficulty resolving aspects of omnipotence in their self-image, which in turn affected their aspirations in relationships to others. Results varied from a propensity toward very effective leadership, to age-inappropriate attempts at aggressive control of others.

Because of the volatile nature of the emotional bonds at the time of marital dissolution, the child was usually imbued with a frightening amount of free-floating aggressive tension, but also often experienced an intensified pleasurable affective bond with one or both parents, who had been long frustrated in the experiencing of pleasure with a mate. In this kind of emotional context it often happened that after coping with the absence of one parent, the child had an additional acute sense of loss and mourning about the home parent as well, as this parent became involved in new adult love relationships. Ways of coping with this additional loss, or loss of "specialness" tended to be indicative of the soundness of the earlier relationships. Though reactions were often acute, their acuteness did not signify lack of resilience in the child. Consider Brian:

Brian, a 12-year-old boy, was describing to me how he felt when he watched his mother relax in laughter with her new man-friend. "It's a little better now," he said, "the Novocain is beginning to take." The needed analgesic in his mind was more effective than it had been the previous month. At that time, when mother had celebrated New Year's Eve by going moonlight skating with Paul, he watched them dance on the ice, and then simply lay down on the edge of the pond on his back, numbing himself with cold. The adults, involved with each other, had in fact not missed him until his 10-year-old sister told mother: "I think you ought to pay some attention to Brian." Having to watch highly pleasurable intimacies between partners, when one has previously shared similar intimacies with one of them, and is now suddenly an outsider, provokes one of the most searing varieties of human pain. During the first 10 years of Brian's life, a quietly unhappy marriage between his parents had left the home devoid of the forces of fresh sexuality. Brian had been a chief source of his mother's excitement and delight, with frequent, shared laughter, and he had had an expectation of being special to people. Now the clarity of his sense of pain seemed to be a mirror of his previous pleasure. But where did his capacity for pleasure go? Brian and I explored his conscious effort to numb himself to his jealousy, in order to see if the numbness was "leaking" into other areas of his life. "School is where I'm happiest now," he told me. For the first time I feel most of the kids *like* me, instead of having just one friend and mostly enemies." "How come?" I asked. "What's turning that around?" "I think I'm making an *effort* for the first time . . . figuring out how to live down being brainy. . . . I take them into consideration more. . . . I don't need to be perfect or lord it over them so much any more, so it's more fun to be with me."

Instead of a constricting depression, Brian had turned to some pubescent, age-appropriate maneuvers—beginning to disengage from the exciting relationship with his mother (and the associated self-image of aspiring to be perfect enough to lord it over others), and investing more fully in his peers. I believe his strength to do that had to do with his assumption that all was not lost when the pleasure in his central relationship was disrupted, that he had it in him to try again, and that the continued interest of his supportive divorced father, whom he saw often, would further sustain him in this process. Brian's plight included a common and poignant difficulty, which colored his sense of loss: When a child who has lived with parents in whom the forces of sexual vitality lay muted during his early development, is then faced, during pubescence, with a parent's second, happier love match, then the fresh and scintillating sexuality provides him with a happier image of what life can be about, but at a time when this is developmentally more difficult to integrate than earlier. His own sexuality is simultaneously stimulated and more urgently in need of deflection.

The crucial role of experiencing a sustained pleasurable affective engagement with one parent is heightened in those cases in which the other parent suffers from the kind of disturbance that is characterized by depressive, manic, or paranoid affective states. Such disturbances are associated with a likely need to either sweep the child into the parents own frightening affective state, creating a sense of dread, or, alternately, to disengage affectively from the child. In either case, the parent becomes unable to respond to the range of affects for which the child has potential. Involvement with the other parent then becomes especially essential in two ways: First, by responding appropriately to the range of affects in the child, the parent encourages richness in the child's development; and second, by sharing pleasurable affects with the child, the parent shows the child that happiness can exist. The child is apt to feel that he or she can't be fully "her or himself" with the disturbed parent, because the only way to feel close is to share the disturbed affect, while the other parent can also respond to what originates in the child. In such cases the child may develop a finely honed ability to split and hide affective states shared with one parent from the other, and to build on the pleasurable affects experienced with the responsive parent, even if the relationship has been disrupted through divorce or death. Guilt over pleasure is then not tied to a particular impulse, but to the object relationship in which there is a taboo on experiencing affective pleasure per se. Under these conditions a quest for the absent parent may play a particularly salient and secret role.

Let us turn to some implications for possible alterations in the course of mourning. In our psychology of the impact of losses we are familiar with the dynamics of mourning and melancholia (Freud, 1915/1957) and, depending on the nature of the loss, as well as developmental status of the bereft, the expected struggle against consequent depletion of emotional life. Not only the loss, but also the profound ambivalence toward the lost person, especially when unresolved, contributes to the impoverishment. It seems, however, that the dynamics of coping with loss, which occurs as an interruption of shared or responded to affective pleasure, involve proclivities toward a different course of resolution and foster different mental mechanisms. When the libidinal engagement, often experienced by the child as shared affective pleasure, had been more prominent than the hostility, previous withdrawal, or rejection, the major reaction (unlike with other varieties of loss) may be to want it to happen again, and to attempt to master the trauma by doing what one can, in deed or symbolically, to bring this about; to somehow create or re-create reminders of the affective pleasure once more. A series of mental processes, including those of a highly inventive nature, are fueled by the unconscious assumption that they will bring one in contact with the affectively pleasurable person again. Creativity in the children of the divorced or deceased was frequently associated with the fervent wish to recreate the lost person in new form, to thereby validate and pay tribute to what could otherwise no longer be seen in the external world. Components of feelings perceived as shared on a level of affecto-motor and sensual interaction provided affective themes that gave form to the creative expression. This aspect of quest for a sense of contact with the wanted person may involve a piece of illusion about the persistence, or even the "permanence" of the past intensely happy moments in one's life. This is different from denial of loss or denial of sadness, but involves a resistance to change in the wanted relationship in the imagination over time.

For example, a daughter's sensitivity to affective pleasure with the father is probably heightened during the Oedipal period, and is associated with a new capacity for rich fantasy and for identification with the feelings of others. Loss of the relationship to the father during the Oedipal period of the girl tended to "fix" the romantic fantasies of the wished-for interaction and the associated quest, without the desexualizing influence of the later reality testing in the more usual father–daughter interaction.

Derivatives of various illusions may have widely differing positive or negative effects on an individual's aspirations or experiences during the life course. For example, adolescent and young adult ego-ideal formation may be eventually consolidated from derivatives of earlier affective engagements with an idealized, emulated parent (Tessman, 1982) and yet become a stabilizing aspect of the individual's identity and aspirations. Thus, whether illusionary aspects of individual motivation are useful to confront may depend on their interference with, or enhancement of life goals.

In late adulthood, however, the individual is faced with a developmental urge toward the deepening of relationships in order to find them rewarding, while simultaneously needing to accept the increasing limitations of the self and reality of the other. At this time, as the individual inwardly eyes the fit between his or her life and innermost version of happiness, a "failed quest," with residues of idealization, that has not been confronted may cause new difficulties. In the words of novelist du Plessix Gray (1981), the task is this: "Love in middle age! A process of hulling, husking, denuding, fleecing, decorticating our early dreams, a stripping away of illusion so radical that we create a new dialectic of passions, a romance of the real" (p. 258).

REFERENCES

Deutsch, H. Absence of grief. *Psychoanalytic Quarterly*, 1937, *6*, 12–22.

du Plessix Gray, F. *World without end*. New York: Simon & Schuster, 1981.

Freud, S. Mourning and melancholia. *Standard Edition*, 1957, *14*, 237–258. (Originally published, 1915.)

Parkes, C. M. *Bereavement: Studies of grief in adult life*. New York: International Universities Press, 1972.

Piaget, J. The development of object constancy. In *The construction of reality in the child*. New York: Basic Books, 1954.

Rochlin, G. *Griefs and discontents: The forces of change*. Boston: Little, Brown, 1965.

Shafer, R. *Aspects of internalization*. New York: International Universities Press, 1968.

Tessman, L. H. *Children of parting parents*. New York: Jason Aronson, 1978.

Tessman, L. H. A note on the father's contribution to the daughter's ways of loving and working. In S. Cath, A. Gurwitt, & J. Ross (Eds.), *Father and child: Developmental and clinical perspectives*. Boston: Little, Brown, 1982.

Wallerstein, J., & Kelly, J. *Divorce counseling: A community service for families in the midst of divorce*. Paper presented at the meeting of the American Orthopsychiatric Association, Atlanta, Georgia, 1976.

Weiss, R. S. *Marital separation*. New York: Basic Books, 1975.

CHAPTER TWELVE

The Impact of Divorce on Children[1]

JUDITH WALLERSTEIN

Although designed as a social remedy, divorce has gradually become a source of grave community concern because of its stressful impact on children and adolescents. The special vulnerability and the particular needs of youngsters in divorcing families at the time of the marital rupture and during the extended aftermath have been reluctantly acknowledged both by the general community as well as by the mental health professions. Partly because of this belated recognition, the problem is upon us with great magnitude. There is grave need for longitudinal research, for a careful consideration of changes in the law and its implementation, and for intervention programs that would provide clinical services, community education, and increased social and economic support. Unfortunately, the delayed recognition of these problems may now lead to hasty efforts to revise family law and court practice and to mount research and intervention programs whose appropriateness to these families in underlying assumptions and in method has been insufficiently examined.

INCIDENCE IN THE GENERAL POPULATION

The incidence of children in newly divorcing families throughout the nation has remained at one million or more since 1972. It is currently estimated that one third of all first marriages contracted in the United States in 1979 will ultimately end in divorce (Norton, 1979). It is also estimated that between 30 and 40% of all American children born during the 1970s will experience

1. Reprinted by permission from *Psychiatric Clinics of North America*, 1980, *3*(3), 455–468. Copyright © 1980, W. B. Saunders Company.

Judith Wallerstein. School of Social Welfare and School of Law, University of California at Berkeley, Berkeley, California, and Center for the Family Transition, Corte Madera, California.

divorce sometime during their growing-up years (Bane, 1976) and that if present trends continue, approximately 45% of children born in 1977 will reside in a one-parent family sometime before they reach 18 years of age (Glick, quoted in *Marriage and Divorce Today*, 1980). These projections depend, of course, on the relative stability of current trends in marriage and divorce. Despite predictions to the contrary, however, it appears that the divorce rate has continued to rise although much less steeply than during the early and mid-1970s.

One major problem in studying divorce has been the relative unavailability of detailed information that might guide the researcher or the community planner. Thus, the number of children involved in separation, divorce, and remarriage can only be estimated until the 1980 census is analyzed. In a significant number of states there is no mandatory reporting of the children in divorcing families, and several states that report the numbers of children fail to report their ages. Moreover, the courts do not, as a rule, report or even tabulate the decrees or modifications requested, or granted, or denied— whether maternal custody, or paternal custody, or joint custody. As a consequence, understanding of the divorced family has been further hampered.

INCIDENCE IN PATIENT POPULATIONS

Clinics and practitioners in private practice alike have, in recent years, reported a substantial increase of children of divorce as patients. A 1975 national survey of children between 7 and 10 years of age in divorcing families found that the number of children in need of psychological help within the divorcing family was significantly higher than among their counterparts in intact families, even after allowance for socioeconomic and educational differences had been made (Zill, 1978). The same report also found that parent–child relationships in divorced families were likely to be burdened by parents' difficulties and tensions. Reports from clinics have placed the child of divorce at between 50 and 80% of the total number of children in treatment (Kalter, 1977). This would far exceed their presence within the general population of children. For example, a 1980 report of a family service agency in Northern California revealed that of a total of 70 children in direct psychotherapy, 58 were from divorced families (Anderson, 1980).

PREVIOUS STUDIES

Early studies in the field of divorce were mainly sociological investigations that utilized questionnaires and group comparison methods to correlate a history of family disruption, whether separation or divorce, with later maladaptive or adaptive behaviors (Burchinal, 1964; Landis, 1960, 1962; Nye,

1957). Findings from these studies are probably of questionable applicability to divorce occurring in the late 1970s and the 1980s. A fairly large literature, drawn mainly from sociology, also addressed issues of the effects of the absence of the father. Many of these studies, reviewed in a by now classic paper by Herzog and Sudia (1970), found major methodological flaws of sufficient magnitude to render findings from this body of research of limited applicability. Socioeconomic factors were poorly controlled. Absence of the father had been treated by many researchers as a unitary phenomenon, whether the absence occurred because of death, separation, or divorce. Moreover, it was presumed that the father in the divorced family was not in contact with his children although there is recent evidence that many fathers keep in close touch with their children over the years.

There is also a significant body of clinical literature consisting of case reports of children and adolescents brought for psychotherapy. These clinical reports point to a variety of psychopathological sequelae. In the main, it has been argued that the absence of the father has rendered developmental resolution of inner conflict more difficult by the unavailability of the reality against which the child could test his or her own idealized image of the father (Neubauer, 1960). Clinicians have warned about the dangers of overidealizing the absent parent and compared the effects of divorce to those of the effects of death of a parent in the grave potential for developmental fixation at the time at which the trauma occurred and the ensuing lifelong search for the lost parent (Tessman, 1977). Other clinicians have maintained that an unhappy marriage or fighting between the parents is more destructive to the child's psychological development than the divorce (Despert, 1953).

RECENT LONGITUDINAL STUDIES

It has been our conviction that the effects of divorce on children and adolescents need to be examined over time and followed within a longitudinal perspective. Case reports alone, although invaluable in developing hypotheses, may fail to shed light on the resilient child or the children in the general population. In part, because longitudinal studies are expensive and difficult to mount and to sustain, and in part because children of divorce have been largely neglected by psychological and psychiatric researchers, only two longitudinal studies are reported in the psychological or psychiatric literature: (1) a Virginia study (Hetherington, Cox, & Cox, 1976, 1978a, 1978b) of 48 preschool children followed for over a 2-year period after the divorce and compared with a control group of 48 children from intact families matched for age and sex; and (2) a Northern California study (Kelly & Wallerstein, 1976, 1977a, 1977b, 1979; Wallerstein, 1977; Wallerstein & Kelly, 1974, 1975, 1976, 1980) of 131 children aged 3 to 18 at the time of the marital separation followed for over a 5-year period from the time of marital separation. A major difference between the two longitudinal studies is that the Virginia study began at the legal divorce and followed the child for 2 years; the California study began at the marital separation, which usually occurred at least 1 year prior to the legal divorce, and followed the children for 5 years from that decisive separation.

The goals of both the Virginia study and the California study were to study the children's responses to the divorce and to examine the course of change and patterns of outcome in the children and in the parent–child relationships during the postdivorce period. Both studies assumed that the family system would undergo a period of acute disorganization immediately after the divorce, followed by gradual reorganization and eventual restabilization.

Although there was considerable difference in project design, methodology, and approach to the families, the similarities in the findings of the two studies are high. This consonance is of considerable interest because of the wide geographical distances between the populations in contrast to their close ethnic and class approximations. Since these represent the only longitudinal studies that have been reported there is no way, at the present, to spell out the expectable responses in the many populations that have not been represented. It may be that the responses of adults and children to marital rupture are more similar than divergent as one crosses across social class and ethnic barriers—or it may be that future studies will reveal major distinctions in initial responses and outcome along many dimensions that reflect socioeconomic differences.

THE CALIFORNIA CHILDREN OF DIVORCE PROJECT

To review the sample and central design of the California study briefly, each of the 131 children and adolescents together with the parents were studied intensively during a 6-week period close to the time of separation. Each family member was re-examined again at 18 months and once again at 5 years after separation. By 5 years, two of the families were lost to follow-up and two others remarried each other and were dropped from the divorce population. The final samples for which there were sufficient data at each point in time to permit a full clinical assessment and diagnosis consisted of 103 children, 47 boys and 56 girls.

In their socioeconomic distribution the families reflected the population of the country in which they resided. The families were largely, but not entirely, within the middle-class range. Of the 60 families, 88% were white, 3% were black, and 9% were interracial with one Asian spouse. They were a relatively well-educated group: 25% of the men held advanced degrees in medicine, law, and business administration. In accord with the Hollingshead two-factor index, 23% were in class one, 20% in class two, 28% in class three,

18% in class four, and 10% in class five. The average age of the men at separation was 36.9, the mean age for the women 34.1. They had been married an average of 11.1 years prior to the final separation. The couples averaged 2.2 children per family.

Prior to the family disruption, all of the children in this study had reached appropriate developmental milestones in the view of their parents and their teachers. They were all performing at age-appropriate levels within the schools and none had been referred for psychological or psychiatric intervention. They therefore represented a group skewed in the direction of psychological health, or at least, psychological normalcy, a population at considerable variance from the clinic population usually reported in the psychiatric literature.

Among the more immediate findings of the study was the number of children in failing, troubled marriages who appeared sturdy and well parented and who expressed relative contentment with their families and the quality of their lives despite the unhappiness of their parents with the marriage. A good 35% of the children in the sample appeared to be functioning very well, indeed, and about 25% were at an age-appropriate average, with 20% each in the moderately troubled and profoundly troubled groups. Many children had clearly been well cared for during the troubled marriage. At least 25% had enjoyed the care of two devoted parents and at least 30% of the children had parents who were fully in accord regarding child-rearing practices and values. At the other end of the spectrum, 40% of the children had relationships with fathers that were impoverished or grossly psychopathological in their overall cast, and at least 25% of the children had impoverished relationships with mothers—parents who neglected them or frightened them with threatened abuse.

The Child's Experience during the Divorcing Period

Children and adolescents experienced the separation and its aftermath as the most stressful period of their lives. The family rupture evoked an acute sense of shock, an intense anxiety and grieving, which many children and many adolescents as well found overwhelming. Few youngsters experienced relief with the divorce decision, and those who did so were in adolescence and had witnessed physical violence between their parents.

The child's early responses were not governed by a balanced understanding of the issues that led to the divorce. Nor were the youngsters much affected by the high incidence of divorce in the community. Actually, at the time of the separation the child's attention is riveted entirely on the disruptive process in his or her family and is intensely worried about what will happen to him or her. The divorce centrally signifies the collapse of the structure that provided support and protection which the child needed and will continue to need.

What Do the Children Know of the Divorce?

It has been maintained by many clinicians that children always have some foreboding of the imminent dissolution of their parents' marriage. There is really little evidence for this among this large group of youngsters who were studied. In the California study, one third of the children had hardly any idea that their parents were unhappy and were taken completely by surprise by the parental decision. And, indeed, it is worth noting that even when children were aware of the marital strife there was no evidence that knowledge of the adult's unhappiness prepared them psychologically for the divorce or diminished their distress when the marital rupture occurred. The expectation of marital separation was a nightmare some youngsters lived with over many long years. Their burden was not lightened by this foreknowledge.

Many children were not directly informed of the parents' plans. Over three fourths of the preschool children in the California study were not provided with an adequate explanation of the divorce that was occurring. They essentially awoke one morning to discover that one parent had permanently left the household. This singular silence of the parents can be regarded as a symbolic marker for what we have conceptualized as the diminished capacity to parent at the time of the divorce.

Ambience of the Divorced Family

There has been insufficient recognition of the disabling impact of divorce itself on the psychological functioning of the adult, and, particularly, on the capacity of the adult to carry on in his or her expected roles and responsibilities during the several months immediately preceding the marital rupture, during the height of the divorce crisis, and during the year or more that followed the marital separation. Many adults who were able to live alongside each other for years without open anger became openly hostile as the marriage ended. Others, who had suffered with chronic or moderate depressions, became severely depressed or agitated. Although in some families the divorce-engendered ambience was continuous with that of the preseparation family, in the greater majority of households feelings of bitterness and scenes of conflict increased at the separation. There is, in fact, evidence that the very structure of the marriage, however happy or unhappy the people are within it, serves as an extended ego control that holds in check a host of primitive angers and sexual impulses that often erupt as the marriage structure topples.

Some of the anger and depression among the parents reflected the fact that very few of the decisions to divorce were truly mutual. Although the adults who were married to each other by and large did not disagree about the sad state of the marriage, they did disagree strongly about the decision to divorce. Mostly, the divorce was sought by one member of the couple and opposed by the other. In the California study, as well as in other studies across the country, the divorce was sought by more women and opposed by more men. This difference between the adults, the intensity of this difference, and the humiliation engendered by this unilateral decision set the stage for much of the interaction at the time of the divorce and during the years that followed.

The children in many of these families had little preparation for the angry, distressed, unhappy behaviors which they witnessed. Many youngsters were bewildered, frightened, or stimulated by scenes of physical aggression between ordinarily circumspect, well-controlled parents, or by verbal attacks which usually included accusations of promiscuity and immorality. Furthermore, children were very worried, sometimes realistically so, about depressed, suicidal parents, especially when the suicidal preoccupation was confided in the child. Almost all of the children worried whether their parents would, indeed, be able to manage along, whether the father would be cared for (who will feed him? where will he sleep?), and whether the mother would be able to maintain the household.

Who Supports the Child?

Thus, contributing to the distress of the children is the fact that many youngsters continue to face the tensions and sorrows of divorce with little help from their parents. And, in fact, many children at this time in their lives often feel that they are losing access to both parents. Characteristically, they experience diminished physical care and diminished emotional support at a time of increased need for adult help.

There is considerable evidence from the California study that children are poorly supported not only by their parents, but also by others during the divorce crisis. Many families live at a considerable distance from extended family members. Within the California study only one fourth of the children were sustained by grandparents or other extended members of the family at the time of the crisis. Fewer than 10% of the California children were helped by adults outside the family, including pediatricians, ministers, rabbis, neighbors, family friends, or other members of the community, many of whom knew the family. The school was helpful to the distressed children by virtue of its continuing presence as a structure in their lives. School also provided a refuge from family difficulties and teachers soon became habituated to children who waited for their arrival early in the morning and begged to remain in the classroom long after the other youngsters had departed. overall, however, only half of the children's teachers knew of the divorce in the family, and several parents, fearing "labeling" of their child, indicated that they preferred that the school not know of the family difficulties. Thus, at the time of the separation and during the several-month aftermath, many children in divorcing families lacked the help of their parents, as well as extended family or community supports which might help them to withstand the stresses of the family disruption.

The Children's Response

Although the child who confronts the disruption of his or her family often feels alone and uniquely burdened, in actuality, children and adolescents share a range of feelings and concerns. Expressed differently by the individual youngsters, certain feelings and responses emerged as the common themes which appeared and reappeared. These themes can be traced from their early appearance in the symptoms and inhibitions of the very young children up the developmental ladder to the often relatively sophisticated utterances of the adolescents. Taken all together, these responses which we have reported may begin to provide a much-needed body of general knowledge about the reactions of youngsters to stress. Specifically, they shed light on the responses of children and adolescents to the particular stress of family rupture in the relative absence of support within the family and the social surroundings.

The children and adolescents were frightened by the marital rupture. They felt vulnerable and exposed to myriad dangers, some real and some fantasied. Mostly they felt powerless to undo the parental decision as well as to take responsibility for their own growing up. In different ways each child worried intensely about who would take care of him or her now that the protective envelope of family had been torn apart.

The children were additionally heavily burdened by a sense of loss and sorrow. They grieved for the intact family and they yearned for the departed parent. The yearning seemed often unrelated to any prior relationship with the parent who was so sorely missed.

The youngsters were further troubled by worries over their parents, by their loneliness, and by their sense that both parents had removed themselves and become more distant. Many youngsters also struggled with the anguish of conflicting loyalties. Although their loyalty conflicts were often exacerbated by parents, the conflict was experienced by children without the external stimulation.

Finally, many children struggled with rising anger and with guilt from a sense of commission and omission which may have caused the divorce.

We were interested to find that the age of the child and his or her developmental stage was the single most significant factor associated with the child's response, and it was possible to distinguish patterns of response in behavior as well as in underlying fantasies which were linked to developmental phenomena. The early history of the child in the family in the preseparation parent–child relationship, while of considerable significance in each child's response, was less salient than the age or developmental stage achieved. How much of this finding is related to the preselection of a particular population of children who had been able to maintain age-appropriate developmental progress during the failing marriage we cannot know without further investigation.

Age-Related Response to Marital Rupture

Generally, the 3- to 18-year-old youngsters in the California study fell into four distinguishable groups in terms of their responses to the divorce-induced stress. While many of the responses are, of course, overlapping or idiosyncratic, the patterns are noteworthy and have some usefulness as predictors. These groups comprised the preschool children, aged 3 to 5½; the early latency youngsters, aged 6 through 8; the later latency youngsters, aged 9 to 11; and the adolescents. The responses of these youngsters have been described in detail (Kelly & Wallerstein, 1976, 1977a, 1977b, 1979; Waller-stein, 1977; Wallerstein & Kelly, 1974, 1975, 1976, 1980).

The preschool children were, by and large, most likely to show regression following one parent's departure from the household. The regression usually occurred in the most recent developmental achievement of the child, for example, in toilet training, in going to nursery school, in venturing into carpools unattended by the parent, in play with peers, in remaining at nursery school unattended by mother. Several youngsters in this group returned to thumb sucking, to security blankets, and to increased mastur-batory activity. Most frequent were intensified fears evoked by routine separations from the custodial parent during the day and at bed time, which the child had been able to achieve without anxiety during the intact marriage. Sleeping disturbances were particularly frequent and appeared linked to the young child's terrifying preoccupation with the thought of awakening to an empty household, abandoned by both parents. The central concern of many of the little children was of abandonment and starvation. Many of the little ones played out elaborate play scenes that portrayed adults caring for adults and children caring for children. Young children were also likely to become increasingly irritable and demanding with parents and to behave aggressively with younger siblings and with their peers.

Children in the 5- to 8-year-old group were most likely to show open grieving, including sighing and sobbing. They were preoccupied with feelings of rejection, with longing for the departed father, and with the fear that they would never see him again. They shared the terrifying fantasy of being replaced, "Will my daddy get a new dog? a new mommy? a new little boy?" were the comments of several of the boys in this age group. Little girls wove what we came to conceptualize as elaborate "Madame Butterfly" fantasies, asserting that the father would someday return to *them*, that he loved them "the best," unable to believe that the divorce would endure. About half the children in this age group suffered a precipitous decline in their school work and reported difficulty in concentrating and worry about their parents. A few children at this age appeared untroubled and were able to maintain their usual composure and their full range of activities.

In the 9- to 12-year-old children, the central response seemed often to be intense anger at one or both parents for the divorce decision. These children were likely to blame the parent whom they singled out as causing the divorce. In addition, these children also suffered with grief over the intact family, with greater anxiety, with loneliness, and a sense of their own powerlessness. These youngsters often cast one parent in the role of the "good" parent and the other as "bad." They were especially vulnerable to the blandishments of one or another of the parents who was actually engaged in fighting with the other and were co-opted as allies in developing complex strategies designed to harass and humiliate the other parent. On the other hand, several children in this group were also very helpful to a troubled parent and showed enhanced maturity and compassion as a response to the divorce. School performances and peer relationships both suffered deterioration in roughly 50% of these children.

And, finally, several adolescents became acutely anxious as they perceived the new vulnerability of their parents. The incidence of disturbance in the adolescents was higher than expected. A goodly number were anxiously preoccupied with their own entry into young adulthood, concerned about the fate of their own future marriages, and the possibility that they, too, might experience sexual and marital failure. They also became concerned with issues of morality and responded in a global way to what they experienced as a need to reorganize their opinions about the world around them and to rethink values. The adolescents seemed more vulnerable than generally recognized. About one third of the adolescents in the study appeared more troubled a year after the separation then they had been at the time of the rupture.

Parents and Children after Divorce

There were many significant changes in the relationship between parents and children following the divorce. The visiting parent's relationship with the children was especially likely to change. Poor, even impoverished, relationships improved, and others which had been close and affectionate during the marriage dwindled unexpectedly. Young children were more likely to be visited over the years than the older youngsters. On the other hand, some of the adolescent boys and girls developed and maintained a close friendship with the father—especially when the mother was depressed. A goodly number elected to follow the father's profession.

Similarly, the custodial parent and children moved into new roles. Many youngsters, some very young, moved closer to their mothers as proud helpers and confidantes. Others moved precipitously away from a closer involvement out of fear of engulfment. Altogether the divorce emerged as a nodal point of change in parent–child relationships in many of the families. These changes are described in detail elsewhere (Wallerstein & Kelly, 1980).

There was considerable evidence that the relationship between child and both divorced parents does not lessen in emotional importance over the years. Although the mother's caretaking and psychological role became increasingly central in the families where the mother had custody, there was no evidence that the father's psychological significance declined correspondingly. Even in remarriage the biological father's emotional significance did not disappear or diminish markedly and the children appeared to have little conflict about creating a special slot for the stepfather alongside of their continued awareness of their relationship with the biological father. And, in fact, throughout the research it has been strikingly apparent that whether the children maintained frequent or infrequent contact with a noncustodial parent, they would have considered the term "one-parent family" a misnomer. The self-image of children who have been reared in a two-parent family appears to be firmly tied to the continuing relationship with both parents, regardless of that parent's physical presence with the family.

Good Outcome at 5 Years Postseparation

Outcome factors point to the desirability during the years after the divorce of children's continuing relationship with *both* parents in an arrangement that enabled each parent to be responsible for and genuinely concerned about the well-being of the children. Children who were well adjusted and happy 5 years after the divorce lived in families who were able to restabilize and restore the parenting after the initial dip during the breakup crisis. Children also improved when a divorce separated a child from a psychologically destructive or incestuous, abusive parent. And children benefited from new parental relationships within remarriages. Children also did well in families where the friction between parents had dissipated. All in all, children who did well enjoyed over the postdivorce years a sense of continuity with both parents and felt that the divorce had contributed to the quality of their lives, both by removing the stress of the failing marriage and by continuing the important gratifications. Approximately one third of the group were psychologically in very good health and content with their lives at the 5-year mark following the divorce.

Poor Outcome at 5 Years Postseparation

At the other end of the spectrum, a considerable number of children—well over half of the group—looked back longingly at the failing marriage and wished for its return. Thirty-seven percent, somewhat over a third of the children in the study at the 5-year mark, were psychologically troubled and distressed. The most frequent clinical finding was that of childhood depression. These were, by and large, children who felt rejected and neglected by either custodial parent or noncustodial parent. Those who experienced repeated disappointment because of the father's infrequent or unreliable visiting, or his disinterest or insensitivity to them during visits, suffered grave unhappiness which did not seem to diminish over the years. Despite repeated disappointments and the passage of time, many children held tightly to the hope that the father would eventually fulfill their expectations. Very few children were able to master their distress at the father's rejection of them. Time did not greatly mute their anguish. A very few were able to counter-reject the rejecting father when they reached adolescence and to look elsewhere for a model and substitute.

Similarly, children who remained in the custody of a lonely, depressed, or emotionally disturbed mother were likely to do poorly. The additional stresses of divorce on an emotionally disturbed or physically ill parent often led to deteriorated parenting which was no longer mitigated by the buffering presence of the healthy or healthier spouse. Children left in the custody of a chronically depressed or disinterested mother were more likely to go downhill rapidly after the divorce, although they might have held their own during the marriage.

Finally, the failure of the divorce to provide its intended remedy was a central cause of children's poor adjustment at the 5-year mark. Where the parents continued to fight, or where the postdivorce bitterness exceeded that of the marital conflict, children were seriously hindered in their efforts to integrate the divorce. It was startling to find that 30% of the children were aware of tension and continued bitterness between their parents at the 5-year mark. Parental fighting which continued was significantly related to poor psychological adjustment among the children.

Factors in Outcome

There is no single theme that appears in the lives of all of the children who enhanced, consolidated, or continued their good developmental progress following the divorce. Nor is there a single theme that appears among all of those who deteriorated, either moderately or markedly. Rather, we confront a set of complex configurations in which the available components are put together in varying combinations in the individual life of each child.

To add to the complexity, the different components of these configurations are intricately interrelated. Thus, children turned more to the noncustodial father for support and yearned for him more intensely when the relationship with the custodial mother was conflicted or impoverished, as well as when they missed him and their relationship with him on its own merits. In this way, the attitude of the child toward the father was both separate from *and* closely related to the child's feelings toward the mother and the degree and quality of the relationship with the home. Or, for further example, the child's capacity to rely on friends and to turn to friends for support during the crisis was also in some measure dependent on the child's relationships within the family. Children with good relationships at home appeared to make friends more easily and to sustain these friendships. Children who were unhappy at home often had trouble making friends and were often manipulative with their peers. Teachers complained about the manipulative, overbearing behavior of children who were often subdued and sad at home. Thus, the fortunate children often felt better at home as well as outside the home; their less fortunate peers were unhappy in both places.

Briefly stated, those components, in varying combinations of importance, which seemed centrally to affect the course and outcome at the 5-year mark included: (1) the extent to which the parents had been able to resolve and put aside their conflicts and angers and to make use of the relief from conflict provided by the divorce; (2) the course of the custodial parent's handling of the child and the resumption or improvement of parenting within the home; (3) the extent to which the child did not feel rejected in his or her relationship with the noncustodial or visiting parent, and the extent to which this relationship had continued on a regular basis and kept pace with the child's growth: (4) the individual assets, capacities, and deficits which the child brought to the divorce; (5) the availability of a supportive human network to the child including siblings and extended family members, and the child's ability to make good use of these; (6) the absence of continuing anger and depression in the child; and (7) the sex and age of the child.

Although the initial breakup of the family is profoundly stressful, the eventual outcome depends in large measure not only on what has been lost, but on what has been constructed to replace the failed marriage. The effect of the divorce ultimately reflects the success or failure of the parents and children to master the immediate disruption, to negotiate the transition successfully, and to create a more gratifying family to replace the family that failed.

Timetable of the Divorce

The timetable of the divorcing process is considerably longer than most people realize. The decision to divorce brought numerous intended and unintended changes in its wake and to the adults and the children and in their relationships with each other. The drama, complexity, and scope of these changes exceeded the expectations of many of the participants. The period of disequilibrium in the lives of the family often lasted several years, and 5 years after the marital separation, divorce-related issues remained infused with strong feelings for children and adults. Perhaps this extended timetable is both realistic and expectable, and we have been naive in expecting quicker resolutions of a major life crisis. Nevertheless, the average time which the newly divorced woman in the California study required to reestablish a sense of continuity and stability in her life was 3 to 3½ years. The men required 2 to 2½ years before they re-established or newly established a sense of order in their lives. The divorce remained a live issue for one half of the adults at the 5-year mark, especially so for the women. Only rarely did both parties to the divorce achieve the same degree of psychological closure, and for at least one partner, the divorce was still very much a very painful issue 5 years later. At that time two thirds of the men and more than half of the women viewed the divorce as beneficial. One fifth of the men and one fifth of the women deplored the divorce as a bad mistake. The remainder had mixed feelings.

Similarly, the children as a group at the 5-year mark remained strikingly aware of their family and its vicissitudes. One of the consequences of divorce appears to be that the family becomes a focus of the conscious—even hyperalert—attention and continuing thoughtful consideration of the children. As the youngster matures, the divorce is looked at anew and the maturing child makes an effort to explain and master the march of family events in ways consonant with his or her enhanced maturity. In this way the intellectual and emotional efforts of the youngster to cope with the family rupture appear to reorganize at each developmental stage and extend throughout his or her growing-up years. Also, in this way the divorce accompanies the child throughout his or her growing-up years, perhaps into adulthood as well.

It is evident that many families need professional advice and guidance in negotiating their way through this complex and tangled pathway of divorce and the postdivorce years. It is important not only to provide the services which they need but to find ways to reach both adults and children at the appropriate time, namely, at the marital rupture, so that we can help to prepare them for the arduous road that lies ahead.

ACKNOWLEDGMENTS

This chapter was written while the author was a fellow at the Center for Advanced Study in the Behavioral Sciences, Stanford, California, 1979–1980. The support of the Spencer Foundation, the Rockefeller Foundation, and the National Institute of Mental Health is gratefully acknowledged. The research was supported by the Zellerbach Family Fund.

REFERENCES

Anderson, L. Unpublished master's thesis based on statistics from the Mid-Peninsula Family Service Agency, Palo Alto, California, 1980.

Bane, M. J. Marital disruption and the lives of children. *Journal of Social Issues*, 1976, *32*, 103–117.

Burchinal, L. G. Characteristics of adolescents from unbroken, broken, and reconstituted families. *Marriage and Family Living*. 1964, *26*, 44–51.

Despert, J. L. *Children of divorce.* Garden City, N.Y.: Doubleday, 1953.

Herzog, E., & Sudia, C. E. *Boys in fatherless families.* United States Children Bureau, 1970.

Hetherington, E. M., Cox, M., & Cox, R. Divorced fathers. *Family Coordinator*, 1976, *25*, 417-418.

Hetherington, E. M., Cox, M., & Cox, R. The aftermath of divorce. In J. H. Stevens, Jr., & M. Matthews (Eds.), *Mother-child/father-child relationship.* Washington, D.C.: National Association for the Education of Young Children, 1978. (a)

Hetherington, E. M., Cox, M., & Cox, R. The development of children in mother headed families. In H. Hoffman & D. Reiss (Eds.), *The American family: Dying or developing.* New York: Plenum, 1978. (b)

Kalter, N. Children of divorce in an outpatient psychiatric population. *American Journal of Orthopsychiatry*, 1977, *47*, 40-51.

Kelly, J. B., & Wallerstein, J. S. The effects of parental divorce: Experiences of the child in early latency. *American Journal of Orthopsychiatry*, 1976, *46*, 20-32.

Kelly, J. B., & Wallerstein, J. S. Brief interventions with children in divorcing families. *American Journal of Orthopsychiatry*, 1977, *47*, 23-39. (a)

Kelly, J. B., & Wallerstein, J. S. Part-time parent, part-time child: Visiting after divorce. *Journal of Child Clinical Psychology*, 1977, *6*, 51-54. (b)

Kelly, J., & Wallerstein, J. S. The divorced child in the school. *National Elementary Principal*, 1979, *59*, 51-58.

Landis, J. T. Social correlates of divorce or nondivorce among the unhappily married. *Marriage and Family Living*, 1960, *22*, 7-13.

Landis, J. T. A comparison of children from divorced and nondivorced unhappy marriages. *Family Life Coordinator*, 1962, *11*, 61-66.

Marriage and Divorce Today, 1980, *5*, 36.

Neubauer, P. The one-parent child and his oedipal development. *Psychoanalytic Study of the Child*, 1960, *15*, 286-309.

Norton, A. A portrait of the one parent family. *National Elementary Principal*, 1979, *59*, 32-35.

Nye, I. F. Child adjustment in a broken and in unhappy unbroken homes. *Marriage and Family Living*, 1957, *19*, 356-361.

Tessman, L. H. *Children of parting parents.* New York: Jason Aronson, 1977.

Wallerstein, J. S., & Kelly, J. B. *Surviving the breakup: How children and parents cope with divorce.* New York: Basic Books, 1980.

Wallerstein, J. S. Responses to the pre-school child to divorce: Those who cope. In M. F. McMillian, & S. Henao (Eds.), *Child psychiatry: Treatment and research.* New York: Brunner/Mazel, 1977.

Wallerstein, J. S., & Kelly, J. B. The effects of parental divorce: Experiences of the child in later latency. *American Journal of Orthopsychiatry*, 1976, *46*, 256-269.

Wallerstein, J. S., & Kelly, J. B. The effects of parental divorce: Experiences of the preschool child. *Journal of the American Academy of Child Psychiatry*, 1975, *14*, 600-616.

Wallerstein, J. S., & Kelly, J. B. The effects of parental divorce: The adolescent experience. In E. J. Anthony & C. Koupernik (Eds.), *The child in his family* (Vol. 3). New York: John Wiley & Sons, 1974.

Zill, N. *Divorce, marital happiness and the mental health of children: Findings from the Foundation for Child Development National Survey of Children.* Paper prepared for National Institute of Mental Health Workshop on Divorce and Children, Bethesda, Maryland, 1978.

CHAPTER THIRTEEN

The Stepfamily: Its Psychological Structure and Its Psychotherapeutic Challenge

NORMAN I. MOSS

Recent national census data indicated that 13% of children under age 18 are living in a home with a remarried parent and a stepparent. This chapter will focus on these families.

Since the industrial age, the nuclear family has been the major buffer against rapid, unsettling, socioeconomic changes. Married and unmarried have viewed the nuclear family as the primary source of emotional warmth and gratification, its establishment as a sign of mature adulthood (Anthony & Benedek, 1971), and its structure as an enduring source of security. The stability of the nuclear family provided a sanctuary for the growing child, the burdened adult, and the aging, infirm grandparent.

In the past 30 years, changes in marital patterns have significantly compromised the prevalence and stability of the nuclear family, and the social values that have been attached to it. Due to the high divorce rate, the large number of never-married and single-parent families, and the increasingly common pattern of both spouses working, only 17% of American families now have the formerly traditional structure of the father working and the mother at home with her child-rearing and household responsibilities.

Observers such as Christopher Lasch (1979) have elucidated this conflict between the individual's sense of his or her personal expectations, versus the sense of value placed on the integrity of the nuclear family. One might argue a culture of narcissism in conflict with the value of identity with, and obligation to, the family. The values of self-actualization and self-fulfillment have synergized with the growing conviction that it is possible to, and perhaps one is even entitled to, find marital compatibility without emotional

Norman I. Moss. Department of Psychiatry, Harvard Medical School, Boston, Massachusetts, and Department of Psychiatry, Beth Israel Hospital, Boston, Massachusetts.

sacrifice or extreme psychological compromise. In my clinical experience I have observed that men more often than women leave marriages because of issues of entitlement and self-gratification.

The increasing liberation of women from what had often been a bitter, oppressive sense of obligation to sacrifice for the welfare of their children, or their duty to their husband or their religion, has also played a major role in the changes of the nuclear family structure. Issues related to the conflicting ambitions of dual-career couples (Rice, 1979) have placed stress on many nuclear families. This most frequently occurs when the husband feels either threatened in the rivalrous sense, or deprived of nurturance, as a result of his wife's increasing involvement in her career. On occasion, as one gathers the history of each spouse and the evolution of the marriage, there is evidence that one or both spouses gradually valued their career development, and enjoyed its gratifications, more than the previously shared value of marital intimacy. Further realization of personal professional potential, as well as the support and approval of professional peers, becomes an ascendant value that adumbrates the value of nuclear family life.

When two people who have been divorced marry, the new families they create have traditionally been called stepfamilies. The term "stepparent" has a negative association in our cultural history, ranging from the bad step-parent of the Grimms' fairy tales, to the news account of the abusive stepparent. Viewed from a family systems perspective, it overemphasizes the adults' parental role. More recent terms reflect a shift in emphasis from the view of the family as having child rearing as a primary role, to the recognition of the family as having more complex intrapsychic and interpersonal functions. The focus in the recent studies of these families is the married couple. Such names as the "blended family," the "remarried family," the "reconstituted family," reflect the growing influence of a family systems theoretical perspective in the study of these families.

The marital relationship is seen as essential to the stability of the family, and as being crucial for it to carry on its child-rearing functions.

The complex structure of the stepfamily presents a challenge for the psychotherapist. Both the therapists who treat the spouses individually, and the marital and family therapists who work with these families, become impressed with their unique needs and their complex communicational patterns. There is a growing awareness of the need to modify therapeutic modalities to better satisfy the adaptational needs of these families. In the last 10 years, there has been an increase in the marital and family literature on the psychological problems and the psychotherapy of the members of divorced families and stepfamilies (Walker, Brown, Crohn, Rodstein, Zeisel, & Sager, 1979). Visher and Visher's (1979) book is an outstanding contribution.

Each stepfamily evolves its relationships in a unique, largely unpredictable manner, and has a distinct history as a family. It is important in studying the stepfamily, and in attempting to help them with their difficulties, to recognize the power of the process of their formation and evolution. In working with a stepfamily, it is important to emphasize to them the value of an openmindedness to personality differences, and to the long time it will take for each member of the family to get to know the new members of the family to whom they have been presented with little preparation. It is useful to emphasize that ideally, each family member will change in some ways, some of which are unpredictable, as the family continues to live together, and that this is a sign of growing strength and maturity in the family. I continually emphasize, in working with remarried families, that the most helpful and accurate view each member of the family can have of their life together is that of a group of strangers on a long voyage. They're all on the same ship; there will be many changes in direction and accommodation, some undesired and frustrating. There will be constant need for each member of the family to try to be flexible and tolerant of the others, recognizing that there will be inevitable disappointments and some unhappy compromises.

I emphasize to the children, in the parents' presence, that they, the children, did not choose their stepparents or stepsiblings, and indeed that this is very unfair. My interest here is to underscore the reality that it is the adults who decided to form the new family. This emphasis tends to reduce the scapegoating of the stepparents and stepsiblings.

TYPOLOGY OF STEPFAMILIES

Death and Remarriage

Stepfamilies formed because of the death of a spouse and the remarriage of the surviving spouse were the most common type until recently. This type of remarried family, because of the historically recent, increasing divorce rate now the statistically less common, may struggle with special psychological problems resulting from the idealization of the deceased parent by both sets of children, and usually, to a lesser degree, the surviving spouses. The degree and rigidity of the idealization determines the degree to which a new spouse and stepparent may be allowed to become an emotional member of the remarried family.

The Inexperienced Stepfather

Stepfamilies with a father who has never married before and who marries a woman with a child or children are handicapped by having one parent with no experience in child rearing. He is relatively advantaged in having no existing loyalties to a surviving spouse or children. Potential problems lie in the possibility that he may have married solely for the intimacy and companionship with this new wife, and have strong needs to be nurtured by her. These emotional needs may make him extremely competitive with, and jealous of, his stepchildren.

Two Sets of Children

Stepfamilies in which both the man and woman have children of their own from prior marriages have the advantage of having two parents with child-rearing experience, as well as an appreciation of the complexity of family life and the need for compromise. However, this advantage may be neutralized by the complexity of rearing two separate sets of children, the relationships with the two surviving spouses, and, often, significant financial difficulties due to the pressures of multiple households requiring financial support.

The Inexperienced Stepmother

Stepfamilies with a stepmother who has no children of her own, who marries a man with a child or children of his own, have the advantage of having a biological father who has had experience in parenting, knows of the rigors of family life, and is not financially burdened by a need to support stepchildren. The stepmother, however, may be disadvantaged by a long-frustrated desire for children of her own. If she hopes to fulfill her frustrated desires by mothering her stepchildren, she is prey to inevitable disappointments.

THE DEVELOPMENTAL ISSUES OF THE STEPFAMILY

The Prior Marriages

This stepfamily has its psychological roots in the nature of the divorces of the newly married couple. The major variable is how successful the divorced adult has mourned the failure of the prior marriage, and psychologically separated from the former spouse. Any failure in this process of separation will result in displacing disruptive feelings from the former marriage to the newly formed family. This may result in (1) unrealistic expectations of the new marriage to make up for the unhappiness of the prior marriage; (2) displacement of hostility to the new mate or onto stepchildren; or (3) a continued emotional enmeshment with the former spouse.

The Single Period

This stage is that period of time in which each adult remained single before the remarriage. It appears to take approximately several months to 2 years for an adult to make enough of a psychological separation to be able to invest in a new family. Remarriage before this time may unfortunately abort the mourning and separation process from the former spouse and the former nuclear family. If this single phase has lasted more than a year, there may be secondary problems of (1) the accumulated frustrations of a long period of emotional and sexual deprivation because of absence of adult intimacy; (2) mounting anxiety about remarriage; and (3) rigidification of single life patterns. However, for many people, this period of singlehood is a unique opportunity for emotional growth and career development.

A prolonged phase of single parenthood may present particular problems for the oldest child living with the custodial parent, particularly that of the adolescent boy living with the divorced mother, and to a lesser degree the preteen or adolescent girl living with her divorced father. In this situation, the oldest child may become both parentified and accustomed to being the surrogate spouse. This often results in marked difficulty for this child in adjusting to the authority of the new stepparent.

Occasionally, during prolonged singlehood, the grandparents, the parents of the now-divorced parent, may assume surrogate parental roles, infantilizing their divorced child and occasionally undermining his or her authority with the children (Hader, 1965). This sets the stage for a power struggle with the new spouse and stepparent.

The Courtship Stage

The time that the couple spends together before their marriage is a crucial time for them to establish the primacy of their relationship in the soon-to-be-established stepfamily. They are often under great pressure from their jealous children, possessive friends, and emotionally attached former spouses.

A common dynamic pitfall in the attraction of the couple to each other is based on a shared Oedipal rescue fantasy. The fantasy is "He (or she) will rescue the unhappy other from the unempathic and deficient former spouse." Here all blame is displaced onto the former spouse, limiting awareness of any shortcomings in the person they are attracted to. The rivalrous feeling with the former spouse and inflated narcissistic sense of being able to bring "deserved happiness" to them both, produces hastiness and shortsightedness.

The overt sensuousness of the new couple's relationship may place great emotional pressure on their adolescent child who, themselves, are struggling to control the powerful sexual impulses of puberty. The adolescent child in the remarried family has a special burden in this regard, because the intensity of the adults' sensuous behavior during their courtship and nesting phase is usually far greater than the adult sexual behavior that an adolescent is exposed to in a nuclear family. This can lead to a great deal of premature and pressured sexual behavior by the adolescent. On occasion, aggressive behavior within or outside the family is used as a defense by the adolescent against his or her heightened and conflicted sexual drives.

The parents of the new couple can possess great psychological power to validate the new marriage by accepting their new son or daughter-in-law with grace and affection. The parents' potent disruptive and divisive power is equally great.

The Early Marital Stage

During the courtship and early marital phases, the newly married couple are often under significant pressure from their separate sets of friends and find themselves caught up in a complex social network of conflicting loyalties. They both hope that their friends will approve of their choice of a new spouse, and validate the new marriage. They hope that their friends will be able, themselves, to work out their own loyalty conflicts to the former spouse to retain the friendships. Both stepparent and stepchild are suddenly thrown together without having the time or opportunity to gradually establish a generational barrier based on a long family relationship (Fast & Cain, 1966). Therefore they must make do with stereotypic intergenerational modes of relating.

The "Our" Child Stage

The next developmental phase experienced by some stepfamilies is that of child rearing, if they choose to have a child of their own. This will be dealt with at greater length later.

The Emptying Nest Stage

Simultaneously with the child-rearing phase, and perhaps even in the early stages of the marriage, the stepfamily may be dealing with the issue of separation of adolescent children, a trying developmental task for a stable nuclear family not also burdened by the complex relationships of step-parenting and custodial issues.

Poignant problems exist in those families in which a divorced spouse is chronically psychotic or severely impaired by virtue of profound depression, addiction, or severe characterologic problems. In this situation, the healthy remarried adult usually feels some guilt about no longer living with and helping the troubled spouse. He or she may remain empathic with the troubled spouse's continued emotional suffering and loneliness. The guilt may be heightened by the obvious sense of relief at no longer having to suffer the emotional turmoil of the former marriage. If the children are in the custody of the troubled parent, the remarried adult may experience pre-occupying concern and guilt about the welfare of the children, being raised in a situation where he or she can no longer temper or neutralize the pathological parenting of the troubled parent. If the healthy parent has gained custody of the children, the children themselves may experience the same mixture of relief and guilt about no longer living with the troubled parent. The new spouse/stepparent may find him or herself burdened by the requirement for interaction with the ill parent, which is usually emotionally draining, if not maddening. These are frequently interminable clashes with the former spouse, if he or she feels abandoned and betrayed, over issues of child care and finances.

PSYCHOLOGICAL ISSUES FOR THE ADULTS IN THE REMARRIED FAMILY

The Dominant Adult

One of the adults may become dominant. This is most often determined by the personality structure of the parent, but occasionally may be determined by relative financial strength, or even the location of the new family's home, for example, if the remarried couple is living in the residence of a former marriage.

An issue of strong agreement among those who work with remarried couples is that they must devote their primary energies and psychological orientation to strengthening and maintaining their emotional alliance. There are many pressures on them to divert their time and loyalties to children, careers, former spouses, in-laws, friends, etc. They need to constantly monitor and keep in perspective these many powerful pulls and drains on their time and energy, to maintain the gratifications in their relationship. The most important function of the therapist in working with a stepfamily is to support the couple in this effort and to help them identify and resolve any psychological blocks they may have to focus their attention and energies on strengthening the marital relationship. In my experience, the remarried couple who have love and good will, have greater success in resolving interpersonal issues than equally troubled couples in their first marriage. Under stress, the couple may try to circumvent their interpersonal problems by scapegoating their children (Kaplan, 1977), or their former spouses. "If only we did not have the children (former spouse), then everything would be good between us." They need help in refocusing on and identifying their areas of conflict (e.g., competition) or needs (e.g., empathy, nurturance).

When interpersonal problems arise in a remarried couple, ghosts of their psychological past may return to haunt them. Have they chosen poorly again? Will this be a second (third, fourth) failed marriage? If the courtship of the remarried couple began while they were still legally married to their former spouses, the fear of infidelity frequently haunts the couple at times of marital stress. Will one or the other spouse have an affair as a way of dealing with the marital unhappiness? It is important for the therapist to be aware of these conscious, or sometimes unconscious, concerns of the remarried couple, and to bring them to the foreground for discussion and resolution.

The Stepmother's Problems

If the stepmother has not had children of her own, she not only lacks experience in child rearing, but she may enter the task of child rearing with resentment that she has to mother the children of another woman. The fact that she has not been a biological mother may result in some lowering of self-esteem that may make her vulnerable to any intimations from her step-children that she is less than an adequate mother. If she herself has strong needs to mother a child, she may unwittingly infantilize an older stepchild who is in a developmental phase in which she or he needs to further separate from the family, not receive greater nurturance (Schulman, 1972). A woman who was deprived of mothering in her own childhood may be motivated to mother the "deprived child" in herself via projective identification with one of her stepchildren. However, this altruistic behavior may be undermined by the awakening of painful, conflicted feelings from her own childhood, which can lead her to chaotically alternate between identifying with (1) the good, deprived child–bad mother dyad, and (2) the overwhelmed, good mother–bad child dyad.

Often unrecognized by the child's biological father, and sometimes the stepmother herself, is the natural wish on her part for expressions of gratitude and appreciation from the stepchildren to whom she has given her care and love. This need may be painfully frustrated in that often the stepchild is resentful, distant, distrustful, and defiant. In the course of work with a remarried family, it is incumbent upon a therapist to bring the stepparents' needs for appreciation to the foreground, explain the psychological basis of the child's "ungrateful" behavior, and focus on the marital relationship as the source of gratification.

The biological father must be consistent and empathic in his support of his new wife's attempts to mother his children, especially being supportive in issues of discipline. He can be most helpful to her if he can articulate the fact that he does not expect her to love his children as if they were her own. Both parents need to be aware that no matter how good the quality of the affection and care the stepmother gives to the stepchild, the stepchild is still likely to feel unloved by the stepmother, and treated unfairly by her. Frequently, it is not until stepchildren have married and had children of their own that they are able to appreciate the quality of the good stepparenting they received.

The Stepfather's Problems

If the stepfather has children from a prior marriage and is not the custodial parent, any guilt he has about not being with his biological children may be significantly exacerbated if he begins to enjoy his stepchildren. In addition, the significant financial drain of supporting two families may lead to chronic physical and psychological stress, and an unconscious tendency to scapegoat his stepchildren.

The stepparent frequently has major problems disciplining the step-children. It is best for the stepparent to move slowly into this area, and always in a well-coordinated effort with the biological parent, both as to the values that are implied by the discipline, rules of discipline, and modes for enforcing the rules. The new stepparent should anticipate at least a several month testing period, especially with adolescent children, on issues of discipline. The adolescent children will often consciously provoke and test the limits of the stepparent, and test their patience and good will. Being fore-warned about this helps the stepparent to take the adolescent's offensive behavior less personally.

Stepparents frequently experience a sense of rivalry with the ex-spouse (biological parent) that can only backfire and injure the stepparent's image in the child's eyes. Ideally, the stepparent should work on developing a positive, an accepting, and a tolerant attitude toward the noncustodial biological parent. This is very important for the child's well-being. In practice, it is difficult to achieve and maintain, and rarely is. In the course of psychotherapy with the remarried family, it is frequently one of the major issues of conflict and one of the areas in which the adults will be most resistant to accepting the therapist's advice and guidance. Often, when I make the recommendation that the stepparent meet with the biological parent and try to achieve at least a distant, if not friendly, respect, it is met with strong resistance, even from psychologically minded step or custodial parents who recognize the usefulness of this for the child. I encourage exploration, often again met with resistance, of the negative feelings for the noncustodial parent, with the hope of some diminution of the envy and competitive feelings. Frequently this exploration will uncover a triangle in which the custodial parent is subtly encouraging a rivalrous relationship between the former spouse and his or her new spouse. If my attempts at working out the psychological relationship with the noncustodial parent fail, I settle for helping the remarried couple focus on the distinction between the former spouse as an adult toward whom they may retain feelings of enmity and as a person who is an ongoing parent of their child and stepchild, and whose cooperation is required for the well-being of the child.

The stepfamily gains needed perspective on their many natural stresses by being reminded that they are living through a process that has multiple inherent difficulties. I discourage a crisis mentality. Most important, the therapist must help the stepfamily mourn the fact that they cannot create the atmosphere of a nuclear family (Visher & Visher, 1979). Many couples strive to accomplish this Herculean task. It can bring nothing but frustration and disappointment to the best-motivated and best psychologically equipped couple. The stepfamily needs help in gradually evolving their own model of family life, with the recognition that their way of living together, if successful, will need to change as their new family enters each new developmental stage.

In my experience, women are better able to make use of the psychological support of friends through their divorce and the single phase between marriages, and while being stepparents. Men may need the help of a structured therapeutic group. The father struggling to gain custody of his children can profit immensely from conversations with men who have successfully fought against the existing social and legal prejudices in this area, and from the fine book *The Disposable Parent* (Roman & Haddad, 1978). In my experience, friends of the divorced couple frequently fail to recognize that the loss of even a hated spouse through divorce can be as traumatic as that of a mostly loved spouse through death. Therefore, both divorced people and their friends fail to recognize the need for a mourning process (Goldman & Coane, 1977) requiring at least a year for the divorced person, and perhaps a lifetime if the divorced spouse was loved at one time, or still is.

Relations with Grandparents

Grandparents can provide a very valuable continuity with the child's past. They are quite often better able than their child to transcend the bitterness of the breakup of the marriage. They frequently are able to continue amicable relationships with their former daughter- or son-in-law, thus providing a needed bridge between the formerly married couple. This bridge is most useful when conflicts around the child arise. They can act as trusted intermediary between the formerly married couple, and provide for the child a model of love that transcends personal conflict.

For the child, attachment to the parents of the absent biological parent may somewhat lessen the emotional loss of the biological parent. From an intrapsychic point of view, the child's love for the grandparents on either side may allow him or her to successfully use the defense of displacement of needs for continuity of an unambivalent, loving relationship, thus lessening the intensity of internal loyalty and identification conflicts. The child's continued relationship with the grandparents offers a stable opportunity to learn about aging, and to begin to work on the lifelong task of accepting disability, and death, with equanimity.

THE CHILD IN THE REMARRIED FAMILY

The Younger Child's Problems

In evaluating the child in the remarried family it is important to know the developmental stage of the child at the time when marital stress began in his or her family of origin and the developmental stage at the time of the divorce. The particular libidinal issues and his or her cognitive capacities will strongly color the child's view of the marital distress, and the notion of what role he or she played in the divorce (Wallerstein, Kelly, 1976a, 1976b); for example, the preschool child whose cognitive style includes magical thinking may frequently fantasize that it was his or her anger that made the parents divorce; the latency-age child may frequently have feelings of guilt of a more complex nature about his or her role in the divorce; the latency-age boy frequently has fierce feelings of loyalty to the noncustodial father, which fosters an intense conflict about forming a good relationship with his step-father. In addition, the developmental stage of the child at the time of counseling also needs to be taken into account, as these issues are frequently in the foreground of the presenting problem.

The children do best psychologically when both custodial and non-custodial parents are part of their weekly life, and they can experience themselves as welcome members of both households. In the best of all possible worlds the noncustodial parent would live within bicycling distance of his or her child.

There will be inevitable periods of scapegoating phenomena, lasting from weeks to months, in combined families, when there are children of two former marriages living together. Parents frequently overreact to these scape-goating phenomena, fearing either that they will become rigidified patterns, or that they will markedly traumatize the scapegoated child. Thee scape-goating episodes cannot be prevented in the early stage, and are likely to resolve themselves if parents take a calm, firm, attitude of guidance, as opposed to punishment. They remain rigid only when actively supported by one parent's neurotic needs. The therapist can reassure the parents frequently about the child's capacity for rapid psychological growth and rebound from the psychological stress of a new family and can counsel them about specific scapegoating issues, expanding their psychological understanding of the dynamics and teaching them a repertoire of helpful interventions.

The child is frequently concerned about the issue of "Is there enough attention, affection, nurturance, to go around?" A secondary concern is that of fairness. How can one be fair? The answer is that one can not be fair in a remarried family, particularly if there are two separate sets of children. It is useful to help both parents and children see that they need to follow different rules and values for their new family, that are adaptive to their new situation. These rules, by necessity, will differ from some of the rules in their former nuclear family. The relativity of these rules is difficult for children to under-stand. This difficulty is particularly great for the latency and younger child who very much depends on clear, consistent rules. A child of 10 or older is cognitively able to re-evaluate and adapt to different circumstances, and even profit from the richness of the different family situation. Both parents and children need help to identify the very difficult task of recognizing the individual differences in age, capacities, interests, and limitations of each child in the family, and attempting to respond to these accordingly. The notion of fairness can best be replaced by the value that the parents will try their best to respond to the uniqueness and special needs of each child in the family.

Children in a stepfamily are usually painfully aware of the practical problems of finding enough time for communication of their needs, the events of their day, and important news from their noncustodial parent and relatives. Because of the large number of people involved in the remarried family system, the task of emotional and factual communication is impossible for the child to accomplish satisfactorily.

The striking increase in the complexity of a child's life in a stepfamily is illustrated by the following example. Jenny's original nuclear family consists of Jenny; her brother, Dana; and her mother and father. The formula for combinations of different relationships (C) taken any number at a time is $C = 2^{n-1}$, where n is the number of people in the system. In Jenny's original, nuclear family, there is a total of eight possible combinations ($C = 2^3$).

Jenny's parents divorce. Her mother becomes the custodial parent. After 1 year she marries a divorced man with no children of his own. After several months, Jenny's father marries a divorced woman with one child of her own. One year later, Jenny's father and his new wife have a child of their own. At this point in Jenny's stepfamily, there are four adults and four children. Using the formula for total number of combinations we have $C = 2^7$, or 128 combinations!

The child in a nuclear family may also have difficulty getting parental attention and time to articulate his or her needs and communicate the exciting events of the day. However, he or she is not handicapped by living in two separate households, with long periods of time often elapsing before he or she can share the news with people in the second household. In addition, he or she is not handicapped by frequently being used as a messenger, carrying information from an adult in one household to an adult in another, or from a child in one household to an adult in another.

If there were even a few good qualities in the original marriage and parenting, children rarely give up their wish and hope that their biological parents will someday remarry one another. Some will suppress this wish, some will articulate it from time to time, and on occasion, a latency-age or older child will make a concerted effort to reunite the biological parents, or even to break up the new marriage with the hope that that will lead to a reunion of the biological parents.

I have treated five adolescent patients—three in individual psychotherapy sessions, the other two in family sessions—who admitted their concerted attempts to break up the remarried family. In two instances the adolescent's efforts were a critical factor in the dissolution of the marriage.

Frequently the child will have a strong sense of both loyalty to, and identification with, the noncustodial parent. This identification may be heightened by actual psychological or physical resemblances to the non-custodial parent, or by feelings of guilt about no longer living with that parent. If the child was physically harmed or psychologically traumatized by that parent, he or she may then struggle with a negative identification, based on the dynamic of identification with the aggressor. It is important for the stepparent to support any positive identification with the absent biological parent. The stepparent will frequently need psychological education and emotional support to be sensitive to and respectful of the subtleties of the child's necessarily long mourning process for the divorce and for the absent parent. Both custodial parents may need help in recognizing the developmental phase-appropriate modalities of mourning and the cognitive processes used by the child in each developmental stage to continue the mourning process.

A universal difficulty experienced by children of remarried families who travel between two homes, is the strain of developing an adaptation to the different rules and values of two households.

The child may be wittingly or unwittingly used as a conveyor of deprecatory or provocative messages from one divorced parent to another, or to the stepparent. If the child begins to develop a close, affectionate bond with the stepparent, conflicts of loyalty may be heightened as the child finds him or herself actually loving this person who is not a biological parent. This conflict may be further exacerbated if the stepparent raises the issue of adoption. On the one hand, the child will experience the stepparent's wish to adopt him or her as further evidence that "he really cares about me." On the other hand, the child who considers this possibility experiences further heightening of guilt feelings toward the biological parent, and increases the anxiety about losing the love of the noncustodial biological parent.

The Adolescent's Problems

The child 13 years and older has a much more difficult time adjusting to the remarried family and the stepparent than does his or her younger siblings. Issues of discipline, control, separation, and sexuality compound the adolescent–biological parent and adolescent–stepparent relationship. The issue of sexuality, in my experience, can be especially charged between a stepfather and an adolescent stepdaughter. This can be heightened by any of the following factors: (1) if there is a troubled sexual relationship between the remarried couple, the stepfather may turn his sexual interests to his adolescent stepdaughter; (2) if the biological mother, due to her own sexual conflicts, gives tacit or even explicit permission for the sexual interest of the stepfather in the stepdaughter and vice versa; (3) if the stepfather is alcoholic, and/or the stepdaughter is retarded.

The increasing sexuality of the adolescent daughter may occasionally elicit feelings of competition in the daughter's biological mother. The mother may respond to this by either withdrawing from the daughter, or becoming hostile, even to the point of making active efforts to expel her from the home.

An adolescent girl may defend against her own feelings of sexual attraction toward her stepfather or adolescent stepbrothers by hostile behavior within the home and by delinquent acts, running away, and compulsive sexual behavior, including pregnancy, with peers outside the home.

The greater psychological and physical independence of adolescent stepchildren, compared with their preadolescent siblings, gives them greater power to intimidate and cause pain in the lives of the custodial parent and stepparent. They may threaten to leave the home as a way of proving that the biological or stepparent is indeed inadequate, and that the other set of parents are better. The parents in a new marriage are often evolving a new value system, and modifying their former self-concepts. This stresses the adolescent who her- or himself is struggling with complex issues of shifting values and identity, and can benefit from a stable parental self- and value system to engage with and then differentiate from.

The "Our" Child's Problems

The remarried couple may decide to have a child of their own as a living representation of their love and their marriage, or by a wish to create an entirely new family, uncontaminated by and disassociated from their painful past lives. There may then be pressure on this child to be a good and happy baby, to fulfill the idealization of the new marriage, and also to compensate for any guilt and disappointment the parents have had about their children from their prior marriages. The "our" child presents a number of problems to his or her half-siblings. At the least, this new child causes a second and serious blow to their self-esteem. The first blow was when the adults decided to marry one another (children of each parent frequently experience the adults' decision to marry as a partial rejection of the adequacy of their own love for the parent). Now, the "our" child further deepens this narcissistic wound, with accompanying anger, sadness, or depression. Feelings of puzzlement and jealousy may occur. The entire remarried family may try to use the "our" child's charm and cuteness as a libidinal binding force to link each member of the remarried family to one another (Whiteside & Auerbach, 1978). The dangers to the child's development in this situation are that (1) he or she may be overly indulged and too highly prized as a narcissistic extension of the parents' entire family, and (2) the child's own sense of self may be further compromised as he or she senses being used by the parents or the entire stepfamily to bind themselves closer together.

PSYCHOTHERAPEUTIC ISSUES FOR STEPFAMILIES

As with other types of families, the therapist's goal may be to have the entire remarried family treated as a unit, and, ideally, this would include the noncustodial family as well. However, as most family therapists have learned from experience, if a family rejects this systems model of therapy, it is best to go along with their definition of the problem and initially treat those members of the family who are defined as the "problem." Often with the growth of trust in the therapist and a broader understanding of the family systems aspects of the presenting problem, the family may be willing to shift to a family systems approach.

I continually emphasize the importance of the strength of the marital bonds to the preservation of the remarried family. I encourage the couple to consider the marriage the most important source of gratification in their lives, more important than the gratification they get from child rearing, or from relationships with extended family members. I urge them to cordon off time for themselves, both during the week and on weekends, and I encourage the stepparent to maintain relationships with former individual friends.

I try to have at least two sessions with the married couple early in the course of evaluating the family, and frequently will work with subgroups of the family (adults, full siblings, stepsiblings, half-siblings, wives, husbands). In the family meetings that follow, I initially use psychodynamic and empathic techniques to clarify the nature of the family's current dilemma, and then gradually introduce systems concepts. I tend to save systems and strategic techniques for the middle and end phase of the therapy. In the course of the evaluation (two to four meetings), I ask each person to say what he or she would like to see changed in the family, and what each is willing to do to promote that change. In addition, I ask each what he or she likes best about the family. Finally (and this is usually most difficult to elicit), I ask each person what he or she needs most from other family members and what each can give in return. I ask all family members to spell this out in detail, emphasizing that they focus on what they want to have, rather than criticize what is. I take careful note of all their responses, and frequently refer to these initial goals in the course of the evolution of the family work, particularly at times of stress, when it is only the initial contract that may tide the family therapy over a time of crisis. The family's initial statements of need and desire to change may be modified as the therapy progresses. However, it remains the most useful tool to focus the therapeutic work, to structure the family therapy, and to prevent aimless exploration into many psychodynamically interesting aspects of the family's life. If a family member has trouble articulating his or her needs, I will return to that person later, either in that or in a subsequent meeting, and try to help him or her deal with any internal resistances or blocks to acknowledging that he or she has needs, while constantly searching for any despair that prevents the family member from recognizing and voicing his or her wishes.

My initial level of interpretations are on issues related to the family's new structure and the family's life phase, for example, an issue related to an adolescent separating from the family, or a situation where the youngest child from a former family now finds him or herself the oldest in the new marriage. Later, I will focus more on interpersonal conflicts, and last, on intrapsychic issues.

Groups of remarried parents are especially helpful. They will initially focus on child-rearing issues, but as the group solidifies and trust grows, issues related to marital conflict will surface. Organizations have been formed by stepfamilies and professionals to specifically deal with the needs of stepfamilies.

Often a remarried family will present a child as the troubled person who "needs to be fixed." Occasionally they are rigid in this perception, and the focus cannot be broadened. The child has been labeled as the deviant one, with a great blow to his or her self-esteem. Individual therapy with the child will frequently be of significant help to the child in dealing both with his developmental problems, and with the specific issues within the family setting (Gardner, 1976). Occasionally, the change in the child may produce a significant positive effect throughout the family system. However, often more is required, especially when the child has been rigidly scapegoated to deflect attention from significant problems in other parts of the family system. Once the child has improved, the therapist can try to negotiate a contract to involve the parents, if not the other siblings. One of the advantages of family therapy, especially with a pre-adolescent child, is that it supports the necessary growing attachment between the child and the stepparent, who will likely be living together for several years. Family therapy, both by its direct statement of the importance of the family as a unit, and its specific help to the stepparent, increases the degree to which the child can be blended into the family.

The occasional "resistances" of the child to having the parent present usually reflect an accurate perception by the child of the parent's anxiety about, and resistance to, being present at the meeting (Weisfeld & Laser, 1977). The child does not wish to offend the parent, and will frequently become a surrogate for the parent, claiming either that he or she doesn't want to be there, or does not need the parent to be there.

In my experience, stepfamilies are eager for guidance from the therapist in their complex task of strengthening a new marriage and of raising children under complex psychological and often economic strains. There are a number of books addressed to the layman on issues related to stepparenting. I have listed six, in addition to the previously mentioned *Disposable Parent* (Roman & Haddad, 1978), in an appendix to this chapter. Stepfamilies are especially eager to hear of the successful models followed by other remarried families.

However, although these can be constructive at times, it is important to remind the stepfamily that they have a unique family structure, with different personalities, a different value system, and a very special history. This will limit to some degree how much they can follow principles that have been successfully used by other families. It is the rare stepfamily member who has had the fortunate experience of him or herself having been the stepchild in a successful remarriage. They, indeed, can provide important leadership and positive feelings about stepfamilies that they can convey to the rest of the family. In the absence of this, the task falls to the therapist to provide a sense of optimism and confidence that by virtue of goodwill, consistent effort, time, and a reasonable appreciation of the difficulties of the task, the family's life can be improved.

APPENDIX: LAY BOOKS ON STEPPARENTING

Atkin, E., & Rubin, E. *Part-time father.* New York: Vanguard Press, 1976.
Galper, M. *Co-parenting.* Philadelphia: Running Press, 1978.
Gardner, R. *The parent's book about divorce.* Garden City, N.Y.: Doubleday & Co., 1977.
Maddox, B. *The half parent.* New York: M. Evan & Co., 1975.
Noble, J., & Noble, W. *How to live with other people's children.* New York: Hawthorne Books, 1977.
Roman, M., & Haddad, W. *The disposable parent.* New York: Holt, Rinehart & Winston, 1978.
Rosenbaum, V., & Rosenbaum, J. *Stepparenting.* Novato, Calif.: Chandler & Sharp, 1977.

REFERENCES

Anthony, E. J., & Benedek, T. (Eds.). *Parenthood: Its psychology and psychopathology.* Boston: Little, Brown, 1971.
Fast, I., & Cain, A. C. The stepparent role. *American Journal of Orthopsychiatry,* 1966, *36*(3), 485–491.
Gardner, R. *Psychotherapy with children of divorce.* New York: Jason Aronson, 1976.
Goldman, J., & Coane, J. Family therapy after the divorce. *Family Process,* 1977, *16*(3), 357–362.
Hader, M. The importance of grandparents in family life. *Family Process,* 1965, *4*(2), 228–241.
Kaplan, S. Structural family therapy for children of divorce. *Family Process,* 1977, *16*(1), 75–83.
Lasch, C. *The culture of narcissism.* New York: W. W. Norton, 1979.
Rice, D. G. *Dual-career marriage.* New York: Free Press, 1979.
Roman, M., & Haddad, W. *The disposable parent.* New York: Holt, Rinehart & Winston, 1978.
Schulman, G. L. Myths that intrude on the adaptation of the stepfamily. *Social Casework,* 1972, *49*, 131–139.
Visher, E. B., & Visher, J. S. *Stepfamilies.* New York: Brunner/Mazel, 1979.
Walker, L., Brown, H., Crohn, H., Rodstein, E., Zeisel, E., & Sager, C. Annotated bibliography of the remarried, the living together and their children. *Family Process,* 1979, *18*, 193–212.
Wallerstein, J. S., & Kelly, J. B. The effect of parental divorce: Experiences of the child in early latency. *American Journal of Orthopsychiatry,* 1976, *46*(1), 20–42. (a)

Wallerstein, J. S., & Kelly, J. B. The effect of parental divorce: Experiences of the child in later latency. *American Journal of Orthopsychiatry*, 1976, *46*, 256–269. (b)

Weisfeld, D., & Laser, M. Divorced parents in family therapy in a residential treatment setting. *Family Process*, 1977, *16*(2), 229–236.

Whiteside, M., & Auerbach, L. Can the daughter of my father's new wife be my sister? *Journal of Divorce*, 1978, *13*, 271–283.

Author Index

Italicized page numbers indicate figures and tables.

Subject Index

Italicized page numbers indicate figures and tables.